The *Open Organization*

This is a rich, well-prepared, well-researched and well-developed book which will become a seminal and foundational work on the Open Organization. *I appreciate the depth and breadth of thought continuity as Philip maintains a focused lens in presenting the tenants, characteristics, realities and possibilities of the* Open Organization. *I look forward to seeing this work become a relied upon source for those developing and studying the* Open Organization.

Diane M. Wiater, Regent University, USA and Editor,
Journal of Practical Consulting

Dr Foster's book The Open Organization *highlights the challenges many 21st century organizations face. Demographics, an aging population, a shrinking workforce, culture, technology, and a world economy are changing the way we engage human capital. In* The Open Organization, *Dr Foster offers solutions to these pressing challenges and challenges leaders to rethink outdated organizational models.*

Skip Prichard, President and CEO, OCLC, USA

The Open Organization *is both an in-depth look at how far we've moved from the closed, bureaucratic systems of the past and a manual for how to operate in a world where adaptability isn't just a competitive advantage…it's a requirement for survival.*

David Burkus, Oral Roberts University, USA
and author of *The Myths of Creativity*

The *Open* *Organization*

A New Era of Leadership and Organizational Development

PHILIP A. FOSTER
Maximum Change Inc., Tennessee, USA

GOWER

Gower Applied Business Research
Our programme provides leaders, practitioners, scholars and researchers with thought provoking, cutting edge books that combine conceptual insights, interdisciplinary rigour and practical relevance in key areas of business and management.

Published by
Gower Publishing Limited
Wey Court East
Union Road
Farnham
Surrey, GU9 7PT
England

Gower Publishing Company
110 Cherry Street
Suite 3-1
Burlington, VT 05401-3818
USA

www.gowerpublishing.com

British Library Cataloguing in Publication Data
A catalogue record for this book is available from the British Library.

ISBN: 978-1-4724-4011-2 (hbk)
ISBN: 978-1-4724-4012-9 (ebk – ePDF)
ISBN: 978-1-4724-4013-6 (ebk – ePUB)

Library of Congress Cataloging-in-Publication Data
Foster, Philip A.
 The open organization : a new era of leadership and organizational development / by Philip A. Foster.
    pages cm
 Includes bibliographical references and index.
 ISBN 978-1-4724-4011-2 (hardback : alk. paper) -- ISBN 978-1-4724-4013-6 (ebook) -- ISBN 978-1-4724-4012-9 (epub) 1. Organizational change. 2. Leadership. I. Title.

 HD58.8.F686 2014
 658.4'06--dc23

2014015798

The *Open Organization* is a registered trademark of Open Organization, LLC. Open Organization LLC is a wholly owned subsidiary of Maximum Change, Inc.

Printed in the United Kingdom by Henry Ling Limited, at the Dorset Press, Dorchester, DT1 1HD

Contents

Foreword   *vii*
Preface   *ix*
Acknowledgments   *xi*

PART I   FOUNDATIONS OF AN *OPEN ORGANIZATION*

1   The History of Leadership and Organizational Structures   3
2   The *Open Organization* Defined   17
3   GitHub: "Creating Awesome" — A Case Study   31

PART II   ELEMENTS OF AN *OPEN ORGANIZATION*

4   The *Open* Ecosystem   41
5   First Principles   63
6   Communication   81
7   Knowledge Commons   89
8   Leading the *Open Organization*   97

PART III   THE TWENTY-FIRST CENTURY ORGANIZATION

9   Cultural Literacy   111
10   Embracing *Open* in the New Millennia   127
11   Should You Go *Open*?   139
12   Beyond *Organization 3.0*   153

References   *159*
Index   *181*

Foreword

What makes certain organizations more successful than others? Why should some organizations benefit from these processes of success and not others? Organizational design and its management has long been the fixation of leaders and scholars alike. Cracking the code to the perfect organizational ecosystem appears to be the dividing line between great success and mediocrity. Added to this pursuit, the twenty-first century launched with great financial volatility, rapid changes, and a level of cultural and global diversity unknown by previous generations. This volatility demands new approaches and methods for the delivery of products, services, and ideas. We no longer can afford to manage organizations with nineteenth and twentieth century models and structures. The pressures of shifting demographics, culture, and technology in this new century require new approaches to organizational leadership and structures. We begin to find that the most successful emergent organizations are agile, self-forming, and self-led. Welcome to the era of the *Open Organization*.

The idea of an *Open Organization* challenges the thinking of many classically trained business school executives. These ideas are in direct conflict with years of nature and nurture within the confines of classical business hierarchies. For organizations to compete in a new world the notions of what is leadership and organizational structure will be challenged and forever changed. Globalism, technology, and a diminishing workforce are all players in the emergence of a more agile competitive structure we call the *Open Organization*.

Philip A. Foster, DSL

Preface

From my very first corporate job in the early 1990s I discovered that the way organizations "do" business is ineffective. In fact, I think the way we "do" business stinks! How we view and treat human capital is not sustainable nor is it any longer realistic for a twenty-first century world. The "way we've always done it" is no longer an excuse for perpetuating outdated and ineffective approaches to leadership and organizational design. What began with my frustration over ineffective leadership and customary hierarchical rituals spans over 20 years of fascination, study and hands-on practical leadership and organizational design; culminating in the solutions I put forth in this book. What I have learned is that solutions for the future viability of any organization must be scalable, agile, self-forming, and self-led. In this new era it is not difficult to find the organizations that are getting it right. But why should only a handful of organizations succeed when there are boundless opportunities for all organizations to embrace a new way of thinking and doing?

Organizational design requires new approaches and innovative ways of thinking. The world is pressed on all sides by a diminishing full-time workforce, differing cultural, generational, political, and religious views and the organization of the twenty-first century must be more agile than the previous centuries. The twenty-first century organizational design will require an ability to share ideas, knowledge, resources, and skills across organizational, generational, and cultural boundaries within and outside of the organizational system for the purpose of achieving desired goals. This book explores the challenge to find an organizational design that will address generational, cultural, industry, and other environmental factors in which the system must operate. This book explores the impact of motivation, culture, and generational differences on the organizational system defined as an *Open Organization*.

Philip A. Foster, DSL

Acknowledgments

Without the help and encouragement of so many friends, colleagues, and family, this book would not have been made possible:

Tom Preston-Werner, Brian Doll, Tim Berglund, and the rest of the GitHub team for opening their doors and sharing their time. In the truest expression of *Openness*, their valuable feedback was essential to the success of this project.

This manuscript was powered by Bluegrass music on Pandora and a whole lot of coffee from Just Love Coffee, Reveille Joe, and Starbucks in Murfreesboro, Tennessee.

My past professors and teachers, Dr Gary Oster, Dr Bramwell Osula, Dr Kathleen Patterson, Dr Jay Gary, Dr Doris Gomez, and Dr Corné Bekker, who taught me how to write and develop my scholarly acumen.

My friends and colleagues, Dr John Lanier and Dr Jeff Suderman, who listened and shared valuable insights toward the concept of the *Open Organization*. Their countless willingness to review drafts and offer feedback was invaluable to me.

Dr David Burkus, my friend and colleague who offered mentorship and motivation to get this book completed.

William Kampbell, MSgt. USMC (Ret.), who proofread and edited the first drafts of my work. He is an invaluable friend and colleague.

Last but never least, my wife Emily who has been my absolute encourager and the love of my life. And two little guys who are the absolute motivation for most everything I do, Conner and Noah—you ROCK!

Philip A. Foster, DSL

PART I
Foundations
of an Open Organization

Chapter 1
The History of Leadership and Organizational Structures

Aristotle once said, "If you would understand anything, observe its beginning and its development." Leadership and organizational structures, for one, have their beginnings symbiotic with humankind. From the beginning of civilization there have been leaders to lead and followers to

> *History cannot give us a program for the future, but it can give us a fuller understanding of ourselves, and of our common humanity, so that we can better face the future.*
>
> Robert Penn Warren

follow them. To borrow from Aristotle, if we look at history we can begin to understand the present condition of leadership and organizational structures as well as anticipate their future evolution.

Beginning around 1500 through roughly 1000 BC, the first known leadership hierarchies emerged as *Caste Systems* which were organized by hereditary distinctions based on one's occupation (Girod, 2013). Before *Caste Systems*, much of society was composed of nomadic tribes. Yet, even in tribes we find distinct structures of leaders and followers influenced through social patterns and norms. These patterns and norms provided the catalyst which eventually moved tribes toward structured monarchies. Around 1000 to 967 BC, monarchs such as King David united their tribes and established capitals (Girod, 2013). Since the time of King David, leadership and organizational systems have greatly evolved. As changes emerged, scholars began to adopt theoretical models to explain the processes and systems of leadership and organizational structures they were witnessing. These theoretical explanations progressed from *Caste Systems* and monarchies to *Great Man Theory* and the classical approaches to leadership we engage today.

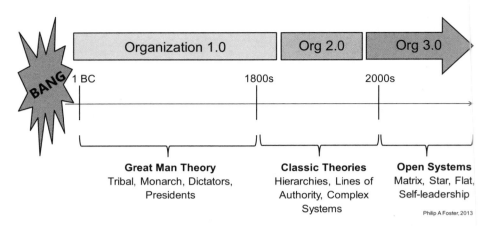

Figure 1.1 **Timeline of *Leadership and Organizational Theory***

Notwithstanding social constructs and norms, leadership is defined as a process used by an individual to influence others toward a common goal (Penn, 2008, p. 1). The act of leadership presumes there are followers to lead and leaders are expected to provide direction, exercise control, and generally execute such functions that are necessary to achieve the organization's objective (Kanungo and Mendonca, 1996, p. 2). While the foundational constructs of followers to lead and leaders to follow have not changed, the overall view of leadership has evolved over time. Early organizations were thought to be led by authoritarian leaders known as *Great Men* who believed followers were intrinsically lazy (Stone and Patterson, 2005, p. 1). This belief transitioned into ways in which we created work environments that were perceived to be more conducive to increased productivity (Stone and Patterson, p. 1). The responsibility of a leader eventually evolved into reinforcing organizational goals through communication, participation, and involvement and to break down old structures and establish new ones (Cummings and Worley, 2001, p. 158; Northouse, 2001, p. 144). In the end, a leader who does nothing more than reinforce organizational goals and objectives is simply a top-down, command-and-control structured leader.

To best understand the evolution of *Leadership and Organizational Theory* we assume three distinct eras of time. The first era, *Organization 1.0*, focuses predominantly on the *Great Man* Theory through the emergence of Fredrick Taylor's *Scientific Management Approach* to production. The *Scientific Management Approach* moved us naturally into *Organization 2.0* and the *Classic Theories* of leadership and organizations. Finally, with increased complexity, globalism, and emerging demographic trends we moved swiftly into the newest era of *Organization 3.0* in which leadership and organizations become flatter and decision-making is driven by members of the organization through self-leadership methodologies. Within this new era, the traditional top-down hierarchy begins to be replaced with flatter structures known as Matrix, Star, and *Open Systems*.

It is important to point out that, while we are advocating the new era of *Organization 3.0*, we recognize that other views of leadership still remain. Certain countries still hold central to the idea of a *Great Man* as leader. This is evident in monarchies and countries ruled by dictators. We further acknowledge that while we see the emergence of *Organization 3.0* as the future of leadership and organization structure, we fully recognize that the classical approaches to leadership and organizational design will be with us for many years to come.

Theory and Systems

The world is undoubtedly complex and from the beginning of time we humans have attempted to make sense of it. Theories are nothing more than our attempt to take a complex world and simplify what is happening in a set of written metaphorical observations (Burkus, 2010, p. 7). Theory places complex ideas in a network of interrelated hypotheses (statements of probable relationships) or propositions (statements of relationships between facts or concepts) concerning an observable fact or circumstance (Vago, 2004, pp. 49–50). We make sense of our world as viewed through our own filters and lenses. These filters and lenses distort our view and we begin to develop interpretations of what is happening to us. Perhaps this, in part, explains why there are literally hundreds of leadership and organizational theories to date. Without theories it would be impossible for us to learn or to act in a consistent fashion; without generalizations and abstractions, the world would exist for us only as a chaotic patchwork of disconnected experiences and impressions (Hans and Wolfgang, 2009, p. 5).

Without an understanding of the world around us, it would be impossible for a leader to make sense of the needs of the follower or the followers make sense of the needs of the leader. The epistemology of leadership theory is simply a process of understanding the limits and validity of a specific action within the context of a system. We look to the study of leadership theories as a process of learning the nature of responses from individuals and organizations with regard to specific actions. It is through the constructs of a theory we begin to better analyze a set of facts and thereby create changes from said process.

Therefore, the need to understand so many leadership theories is a result of the process of analysis and learning. In the end, the purpose of *Leadership Theory* is simply to find understanding of human nature as it relates to the interaction with human capital in an organizational system.

General Systems Theory

The study of theory is incomplete without an understanding of systems. Ludwig von Bertalanffy (1968), the father of *General Systems Theory*, noted there are models, principles, and laws that apply to generalized systems or their subclasses to present a universal set of principles. Bertalanffy set out to develop a universal systematic, theoretical framework for describing relationships in the real world. His objective was to search for parallelisms in disciplines that would give rise to a general theoretical framework. Bertalanffy noted certain characteristics similar in all sciences: (1) the study of a whole, or organism; (2) the tendency of organisms to strive for a steady state or equilibrium; and (3) the "*Openness*" of all systems, that is, an organism is affected by and affects its environment (Wren, 1994, p. 402).

What we begin to observe from the *General Systems Theory* is that all systems have boundaries and that over time most systems will naturally develop some form of structure (Advameg, 2011). Organizational systems display a hierarchical ordering in which each of its higher level of systems comprise of lower-level systems such as: systems at the level of society comprise of organizations; organizations comprise of groups or departments; and groups comprise of individuals (Cummings and Worley, p. 85). When we consider *General Systems Theory*, we begin to see organizations as living entities and the very idea of boundaries changes profoundly in that they become the place of meeting and exchange (Barbour and Hickman, 2011, p. 34).

Theories X, Y, and Z

There are two distinct sets of assumptions that managers, in general, have about their employees and which often turn out to be self-fulfilling prophesies. These assumptions are represented by *Theory-X* and *Theory-Y*.

Theory-X assumes: (1) most people dislike work and will avoid it to the extent possible, therefore (2) they must be continually coerced, controlled, and threatened with punishment to get the work done, and that (3) they have little or no ambition, prefer to avoid responsibility, and choose security above everything else (WebFinance, 2013). *Theory-Y* assumes: (1) physical and mental effort are natural and most people (depending on the work environment) find work to be a source of satisfaction, (2) they generally, on their own motivation, exercise self-control, self-direction, creativity, and ingenuity in pursuit of individual and collective (company) goals, (3) they either seek responsibility or learn to accept it willingly, and that (4) their full potential is not tapped in most organizations (WebFinance).

These assumptions serve as powerful behavioral models reflected in the way an organization is structured. Management that believes in *Theory-X* assumptions create stick-and-carrot approach-based firms with restrictive discipline and pervasive controls. *Theory-Y* believers create trust-based firms with empowered employees (WebFinance).

We said that there were two distinct sets of assumptions that managers have about their employees. There is, however a third assumption that most resonates with the twenty-first century approach to leadership and organizational structures. *Theory-Z* introduces consensus management style based on the assumptions that (1) employees want to build cooperative relationships with their employers, peers, and other employees in the firm; for this they (2) require a high degree of support in the form of secure employment and facilities for development of multiple skills through training and job rotation, (3) they value family life, culture and traditions, and social institutions as much as material success, (4) they have a well-developed sense of dedication, moral obligations, and self-discipline, and (5) they can make collective decisions through consensus (WebFinance).

Organization 1.0 | 1 BC through the early 1800s

The earliest studies of leadership focused on the characteristics and behaviors of successful leaders; while later theories consider the role of followers and the contextual nature of leadership (Bolden, et al., 2003, p. 6). In such case, the *Great Man Theory* of *Organization 1.0* essentially presumes that all great leaders are born or rather somehow biologically gifted as leaders. The *Great Man Theory* was developed in the early 1900s as leadership traits began to be studied to better determine what made certain people great leaders (Northouse, p. 15). The *Great Man Theory* predominately focused on identifying innate qualities and characteristics possessed by great social, political, and military leaders as it was thought that leaders possessed certain attributes that distinguished them from people who were not leaders (Northouse, p. 15). Up until this point in history, most all leaders were seen in the context of *Great Man Theory*.

The *Great Man Theory* fits well with a top-down hierarchy approach to leadership in that it assumes the leader at the top has a natural instinct for leadership and is placed in such a position out of some observable greatness. Top-down leadership follows the *Great Man Theory* in that a top-down organization is a traditional model whose concept is borrowed from centuries of war, military hierarchy, dictatorships, and monarchies. The focus of such an organization is on the leader at the top of the chain of command. For example, the CEO is in command and there are many layers between them and the customer. In a top-down organization, everyone focuses on the boss and away from the customer (Homula, 2010).

Toward the end of the *Organization 1.0* era, early in the twentieth century, management emerged as a field of study introduced by Frederick W. Taylor (Gordon, 1991b, p. 16). It is during this era the United States saw mass immigration and the workplace was being flooded with unskilled, uneducated workers (Walton, 1986, p. 8). Taylor, a foreman at the Bethlehem Steel Works in Bethlehem, Pennsylvania introduced the *Scientific Method* which was believed to be an efficient way to employ larger numbers of labor as well as reduce conflict and eliminate arbitrary uses of power by managers (Gordon 1991b, p. 16; Walton, p. 9). Taylor and others began to believe that management could be studied and applied through scientific process (Walton, p. 9). Taylor's structure and design of management activities stated managers and employees held clearly specified yet different responsibilities and Taylor's approach required managers to develop precise standard procedures for doing each job; select workers with appropriate abilities; train workers in the standard procedures; and carefully plan out all their work and provide wage incentives to increase employee output (Gordon 1991b, p. 16; Daft, 2004, p. 25). Hence the rule-bound, top-heavy American corporate structure was born (Walton, p. 9). While Taylor's system did produce larger quantities of output; the process was cumbersome, rigid, and therefore slow to adjust to changing market conditions (Walton, p. 9). The process created the assumption that the role of management was to maintain stability and efficiency, with top managers doing the thinking and workers doing what they are told to do (Daft, 2004, p. 25).

Taylor's approach to leadership and organizational structure naturally gave rise to other theorists and the emergence of the *Classical Theories* of leadership and organizational structure we find in the era of *Organization 2.0*.

Organization 2.0 | Early 1800s through the late 1990s

Entering the era of *Organization 2.0* we find several schools of thought or perspectives related to leadership and organizational theories. Toward the end of the *Organization 1.0* era, Taylor's theories created an interest in understanding the way leadership and organizations should behave. With this growing emphasis we began to witness a shift toward the structural perspective of theory we call *Organization 2.0*. This era can best be described as the era of *Classical Theories* of Leadership and Organizational structure which spanned most of the twentieth century.

Included in this school of thought we find the *Classical School* Theory in which employees have specific but different responsibilities; are scientifically selected, trained, and developed; and division of work between workers and management is equal (Gordon, 1991b, p. 15). In addition, the *Bureaucracy* school of thinking emphasized order, systems, rationality, uniformity, and consistency in management; these attributes led to equitable treatment for all employees by management (Gordon, 1991b, p. 15).

By the 1920s however, structural perspectives of administration gave way to behavioral perspectives of leadership and organizational thought. Beginning with *Human Relations*, organizations began to focus on the importance of the attitudes and feelings of workers and it was determined informal roles and norms influenced performance (Gordon, 1991b, p. 15). The *Classical School* briefly reappeared as a reemphasis on the classical principles of chain of command and coordination of activities previously developed in the 1910s (Gordon, 1991b, p. 15). By the 1940s *Group Dynamics Theory* began to encourage individuals to participate in decision-making and by the 1950s the *Leadership School* stressed the importance of groups having both social and task leaders (Gordon, 1991b, p. 15).

Decision Theory (behavioral perspective), *Sociotechnical School*, *Systems Theory and Environmental and Technological Analysis Theories* (Integrative Perspective) emerged in the 1960s. *Decision Theory* suggested that individuals "satisfice" when they make decisions (Gordon, 1991b, p. 15). *Sociotechnical School* called for the consideration of technology and work groups when understanding the work system in which we operate (Gordon, 1991b, p. 15). *Systems Theory* offered the first glimpse of an emerging *Organization 3.0* era as it represented an organization as an *Open System* with inputs, transformations, outputs, and feedback where systems strive for equilibrium and experience *Equifinality* (Gordon, 1991b, p. 15). Next, *Environmental and Technological Analysis Theories* described the existence of mechanistic and organic structures and stated their effectiveness with specific types of environmental conditions and technological types (Gordon, 1991b, p. 15). Finally, in the 1980s, the emergence of the last Integrative Perspective known as *Contingency Theory* emphasized the fit between organizational processes and characteristics of a given situation (Gordon, 1991b, p. 15).

The distinction between *Organization 1.0* and *Organization 2.0* was in the movement away from an emphasis on the manager and toward an emphasis on the employees. However, influence still played a role in how managers were able to lead others. In modern application leaders are to be competent in that they hold knowledge of a given topic, intelligence, expertise, skill, or good judgment (Hackman and Johnson, 2000, p. 163). When competence is found, a leader can then influence a group of individuals to achieve a common goal (Northouse, p. 3). In fact, in the era of *Organization 2.0*, leadership occurred in groups and involved influencing groups of individuals (Northouse, p. 3). The *Classical Theories* of *Organization 2.0* forward the thought that for an organization to thrive, leaders and employees need to understand how structure and context (*Organizational Theory*) are related to interactions among diverse employees (organizational behavior) to accomplish the goals and objectives of the organization (Daft, 2004, p. 34).

In the *Organization 2.0* era, leadership might be defined in terms of the power relationship that exists between leaders and followers (Northouse, p. 2). Leaders exert their power and influence on the environment through: (1) goals and performance standards they establish, (2) the values they establish for the organization and (3) the business and people concepts they establish (Clark, 2004). Organization values began to reflect concern for employees, customers, investors, vendors, and the surrounding community (Clark).

Historically we find many theories which deal with leadership and its influences over subordinates in varying degrees. It is during the *Organization 2.0* era that leaders began to seek the "secret formula" of *Leadership Theory* in their pursuit of effective organizational transformation. One viable option was the *Leader–Follower Theory* which implies a system of two or more persons working together at any one time, where leaders assume followers' roles and followers assume leadership roles (Pitron, 2008; Gilbert and Matviuk, 2008). Unlike traditional definitions of leadership, this approach claims followership and leadership are not so much about position, but about their ability to influence through behaviors and self-concept (Gilbert and Matviuk). Followers and leaders orbit around the purpose rather than followers who orbit around the leader (Chaleff, 2003). The concept of *Leader–Follower* contrasts with traditional approaches to leadership such as *Great Man* and *Top-Down* Theories. The *Leader–Follower Theory* pushes followers beyond the context of subordinate and obedience and opens the opportunity for innovation and change within an organization otherwise unrealized in the *Great Man* and *Top-Down* organizational models. Evidence shows those organizations where the *Leader–Follower* methodology is in use yield individuals who desire investment in their jobs and the organization as a whole.

Beyond theory and structure, *Organization 2.0* introduced the need for critical thinking, which examines assumptions, discerns hidden values, evaluates evidence, and assesses conclusions (Myers, 2007, p. 24). Critical thinking requires distinguishing between strategic planning and strategic thinking. Strategic thinking requires thinking through the plan to determine likely unintended consequences. Values and ethics also grew in importance during this era. Values and ethics or trust is based on an employee's perception of the leader's reliability and dependability as a result of past follow-through on their commitments (Davis and Rothstein, 2006, p. 408). Trust and credibility is tied to psychological contracting which is a perceived (either verbal or implied) agreement between two parties and is born from a belief that a promise of some future return has been made and that an obligation to future benefits has been created (Davis and Rothstein, pp. 408–9). Leaders become part of the *soul of the organization* as they set the tone as to how things were to be done around the organization (Foster, 2011c). For example, if a leader is consistently late, it is difficult for them to effectively require their followers to adhere to company attendance policies. *Behavioral Integrity* is therefore perceived to be low because of a mismatch between expressed values and the values expressed through actions (Simons, 1999, p. 90). It was found that leaders developed trust by their consistency in moral judgments, values, and character. Character is something that must manifest not only in the leaders public life but throughout their entire life (HRMID, 2011, p. 6).

Values formation is an approach to life that impacts all members within the organization (Grace, 2011). Moreover there appears to be a correlation between effective leadership and how much autonomy is given to the followers. A leader who does not trust their followers appears to have the most trouble with change. Such a resistance to change appears linked to a shared commitment of beliefs which encourages consistency in an organization's behaviors, and thereby discourages change in strategy (Mintzberg, et al., 1998, p. 269). When change fails to occur within the organization as planned, the cause is always to be found at a deeper level, rooted in the inappropriate behavior, beliefs, attitudes, and assumptions of would-be leaders (O'Toole, 1996, p. x). Organizations can benefit greatly from a leader who understands the influence they hold on the values of their organization. Unfortunately most organizations are led by leaders who only know how to be administrators (Hamel, 2002, p. 22). Leaders who do not understand the role they serve create a misalignment and instill inappropriate values in those they lead. An effective leader would almost always begin with a commitment to the moral principles of respect for the followers (O'Toole, p. 34). Ultimately, followers create a perceived notion of the leader's character. Character is what makes a leader worth following (Stanley, 2003, p. 131).

Before the 1960s, traditional theories only looked at organizations as closed, isolated systems. However over time theorists added humanistic and holistic ideologies to the mix (Griffin, n.d.). Predominantly, these traditional theories ignored outside environmental influences such as natural disasters, social changes, political changes and even employees' personal problems (Griffin). With that, *Organization 2.0* began to produce a greater emphasis on organizational structures, systems, and environments and our understanding of organizational structures, boundaries, and communication from within and sometimes outside the confines of the organization. What began to emerge was a sense that leaders and organizations must be flexible and adaptable enough to enable managers to forward plans in context of constantly changing operating environments (Stanford, 2009, p. 69). Toward the end of the twentieth century, as the economy attempted to recover and organizations maintained relatively smaller staff, organizations began facing globalization, advances in technology, a diverse workforce, greater segmentation in the customer base, attuned investors and competition from both traditional global players and smaller innovators (Hesselbein and Goldsmith, 2009, p. 15).

Organizational capabilities emerged as the last true sustainable source of competitive advantage (Nadler and Tushman, 1997, p. 226). Organizational design required an assessment of the current structure and its ability to deliver future results and which are in alignment with other organizational attributes (Stanford, p. 46). Such designs must direct sufficient attention to the sources of the organization's competitive advantage in each market in which it serves (Stanford, p. 46). Organizational design was not limited to structure as leaders were also considered as part of the design that keeps the structure in alignment (Branch, 2011). In context of organizational design, leaders must: balance the demands of daily activities with the demands of specific projects; manage competing priorities, tasks, and activities; assist followers to cope with inevitable change; satisfy business needs quickly while getting it done right; get the timing right on leadership issues; motivate all stakeholders whose input is critical to the project; demonstrate the ability to work effectively with other leaders within and without the project and/ or organization (Stanford, p. 189). As we neared the end of the twentieth century, non-traditional organizations began to break free of their former rigidity and developed different shapes, working habits, age profiles, and differing traditions of authority (Handy, 1989, p. 15).

Pressures on organizational design increased and the view of centralized systems began to shift. While a centralized system has a clear leader who is in charge and a specific location where decisions are made, a decentralized system has no clear leader, structure, or central location (Brafman and Beckstrom, 2006, p. 19). The benefit of a decentralized system is its agility under pressure. When a decentralized system is attacked it becomes more decentralized and more difficult to stop (Brafman and Beckstrom, p. 21). The decentralized system is not necessarily a better organization or better at making decisions insomuch as it is able to more quickly respond to changing conditions because all members of the system have access to knowledge and hold the ability to make decisions (Brafman and Beckstrom, p. 39). The true role of organizational design is to develop adaptability, flexibility, and profitability in the most efficient and effective manner available, given the resources available to it. Organizations of the future will continue to adapt and develop a spirit of learning and growth. The organization of the future will need to focus on creativity and innovation to meet the constant changing needs of the world in which it serves.

Leaving the twentieth century we find a time of unprecedented globalization of organizations and economies. Understanding the effects of culture had a large impact on an organization's ability to achieve success. Organizational decision-making styles began to be influenced by generational and cultural attributes of the individuals from within the organizational system. The advent of the Internet and other technologies began to link individuals across cultures; creating collaborations unheard of in centuries past. Through this reality, leaders began to understand the impact a globalized economy brings to the doors of their organizations. Accessibility of information and goods via the Internet opens doors for nearly every business to compete globally. In fact, if an organization has an Internet presence, they are, by its very definition a global organization. As the global economy arrives and leaders step forward into the global arena, they must understand geography, language, customs, values, ethics, varying laws, and national psychologies. These skills will determine their level of success within the global marketplace. Leaders and their organizations must learn to move beyond their own worldview and open themselves to the complexities of cultures, geography, laws, customs, and languages that await them. Leaders who take the time to become culturally literate will best develop relationships that positively impact their organization. Developing relationships is essential to the success of any leader who seeks to operate in the global context. Developing relationships builds respect, trust, and creates understanding. Developing relationships of trust creates freedom amongst the followers to self-initiate solutions to problems without delay or confusion. These cultural nuances become essential to the overall success of the leader from within the culture they operate.

Organization 3.0 | 1990s through the 2000s

While the *Organization 1.0* era focused entirely on the leader and *Organization 2.0* on the *Classical Theories*, the era of *Organization 3.0* began to focus on organizational design and its effects on employee behavior. In this new era, we no longer rely on the traditional models of structure, function, and employee interaction. The business climate of the early twenty-first century almost instinctively requires organizations and its members to become more agile in their response to ever-changing economic conditions. The classical approaches of *Organization 1.0* and *2.0* evolved over time. In fact, there was no Internet, cell phones, or social media which to communicate through 100 years ago. If you wanted to push out a message to a large staff you needed a lot of people to help communicate a message. Today, we can communicate with one person or millions of people with little to no help at all. Organizations must now learn to develop processes to share knowledge and resources across boundaries to achieve stated goals. The organization of the twenty-first century must be more agile than its nineteenth and twentieth century ancestors. Organizational design is essential to how the organization deals with the challenges it now faces.

In the early part of the twenty-first century, organizations engaged in a frenzy of structural realignments that led to acquisitions, divestitures, joint ventures, outsourcing, and alliances (Ashkenas, et al., 2002, p. xxvii). *Organization 3.0* has already witnessed change at a historically unprecedented rate. In this new era, organizations must find ways to adapt to the changing world. In 1989 it was predicted that by the year 2000, less than half of the workforce in the industrialized world would be in "proper" full-time jobs and that before long full-time employees would be the minority (Handy, pp. 31, 34). The organization of the future must structure itself around new realities of globalization, technology, diverse employees, and customer demands (Hesselbein and Goldsmith, p. 15). More than ever, organizations must find organic approaches to dealing with change and innovation. One such emerging concept is that of a decentralized Matrix-style organization, otherwise defined as the *Open Organization*. The end result is not to abolish organizational structures but to create a more flexible flow of ideas and processes that meets the needs of each individual within the organization as they pursue the goals of the organization and its stakeholders.

Within the *Organization 3.0* era, traditional hierarchical structures are becoming flatter as the emphasis of structural design is placed on specialization, shape, distribution of power, and departmentalization and its impact on the leaders, followers, and clients (Galbraith, 2002, p. 17–18). In this era, decentralized organizations have a better chance of surviving and more effectively adapting to the culture, current business climate, increasing competitiveness, and attacks in general because it is autonomous and is more agile in its ability to react to changing conditions (Brafman and Beckstrom, p. 48–49).

In this era, we find organizations increasingly comprised of individuals from differing cultural origins. Therefore, understanding the effects culture has on an organization is important to the success of it becoming more *Open*. Not only can culture act as a prism that blinds organizational leaders to changing external conditions, but even when those leaders overcome their cultural myopia, they respond to changing events in terms of their own cultural lens and they tend to stick with the beliefs that have worked for them in the past (Mintzberg, et al., p. 270). Culture remains complex because it is essentially composed of individual interpretations of the world and the activities and artifacts that reflect these interpretations (Mintzberg, et al., p. 265). The organization of the twenty-first century must contain collective beliefs for the argument of all cultural elements to be self-evident (Mintzberg, et al., p. 265). Resistance to change appears linked to a shared commitment to beliefs which encourages consistency in an organization's behaviors, and thereby discourages any changes in strategy (Mintzberg, et al., p. 269). Culture acts as a perceptual filter or lens in which individuals establish the premise for their decisions (Mintzberg, et al., p. 269). Arguably, it boils down to how a person's worldview may influence organizational thinking.

Organization 3.0 operates in a globalized market. Globalization forces us to consider worldviews and cultural difference which are determined by the psychological distance or cultural distance between the home or existing geography and the new geography (Galbraith, 2002, p. 49). Cultural difference is greater for countries with different language, religions, political systems, economic systems, legal systems, levels of development, and education (Galbraith, 2000, p. 49). Simply put, it is easier for organizations to operate within countries that have the smallest cultural distance and the lowest learning curve (Galbraith, 2002, p. 49). This prompts us to consider our own worldview or presuppositions which we hold about the basic makeup of the world around us (Sire, 1997, p. 16). Considering our own worldview helps us to understand the challenges multinational companies have in their integration of activities that take place in different countries (Galbraith, 2002, p. 3). There are societal/cultural risks associated with operating within differing sociocultural environments (de Kluyver and Pearce, 2009, p. 200). Considering your own worldview or cultural influence therefore is an essential element of an *Open Organization's* success. When autonomy and self-management are important aspects of the organization, matters of culture are less of an issue.

As we begin to explore this new era, we find eight functional rules of an *Open Organization*: (1) it has a written *Charter* or *Governance*; (2) *Open* participation amongst members; (3) self-management; (4) best practices are explicitly defined; (5) absolute respect for skills and knowledge; (6) public ownership of knowledge; (7) diversity; and (8) affirmative or positive environment.

Chapter 2

The *Open Organization* Defined

An *Open Organization* is defined as the sharing of ideas, knowledge, resources, and skills across organizational, generational, and cultural boundaries within, and in some cases outside, a highly adaptable, *Flat*, agile, self-led formal organizational system

> An Open Organization *is simply a method of self-leadership in which individuals participate in the movement of an organization from their strengths.*

for the purpose of achieving a stated outcome (Foster, 2011a). Knowledge resides where it is most useful and at the moment it is most needed. The *Open Organization Model* permits teams to carry out several projects at once through the use of differing approaches and agendas in an effort to expel the use of centralized models and hierarchies (Open Organizations, 2006).

The main attribute of an *Open Organization* is in the peer interaction which crosses organizational, generational, and cultural boundaries to collaborate with others for the expressed purpose of producing an end-product and sharing the source-materials, blueprints, and documentation freely within the organization (Open Organizations). An *Open Organization* is about transparency and clarity in a very structured and ordered environment with expressed and explicit rules so that no one has to guess and everyone is on the same page (Bowers, 2014).

The *Open Organization* begins to recognize that individuals, groups, and organizations have needs that must be satisfied. It is this thinking that underpins the idea of the *Open Organizational Approach* which takes its inspiration from the work of Ludwig von Bertalanffy. Bertalanffy's approach builds on the principle that organizations, like organisms, are "*Open*" to their environment and must achieve an appropriate relation with that environment if they are to survive (Morgan, 2006, p. 38). As the *Open Organization* concept gains attention, it enables teams to develop products and services within diverse production models, communication methodologies, and interactive communities (Elmquist, et al., 2009, p. 329; Open Organizations).

Some will argue that you cannot mix *Leadership and Organizational Theory* because they are two different animals. In fact, an *Open Organization* begins to blur the lines between the two. An *Open Organization* is simply a method of self-leadership in which individuals participate in the movement of an organization from their strengths. The *Open Organization* is a decentralized structure which trends away from authoritarian management styles, separatist titles, and privileges of multilevel hierarchies found mostly in *Organization 1.0* and *2.0* (Galbraith, 2002, p. 17). As a non-traditional organization, the *Open Organization* leads to faster decision-making, lowers overhead, is considered more flexible, has followers who are generalists and leaders who are more in touch with their followers (Galbraith, 2002, pp. 13, 20). Unlike the centralized system of eras past, an *Open Organization* may at times appear to not have a clear leader who is in charge or a specific location where decisions are made (Brafman and Beckstom, p. 19). An *Open Organization* is a more agile structure that is able to more quickly respond to changing conditions because all members have access to knowledge and can make decisions (Brafman and Beckstrom, p. 39).

While there is no one-size-fits-all approach to organizational design, we can argue that an organization behaves the way it has been designed to behave (Stanford, p. 3). An *Open Organization* requires that everyone in the organization have some control over what is going on and it requires all members have an equal voice in the process (Stanford, p. 28). As a result of everyone holding equal voice in the process, you will find a strong level of accountability by all members within an *Open Organization*. The process of being accountable makes it necessary for all members to intervene in the decision-making process when another member does not meet their obligations. This requires all members to let go of their preconceived notions of how people operate and essentially trust that the people to whom power is given will act responsibly (Li, 2010, p. 18). The biggest indicator of success of an *Open Organization* comes from an open-mind and the leader's ability to give control over to the followers at the right time and place and to the extent which people need the discretion to get their job done (Li, p. 8).

An *Open Organization* structure in no way signifies that it is void of formal structure or leadership. In fact, an *Open Organization* very much relies on a framework on which to build and the leadership element very much remains a central requirement of an *Open System* (Yehuda, 2001). While organizations may vary in how *Open* they are to their environments, even an *Open Organization* will display a hierarchical ordering in which each of its higher level of systems comprise of lower-level systems such as: systems at the level of society comprise of organizations; organizations comprise of groups or departments; and groups comprise of individuals (Cummings and Worley, p. 85).

An *Open Organization* will not only maintain a structure but also utilizes a set of standards called an organizational *Governance* or *Charter*. An *Open Organizations Governance* explicitly lays out how members within the system will work together without having to negotiate individual agreements with each member (Li, p. 34). The structure which emerges must exist independent of any organizational compensation or rewards systems that seek to reward individuals disproportionately and most are often associated with a formal business model (O'Mahony, 2007). To accomplish this framework requires the organization to develop formal written *Governance* that ensures that the interest of all members is represented and provides independent decision-making at all levels of the organization free from any single external controlling influence (O'Mahony). A formal *Governance* or *Charter* provides operational standards which aim to facilitate the dissemination of information and content throughout the *Open Organizational System* (Open Archives, 2011).

While *Open Organizations* are not leaderless, they are very much lead in such a way that leverages new behaviors within the system (Yehuda). In fact, it could be argued that an *Open Organization* is an organization of leaders. Beyond self-leadership, leaders are still required to manage, measure, correct, take control, and be accountable for given results (Yehuda). The level of *Openness* within the organization will determine to what extent the leadership will operate. An *Open Organization* is much like the *Leader–Follower Theory* in that the leader in no way abdicates the role of leadership within the organization. Instead, an *Open Organization* leader explicitly empowers their followers through the mechanism of a *Governance* to get things done.

The structure of most traditional businesses in the *Organization 2.0* era are typically recognized as having closed decision-making models and individuals who are un-accountable, knowledge is hoarded and there is likely to be some kind of abuse of power (Open Organizations). Counter to the traditional organizational mode, *Open Organizations* typically rely on trust and the free flow of ideas amongst the members within the confines of the organizational structure and *Governance*. It is generally accepted that organizations have some kind of formal lines of communication and dissemination of work assignments is directed and does not necessarily account for individual motivational needs. When organizations do consider motivational needs of the followers, there remain rigid organizational mandates before any of the needs of the individuals will be considered. The best scenario for success would be an organizational model that champions the intrinsic motivational needs of the individual while facilitating the expressed needs of the organization. Creating a flexible environment that meets the needs of both can be a challenge for leaders.

The best option for success rests in a more organic organizational approach. For example, a vine has structure but is flexible and can make changes as challenges arise. Such flexibility affords the vine the ability to navigate around obstacles, yet maintain the structure required to move nutrients throughout the entire system of the vine. The challenge is to translate the vine analogy into an organizational mechanism that permits the structure to reach specified goals.

In considering an organic approach to sourcing information, an *Open Organization* offers a solution that will meet the needs of an organization. The *Open Organization Model* includes the concept of concurrent yet different agendas and differing approaches in production, which is in contrast with more centralized models of development such as those typically used in hierarchical teams. A main principal and practice of *Open Organization* teams is the peer interaction across organizational boundaries through collaboration with the resulting product, source-materials, blueprints, and documentation made freely available to all members of the organization (Open Organizations). *Open Organizations* create structures that are less rigid than their more formal structured hierarchical counterparts. The end result is not to abolish organizational structure but to create a more flexible flow of ideas and processes that meets the motivational needs of each individual within the organization as they pursue the goals of the organization. Within an *Open Organization,* the decision-making process must be highly inclusive and it must allow consensus to emerge where it exists (Ousterhout, 2009).

The idea of an *Open System* reveals a fundamental truth that the best person to complete a given task is typically the one who most wants to do that task and the best people to evaluate the individual's performance are those who will enthusiastically pitch in to help improve the final product out of the sheer pleasure of helping one another achieve something from which they all will receive benefit (Howe, 2008, p. 8). The nature of an *Open Organization* has revealed that, contrary to conventional wisdom, individuals do not always behave in so-called predictable self-interested patterns (Howe, p. 15). Individuals will typically participate for little or no money; laboring tirelessly despite financial reward through the mechanics of collective intelligence to contribute and aggregate information to come up with better solutions (Howe, pp. 15, 54, 180). Wikipedia offers an excellent example of an aggregated solution. Individuals may, within guidelines, participate in the writing, editing, and monitoring of material placed on the Wikipedia website.

An *Open Organization* does not mean that the members are able to make better decisions, but that they are able to respond more quickly because they have access to a collective knowledge and the ability to make use of it (Brafman and Beckstrom, pp. 39–40). Wikipedia is not necessarily a better form of Encyclopedia as it is proven to have less than accurate information. However it offers a real world example of collective knowledge and the desire to create an accurate communal database of information.

Closed

Most organizations are considered closed structures. Not just closed to the outside world but also closed internally as well. Information is closely guarded and disseminated on an as needed basis. A closed organization doesn't make any distinction between the laws of nature and social rules, and it assumes that both are unchangeable (Bodo, 2004, p. 6). In a closed organization each department or silo has its own predetermined duties and within those silos individuals carry out their own assigned tasks. Many times members of a given silo are discouraged from crossing organizational boundaries to interact with individuals in other silos. Cross-silo communication is structured and typically must cross through the chain of command.

A closed organization has many policies and procedures dictating the way individuals within each silo and the organization as a whole will operate. The result of this invariability and determination of the organization's reality is that, on the one hand, members of the organization can rely on existing order, but on the other hand are rendered helpless if threatened by rules (Bodo, p. 6). Members of the organization become prisoner to the rules and regulations; while political infighting becomes the focus as individuals jockey for the best possible position. The closed organization offers its members a deterministic view of the ideal norms and values that regulate its members lives (Bodo, p. 6).The focus of the organization thereby becomes self-preservation over anything else.

Because individuals within a closed organization are seen with a predetermined view of responsibilities, they are rarely encouraged to stray beyond the borders of their position or departmental silo without repercussions. If we were to compare an organization to an organism, each organ has its own duties, and stands in a complementary relation to others (Bodo, p. 6). Unfortunately organizations do not act like an organism and a predetermined view of individuals very much stifles creativity and intellect.

The closed organization is often viewed through a utopic lens as it is believed there exists no conflicts between the different classes and because every member works for the benefit of the whole organization (Bodo, p. 7). In fact, the closed organization is not always as collective in its interests as the presupposition presents. Closed organizations create a false feeling of safety and harmony but do not deliver on its idealistic philosophy of human nature. The closed philosophy argues that human knowledge is more or less free of errors and it is assumed that there is a possibility to discover the plain truth through proper research and proven knowledge (Bodo, p. 7). The closed organization creates classes within the organization and determines the roles individuals will play despite their knowledge, skills, or abilities beyond the position they are given.

Over time, closed organizations develop artificial barriers within the system that diminish the organizations throughput abilities. If permitted to continue, infighting and inefficiencies are no longer contained and will bleed out beyond the borders of the organization presenting outward dysfunction to clients and competitors alike. While proponents of a closed organization argue the natural status of the system, closed organizations are nothing of the sort. In fact, closed organizations have an intentional design, created to focus solely on an expressed mission, vision, and strategy within the confines of a business structure (Stanford, pp. 32–33). Creating artificial boundaries creates artificial results.

Open

The state of *Open* has received a great deal of attention in the past few years. Many classically trained managers however look at the idea of an *Open Organization* and shake their heads with disapproval. For many, wrapping their minds around the state of *Openness* is counterintuitive to their years of training and experience. They begin to ask questions about how one decides to go *Open* or what should be *Open* or kept secret? An *Open Organization* is far beyond a simple structure and more of a state of organizational being. The central dilemma of participatory process (*Openness*) is clear enough: How do you get everybody in on the act and still get some action (Cleveland, 2002, p. 225)?

In this new era, the term *Open* is viewed as loaded with a rich meaning and, among other things, is associated with candor, transparency, freedom, flexibility, expansiveness, engagement, and access (Tapscott and Williams, 2008, p. 20). Wayne Elsey (2013), founder of Soles for Souls and The 501c3 University sums up the essence of an *Open Organization* as being all about the people that are involved in all roles—from the bottom to the top. An organization is *Open* because of its dependency on and continual interaction with the environment in which it resides while closed systems exist only in the world of nonliving matter (Burke, 2002, p. 43). The simplicity of *Openness* is what many leaders stumble over. It is not just an adjective used to describe an organizational structure but a process that affects a number of important functions, including Human Resources, innovation, industry standards, and communications (Tapscott and Williams, p. 20–21). In summary, *Openness* becomes the degree to which individuals hold a broad range of interest and are imaginative, creative, and willing to consider new ideas (Daft, 2002, p. 121). The idea of being *Open* is focused on ideas and human capital rather than on process and structure.

In the context of organizational structure and leadership, an organization with *Open* tendencies believes that it is able to actively influence the market, to select between different alternatives, and to draw up plans that fulfill the stakeholders of the organization (Bodo, p. 9). Beyond influence of markets, an *Open Organization* would be an enterprise that desires to accommodate the needs of its members, treat them equally within the enterprise, and to protect them (Bodo, p. 9). The focus of an *Open Organization* is first and foremost of the members of the organization and second to the mission and task presented. The *Open Organization* is in a permanent search for knowledge, trying to improve what it has already attained with new ideas and innovations, or by organizational development and team building (Bodo, p. 10). An *Open Organization* seeks knowledge and the best possible solution for the betterment of the organization and its stakeholders while seeking to maintain the integrity of the organization's core values and mission.

Open and Closed

Rather than take the view that an organization is either *Open* or closed, we discover that systems can be *Open* and closed. In fact, a system such as the human body is considered both *Open* and closed. *Open*, because it interacts with the environment in which it resides and closed because there are organs enclosed within the system that cannot be seen or touched without opening the system. Opening the human body outside of the confines of a sterile setting can be detrimental to the closed system. Organizations are similar in nature. They can be both *Open* and closed at the same time (Li, p. 18). Organizations, like the human body, are *Open* because they interact with the environment in which they reside and are closed because there are certain aspects of an organization, such as trade secrets, that are not available to their environment. Therefore, systems are both *Open* and closed—*Open* structurally and closed organizationally (Burke, p. 54). Even organizations that are normally considered command-and-control hierarchies can have elements of both *Open* and closed at the same time.

Open Systems Theory

Open Systems Theory begins to offer a structure and language which can be used to explain the *Open Organization*. As noted in Chapter 1, we engage theory to help metaphorically explain what we are witnessing in the natural world. *Open Systems Theory* views organizations as highly complex entities, facing considerable uncertainties in their operations and constantly interacting with their environment (Burton, et al., 2006, p. 37). Constant interaction with the environment requires an unfettered workforce. *Open Systems Theory* changes our diagnostic focus from the individual (leader) to the system (employees) (Beitler, 2006, p. 15). The concept of an *Open System* begins to explain the interaction that the organization and its members have with their environment. An *Open System* is one that interacts with its environment; it draws input from external sources and transforms it into some form of output (Nadler and Tushman, p. 26).

The *Open System* requires new approaches to the environment in which the organization operates. Theorists and practitioners alike have previously devoted relatively little attention to the environment (Morgan, p. 38). The *Open System* view has changed all this, suggesting that we should always organize with the environment in mind (Morgan, p. 38). While focus on the environment is important, The *Open Systems Theory* is multifaceted. *Open Systems Theory* begins to also explain the intrinsic motivators of those in the system. The emerging theory helps us to recognize that individuals, groups, and even organizations have needs that must be satisfied (Morgan, p. 38).

An *Open System* in its natural state must interact with the environment to survive as it both consumes resources and exports resources to the environment (Daft, 2004, p. 14). An *Open Organization* by its very nature will seek to interact with the environment and as a result will continuously adapt to the environment (Daft, 2004, p. 14). Survival of an *Open System* is obtained through continuous interaction and adapting to the environment.

Why an *Open Organization?*

While the concept of the *Open Organization* is an emerging field of study, *Open Systems Theory* was found to be applicable across all disciplines as it acknowledges that the environments surrounding and permeating organizations had important effects on organizational behavior and structure (Rollag, n.d.). As the landscape of employment changes, organizations must consider structures that account for decreasing numbers of full-time employees and increasing numbers of part-time, temporary, and consultant/contract labor. This alone will have a lasting and profound effect on how organizations operate.

Transferring the application of *Open Systems Theory* to leadership and organizational design; the concept of an *Open Organization* emerges as a viable and sustainable solution to the ever-changing business landscape. While the concept of *Open Systems* has most recently been associated with the software industry (*Open Source Software or OSS*) and in research and development (*Open Innovation*); there remained up until now a lack of framework in vocabulary, processes, and developed models for which we can hold discussions and make decisions around the metaparadigm of *Openness* because of the many differing opinions on the idea (Li, p. 18). However, with the advent of OSS solutions such as Firefox, WordPress, Wikis, and the Internet, we begin to find emerging literature expresses *Open Source* as practices in production and development that promotes access to end-products and source-materials (Open Organizations).

As OSS disperses more widely, we begin to find blogs, articles, and discussions focused on the articulation of *Openness*. These resources highlight how an *OSS* enables a team to develop products and services within a diverse production model, communication methodologies, and within interactive communities (Open Organizations). What we begin to unpack is the notion that this model is transferable across industry platforms as we begin to homogenize the idea of an *Open Organization*.

To mainstream an *Open Source* solution across general industry, we must begin to understand that most of what we understood about leading and structuring organizations must change. To begin, an *Open Organization* requires all members to let go of their preconceived notions of how people operate and trust them to act responsibly (Li, p. 18). Changing human nature is not always an easy task. We find that the biggest indicator of success of an *Open System* comes from an open-mind and the leader's ability to give control over at the right time and place (Li, p. 8). This is a challenge for most leaders that are classically trained in the virtues of command-and-control systems.

The idea of the *Open Organization* may appear to be a one-size-fits-all approach to organizational design; we fully acknowledge there is no such beast. While the structure of an organization would appear to affect both the members within the organization as well as the clients it seeks to serve, even as traditional hierarchical structures of organizations receive harsher criticism, we will likely see them around for the foreseeable future (Galbraith, 2002, p. 17). However, organizations are beginning to trend away from authoritarian management styles, separatist titles, and privileges of a multilevel hierarchy (Galbraith, 2002, p. 17). Emerging are these non-traditional *Flat* flexible organizational structures known as the *Open Organization*.

Open Organizations Require Structure

Bertalanffy's *Open Systems Theory* shows that all systems have boundaries and most will agree that over time most organizations will naturally develop some form of structure (Advameg). While there remains a natural tension between *Open* and closed, an *Open Organization* in no way signifies that it is void of formal structure or leadership. In fact, an *Open Organization* very much relies on a framework on which to build and the leadership element will very much remain a central requirement of an *Open System* (Yehuda).

We now know that organizations will vary in how *Open* they are to their environments and to what extent they display a hierarchical ordering. In an *Open Organization*, leadership and structure begin to intersect and new efficiencies emerge. If done correctly, an *Open Organization* structure can be quite liberating to all those connected (Signore, 2013). The *Open Organization's* central purpose is in moving ideas to reality in the most effective way possible without delay. But more so, an *Open Organization* is the method leaders utilize to replicate themselves, build high-performing teams, expand market share, and hone their competitive edge (Signore). *Open Organizations* are emerging as the most effective method for dealing with a complex, volatile environment in which decisions have to be made quickly.

Organizational structures traditionally have become more focused on the leadership and less on the clients and the organization's purpose. It is then no surprise that traditional organizational structures by their very nature facilitate power struggles and fiefdoms. An example of such power struggle is found in organizations with a *product structure* or diversified product line (Galbraith, 2002, p. 25). Within a *product structure* or product silo, the product general managers typically want autonomy which creates duplication of efforts and missed opportunities to share in opportunities and economies of scale (Galbraith, 2002, p. 26). In this setting we rarely find general managers that share information, resources, and clients across product lines. Customers create challenges within a *product structure* in that they have come to expect direct relationships with their manufacturing sources and reject centralized relationships (Galbraith, 2002, p. 27). The inefficiencies of a structure such as this becomes obvious to the outside world. The danger is in building higher levels of frustration among clients that have to deal with multiple contacts at a given company because the internal politics does not allow for such.

The structure of an organization also has an effect on the employees. For example, flexible organizations require cross-functional teams with individuals who are generalist and are able to cooperate with one another (Galbraith, 2002, p. 13). *Open Organizations* require a greater emphasis on hiring skilled labor that is capable and willing to work in a rapidly changing environment. Because of the emerging market forces and demographics, traditional hierarchical structures are becoming flatter and consideration of the structural design of an organization is placed on specialization, shape, distribution of power, and departmentalization and its impact on the leaders, followers, and clients (Galbraith, 2002, pp. 17–18). Traditional hierarchies are emerging ill-prepared for the realities of a twenty-first century marketplace. They must begin to embrace those virtues that will best help them survive a flatter world.

The classically trained leader appears endeared to the more centralized systems of control. Because the traditional centralized system has a clear leader who is in charge and there is a specific location where decisions are made, this becomes a challenge for the classically trained leader who observes decentralized *Open Systems* as having no clear leader, structure, or central location (Brafman and Beckstrom, p. 19). In fact, many classically trained leaders reject the idea of an *Open Organization* as being a centrifuge of chaos. The challenge is in helping the classically trained leader see the great benefits of an *Open Organization*. When a decentralized system is attacked it becomes more decentralized and more difficult to stop (Brafman and Beckstrom, p. 21). The best example of a decentralized system under attack is that of the Minutemen during The American Revolutionary War. The British Red Coats conducted warfare in the classically trained format, lining up in formation in the open. The Minutemen were disbursed and more difficult to detect. Because the Minutemen were decentralized they were much harder to attack and capture and thus one of the main reasons the Colonists were able to take on the best military in the world at that time.

The decentralized system is not necessarily better at making decisions. It is however more able to respond quickly to changing conditions because all members are given access to knowledge and are able to make decisions (Brafman and Beckstrom, p. 39). The Minutemen were clearly able to overcome the Red Coats, not necessarily by cunning intelligence insomuch as they leveraged their power of decentralization to overcome their enemy. The emerging market of the future requires this same level of dispersion and agility to meet the challenges ahead.

Humans are creatures of habit. We seek out those things that create the path of least resistance. Centralized organizations have been the norm simply because individuals naturally gravitate toward a tribe mentality that connects them through a common leader and/or idea (Godin, 2008, p. 1). While it is nice to think that someone will take care of you, what this mentality creates is a community reliant on one person to make decisions for them. Over time, systems, such as the centralized organization, no longer are able to support people, but rather take the lead over them commanding more attention than the human capital that supports it (de Bree and de Wiel, 2011). The Red Coats were rigid and followed a central command-and-control methodology of warfare. We are beginning to discover that decentralized organizations have a better chance of surviving and more effectively adapting to culture, shifting business climates, and increasing competitiveness because it is autonomous and is more agile in its ability to react to changing conditions (Brafman and Beckstrom, pp. 48–49). Traditional organizations that are slow to adopt attributes of *Open* will find a formidable opponent in the marketplace.

Those who moderate traditional structures persist in trying to adapt the world to their organization rather than adapting their organization to the world (Handy, p. 4). As the Red Coats discovered, this worldview is no longer sustainable. A traditional organization creates a comfort and predictability that ensures that control is maintained (Handy, p. 10). However, in times of complexity and rapid change, slow and steady is no longer an option. Traditionally, leaders tend to think of organizations in terms of their structure, such as an organization chart which creates a narrowing focus that may overlook alignment issues amongst other things (Stanford, p. 20). The new reality is that the kind of work being produced is radically different from the routine work of the Taylorian organizations of the past (de Bree and de Weil). *Taylorism* focuses on formal processes which creates false efficiencies. When we use false indicators in our decision-making process, we create a system of lag-thinking. Lag-thinking is nothing more than using information about things that have already happened to make decisions about things that will happen. We do this when we engage financials and other organizational metrics. Traditional organizations lag in their ability to keep up as organizations must more rapidly adapt themselves in order to survive and can no longer be organized around predictability and liner processes (de Bree and de Weil).

Non-traditional organizations, however, tend to focus on the here and now to anticipate the "what's next" in a highly volatile setting. Non-traditional organizations are now considered more flexible as they introduce situational organizing and destroy bureaucratic red tape (Galbraith, 2002, p. 13; de Bree and de Weil). Situational organizing creates a level of ambiguity that cannot be prepared for in advance. Regardless of the design, these more flexible non-traditional structures will become our contemporary traditional styles of organizational design. Non-traditional organizations are typically those that espouse people as assets, requiring maintenance, love, and investment rather than costs to be reduced wherever and whenever possible (Handy, p. 24). The management in a non-traditional organization is situational and self-governed rather than the role of a select few. While there is freedom of self-management it is not without responsibility. Once there is a commitment to a project, it is important for the individual to maintain their commitment, live up to their appointments, and deliver output and reach their deadlines (de Bree and de Weil).

An *Open Organization* will not only maintain a structure but it will also utilize a set of standards called a *Governance*. The *Governance* is the mechanism that creates the formal structure of an otherwise assumed structureless system. The *Governance* may contain few formal rules, but those rules are rock solid and easily understood. The *Governance* formally dictates how leadership engages the workers and how workers engage their work. The leader is not without a role in the organization. An *Open Organization* in no way abdicates the role of leadership within the organization. The *Open Organization* is arguably an echo of Peter Drucker's *Decentralized Authority Model* (1946), Robert Greenleaf's *Servant Leader Model* (1970), and Tom Peter's *Employee-led Teams Model* (1982) (Yehuda).

The structure of most traditional business models are typically made by a few individuals at the top of the hierarchy. Like the Red Coats, decisions in a formal structure are typically slow moving and bureaucratically regulated. Individuals within the organizations are un-accountable, knowledge is hoarded, and there is likely to be some kind of abuse of power (Open Organizations). Counter to the traditional organizational mode, *Open Organizations* typically rely on trust and the free flow of ideas and information amongst the members within the confines of the organizational structure and *Governance*. In an *Open Organization* structure, decisions are rarely made by the leader alone. The essence of *Open* relies heavily on decisions being made at all levels of the organization. The free flow of ideas encourages the ability for members to creatively solve problems that will arise in the course of a business cycle (Simoes-Brown, 2009, p. 51). This creativity may even result in the *Open System* developing a flow of ideas and information between the organization and its clients. Such creativity will require all members of the system to suspend judgment and allow for new ideas and opinions to be expressed (Simoes-Brown, p. 51). The result of a free, unencumbered sharing of ideas allows for unconventional and innovative approaches to develop and grow (Simoes-Brown, p. 51).

Open Source

The idea of the *Open Organization* has its birthing in the high-tech industries. It borrows from *Open Systems Theory* and was founded in the 1960s on collectivist ideals and in reaction to behemoth corporate software programs like the UNIX computer operating system (Hayes, 2008, p. 126). *Open Source* was designed to create efficiencies in complex environments. What evolved was an idea in which people volunteer to work on projects for the public good (Goldman and Gabriel, 2005, p. 15). More than that, *Open Source* is a philosophy which holds that knowledge should be shared and work improves with collective effort (Hayes, p. 126–127).

The term *Open Source* was originally created in 1998 and has come to mean many things: a type of software license, an approach to software development, a type of community, and a type of business model (O'Mahony, p. 140). Moreover the idea of *Open Source* has evolved to describe a cultural approach to how an organization operates. *Open Source* organizations are self-organized groups that work together for a common cause or outcome. Despite its "*Open*" nature, *Open Source* communities adhere to strict quality control mechanisms (Aitken, et al., 2003, p. 1). *Open Source* communities are typically connected through technology and are governed by consensus. *Open Source* is a philosophical movement that moves far beyond a given industry silo. Proponents of the *Open Source Model* value transparency for its own sake, not simply because opening up the development process to outsiders happens to produce better code, but because of the efficacy of the *Open Source Model* that drives organizations to adopt it as a way to save money and develop better products (Howe, p. 54).

What makes *Open Source Models* so efficient is the ability for larger numbers of people to contribute and come up with better solutions than the most talented, specialized workforce (Howe, p. 54). *Open Source Models* depend on economies of scale in which information and processes are shared equally by all members of the organization.

Chapter 3
GitHub: "Creating Awesome" —A Case Study

In this case study we examine GitHub, an *Open Organization*. Through research, interviews, and first-hand observations we identified certain cultural attributes as well as the decision-making, communication, and leadership required to sustain an *Open Organizational System*.

Company History

GitHub Inc. began in 2007 as a part-time venture between Tom Preston-Werner and Chris Wanstrath as a way for *Open Source* software writers to rapidly create new and better versions of their work (Hardy, 2012). GitHub is an online repository for developers to post, borrow, and collaborate on code together and has over four million users as of September 2013 (Lunden, 2013). GitHub helps companies and developers build software using a software version control system utilized by just about all the major Web companies—Google, Facebook, and Netflix all have a presence on GitHub where they share their *Open Source* code with the public and give their internal engineers a place to collaborate (Vance, 2013). "Git" is best described as Wikipedia for programmers, as it creates a virtual environment where participants can edit files, see who has made changes, view older versions of files, and access this information from anywhere in the world (Linderman, 2010). However, the main difference is that members are working on software source code instead of encyclopedia entries and the information provided is used by companies to build software and websites in a more *Open* format (Linderman). When Tom and Chris began GitHub in late 2007, the process of "Git" was largely unknown as a software version control system and essentially there was no market for a paid version. GitHub currently provides code hosting services which allows users to share coding with friends, co-workers, classmates, and strangers all while offering collaborative management for the development of software. GitHub operates under a *Freemium Model* in which most of the system is *Open* and free, while certain tools and robust processes are a pay-for-usage framework. GitHub is far more than just a software developer's toolbox. It is a living philosophy for operating an organization.

Culture

Tom and Chris did not originally set out to create any particular type of organizational culture. If you were to ask either of them they would say it evolved. The key to the GitHub culture is their pursuit to be deliberate in all they do. Because GitHub started as an *Open Source* team they work hard to be true to that idea. Decisions are made in groups by the people who are most involved in the daily process of developing code. Organizational behaviors are fractioned and they are quick to point out that they do not have employees or remote workers—but a distributed workforce. GitHub is a purpose built self-managed organization rather than an organization focused on the philosophy that people need to be managed (*Theory-X* and *Theory-Y*). The culture of purpose is focused on what "GitHubbers" call their *First Principles* in which goals, purpose, focus, or what they call the "main thing" is raised each and every day. With *First Principles*, members are constantly asking fundamental questions such as: "What are we trying to do? What is our core reason?" and they are measuring the answer against *First Principles*.

According to GitHubber Brian Doll, when GitHub first started, they just had a row of tables and everyone worked at the tables. As they grew, they just kept adding tables until one day they thought ... "Why are we just setting up more tables in a line?" So they sent out a company-wide email and asked if everyone wanted the tables or something else. That is when they realized their work environment was different. Today the office is full of couches, tables, a bar, video games, clusters of chairs, a few private offices (with windows and glass doors) and one conference room. The employees can pick and choose where they want to sit and work. Some even work from home in distant countries. The office has a fully stocked kitchen with food, drinks, and even a seltzer water fountain attached to the sink.

The culture at GitHub resonates with a desire to be optimized for *Happiness*. Meaning they don't have meetings, set work hours, or even work days. They don't keep track of vacation or sick days and they don't have managers or even an organization chart. Tom is quick to point out that they don't have a dress code, expense account audits, or even an HR department. At GitHub they believe that hours are not a great way to determine productivity, in fact, they point out that you can't throw more time at a problem and expect it to get solved. Intentionality and *Happiness* means that GitHub wants their employees to be in the zone of creativity as often as possible.

By allowing for a more flexible work schedule, an atmosphere is created where employees can not only be excited about their work, but also work at their most optimal personal best. Flexible schedules at GitHub generally lead to more hours of productive work. For many employees, working weekends blur into working nights and weekdays, since none of the work feels like work to them (Holman, 2011e). Because of the flexible work schedule, there are employees who start work around 7am, and some who come in at 3pm, while others are more productive at home (Holman, 2011e). The reason GitHub can operate in such a loose environment is based on an intense focus on communication via chat rooms which allows the team to work when and where they want (Holman, 2011e).

There is however a caution to *Happiness* optimized flexible work environments. Because employees typically work in a self-organized, self-led environment, it is easy for them to lose themselves in their work. Many observing from outside will look at this and say it doesn't work because our culture promotes the idea that employees must work 40 hours a week. Unfortunately our society has trained us to think in terms of black and white or work and life. GitHub has ditched the idea of work/life balance because it just doesn't make sense to them (Neath, 2009). To help with life balance, GitHub allows employees to work from home (wherever in the world that may be); hack (work on) side jobs or just plain have fun when and wherever possible. Whether employees are *hacking* on the 3D printer or writing code, the focus is on being creative. Employees need to make sure their life promotes creativity. In a creative environment there is no magic formula or number of hours required to work. Each employee must find what works best for them (Neath, 2009). A creative environment requires individuals who are passionate about what they do. This passion comes from an environment optimized for *Happiness* which requires individuals find what they are passionate about in life and then empower them to go and do it. The GitHub culture promotes autonomy, *Happiness*, creativity, and a level of *Openness* that creates an exciting work environment.

Happiness

The culture of GitHub is focused on *Happiness*. Everything that GitHub does it attached to the idea of *Happiness*. Optimizing for *Happiness* means that the organization is more focused on creating *Happiness* than in creating wealth. The normal work day at GitHub finds employees working whenever and wherever it is most comfortable for them; be it on the couch, at tables, in chairs, in an office or even at home. Optimizing for *Happiness* means that employees at GitHub are the happiest when they're building things of interest and value. From this we find that *Happiness* is not always about creating tangible things of value. One of the cool things about this *Open* creative environment is something the tech industry calls *hacking*. *Hacking* is a term used to express the action of working on something that interests you just for fun. *Hacking* may or may not result in a market viable product, but may just be something for fun. At GitHub, *hacking* may take the form of working on a side coding project for an entirely different product or even playing with the 3D printer in the office. *Hacking* is really about tapping into the whole person and engaging their minds in creative endeavors outside of their normal work processes. *Hacking* may offer some side benefits in that it helps the employee take their mind off what they are working on. Sometimes when we are working so intently on something we enter into *can't see the forest for the trees* syndrome. When we relax our minds through other means, such as *hacking*, we free our subconscious brains to go to work on the problem at hand. Consider *hacking* a mental vacation. Overall, *hacking* is about engaging the creative minds of the followers.

There are other really great things you can do when you optimize for *Happiness*. According to Tom you can throw away things like financial projections, hard deadlines, ineffective executives that make investors feel safe, and everything that hinders your employees from building amazing products. GitHub pays their employees well and gives them the tools they need to do their jobs as efficiently as possible. Beyond that, they let them decide what they want to work on and what features are best for the customers. As a result of this focus, GitHub is able to offer clients the products and services they want and therefore revenues are generated by meeting the market demands.

Decisions

Decisions are all based around what is the right thing to do. Because of the flexible work environment, people can work on the things that interest them. This is the essence of Optimized *Happiness* at GitHub. What we have found is that *Open Organizations* flourish when people are permitted to work on certain things, not because they are told to but because they want to. *Open Organizations* hire knowledgeable, skilled human capital, empower them and then set them free to create "Awesome."

Tom believes the GitHub way of *Open Source* requires a high degree of trust and collaboration among relative equals and he strongly feels that it can be extended more broadly into general industry, even government. Through internal processes, communication, and creative or *Knowledge Commons*, organizations can capture the process of decision-making in real time. As complex as an *Open Source* project may be, it is also based on a single, well-defined outcome, and a task that is generally free of concepts like fairness and justice, about which people can debate endlessly. Without the freedom to make decisions in real time, members of the organization are not optimized for *Happiness*, nor are they truly free to do as they see fit.

Communication

You cannot have effective *Open* decision-making without really good communication. In observing the process of conversations and internal dialogues at GitHub, it becomes clear that the participants are more interested in the conversation than in the actual result of the conversation. No one appears to take the conversations personally. The bottom line to a conversation is in the curiosity of finding the answers over defending turf or ego.

While GitHub does not have meetings, each Friday the organization comes together in what is termed *Beer:30*. These gatherings are not about having a company-wide meeting insomuch as it is for celebrating wins and to make adjustments to the organization's course. Because GitHub is a learning organization, *Beer:30* becomes an important time to share intelligence, ask tough questions, and just plain have a fun time with friends. *Beer:30* is video-streamed live so that employees can link in and be part of the gathering. The sessions are archived as part of the company's *Knowledge Commons* so that they can be later referenced and viewed by those who could not attend the live event. *Beer:30* is a time for Tom and others to have fun with shout-outs and celebration of new "on-boards" (employees). During these gatherings it is common for employees to have a beer or mixed drink and the atmosphere is relaxed and informal.

GitHub is all about communicating with others. They are fairly public about how the organization works and they even go so far as to write, tweet, and give talks about how they operate as a company. It only takes a few minutes to realize that GitHub does things differently. Because of the distributed workforce that makes up GitHub, employees work mostly in chat rooms with zero supervision. And because they are self-managed, they work on what they want to work on. GitHub has natural or self-organizing groupings, so there aren't a lot of barriers between teams which means there is a lot of movement and communication within the organization (Holman, 2011c).

As a byproduct of *Openness*, automation becomes essential to how these organic self-forming teams communicate. Automation reduces institutional knowledge that would normally lead to a minority group inside of the company retaining information and answers (Holman, 2011c). With automation, chat trumps meetings and instead of a large office complex, the GitHub office is found predominantly in chat rooms and email rather than development meetings and in-person code reviews (Holman, 2011c). In this organizational context, text is seen as explicit and forces individuals to better formulate their ideas before posting them (Holman, 2011c). Focused text is seen as skimmable, quicker to mentally process, and leaves less room for ambiguity of thought (Holman, 2011c). Another benefit of the GitHub communication process is that written text is on-record. Everything said is being logged in chat so that people working remotely do not miss out on what was happening in the office. This makes communication in the company searchable and accessible (Holman). GitHub uses chat to gain more insight about previous decisions (Holman, 2011c).

Writing down ideas is encouraged. GitHub's internal wiki (a kind of online bulletin board) is filled with ideas. Many of the ideas are not necessarily new ones as they have been likely discussing them in person, seen in another product, or maybe even thought about internally (Neath, 2011b). Writing down an idea is really only half the point—seeing someone else write down the same idea you've had makes you twice as excited about the idea and, as others chime in saying they'd love to see the feature, excitement about it grows and grows (Neath, 2011b). This is the power of self-organized *Open Systems*; eventually you've got four developers *hacking* on something at 11:30pm because they want to see it happen so badly (Neath, 2011b).

An *Open Organization* may require a whole lot of arguing. GitHub is not a quiet place to work. I've been told that new hires right through to Tom argue in bars, in emails, and even in chat. The beauty of the argument is that it's not personal—it's about making their product better and it forces them to rationalize product choices, and whether they are making good decisions (Neath, 2011b). Arguing with co-workers isn't a bad thing. It's not creating a negative work environment—it's a tool to help you make good decisions (Neath, 2011b). GitHubbers see arguing as the process to making good decisions.

Leadership

GitHub acts very much like a distributed organization. There are no managers and no one to tell people what to do. In fact, they vehemently avoid the action of telling people what to do (Tomayko, 2012). GitHubber Ryan Tomayko believes that

> *You need to lead by example as loud as possible!*
>
> Ryan Tomayko

telling people what to do is lazy. Instead, he prefers to try and convince others with arguments as this is how humans interact when there's no artificial authority structure and it works great.

GitHub creates the truest essence of empowerment. In fact, they purpose to create mini-managers, each responsible for managing a single person: themselves (Tomayko). Part of the process of empowerment is leading by example and as Ryan says, "You need to lead by example as loud as possible!" The only thing that might be unique or interesting about the way he does this is that he insists on being extremely visible; meaning removing sidebar conversations, private meetings, Face Time, IM private messaging, and anything else that limits the visibility of work and process. The power behind the *Open Organization* at GitHub is the nature that people already tend to self-manage when everyone else can see what they're doing. Ryan notes, "*Open* allows other people to jump in when they notice something amiss and of course everyone learns when anyone makes a mistake or does something brilliant."

The magic, if there is any at GitHub, is to get people contributing as soon as possible When they on-board (hire) someone new, there is a conscious effort to mention them on issues, comments, and commits to bring them into a bunch of different projects and discussions (Tomayko). When they first have an idea or feedback on something, Ryan will turn it around on them and ask: "Where's your patch?" … In other words, go build the thing in your head, show me how you got there, and then sell it to me and all your peers (Tomayko). The bottom line of leadership at GitHub is that everyone is a manager. Instead of assigning 100 percent management duties to individuals, the basic role of management is spread between (1) every single employee, and (2) a set of custom in-house tools that serve to keep everyone in the know with regards to other projects (Tomayko).

GitHub is a powerful example of an *Open Organization*. Their tools document changes, let developers chat with each other, and make it easier for people to combine their various bits and pieces into a working whole (Vance). The company plans to open its collaboration tools up beyond the software industry (Vance). In fact, Tom believes that the idea of an *Open Organization* is transferable to many industries including government. His desire is to carry this structure to other industries and more mainstream professions to create plenty more "Awesome." Tom believes there will come a day when lawyers, people in government, everyone will engage in the use of *Open*.

PART II
Elements of an
Open Organization

Chapter 4

The *Open* Ecosystem

In Chapter 2 we defined an *Open Organization* as the sharing of ideas, knowledge, resources, and skills across organizational, generational, and cultural boundaries within, and in some cases outside, an organizational system for the purpose of achieving a stated outcome. We also learned that an

> *When you give smart talented people the freedom to create without fear of failure, amazing things happen.*
>
> *Valve Corporation*

Open Organization is in no way void of structure. The ecosystem of an *Open Organization* can best be described as a framework of agility and empowerment. While the structures of classical business models are hierarchical in nature, the organizational structures of the future are emerging as anything but. What we find are new organizational ecosystems producing a strong diverse organization of adaptability, culture, *Happiness*, and innovation.

Structure and Complexity

There appears an assumption or myth amongst many classically trained leaders that if something is described as *Flat*, *Open*, leaderless, or self-led that it somehow has no structure or rules. The *Open Organization* is far from this. In fact, the *Open Organization* is very much an ecosystem with structure and complexity. An ecosystem, such as an *Open Organization*, is a system formed by the interaction of a community of organisms (employees) within their environment (Ecosystem, 2001, p. 619). Organizations, like communities of organisms, are complex and cannot be managed effectively through rigidity and constraints on its natural environment. An *Open Organization* has a natural balance between chaos and order. The natural balance of the *Open Organization* pivots on the organization's ability to flex, bend, and accommodate shifts and changes within its environment. Its flexibility is rooted in the organization's ability to respond immediately to environmental challenges in real time and without bureaucratic "red tape."

The twenty-first century organization will continue seeking greater flexibility as its access to full-time human capital diminishes. This means that the need for flexibility and continuous resource reconfiguration and management of collaborative networks will lead to newer levels of complexity not yet seen in organizational structures (Prahalad and Krishnan, 2008, p. 29). The benefit of an *Open Organization* is that its structure is less rigid and more flexible than its traditional counterparts. It is this flexibility that permits an *Open Organization* to compete in complex evolving environments.

An *Open Organization* will require management of its complexity through a sophisticated system of technological architecture called a *Knowledge Commons*. This level of complexity also calls for all employees to recognize the need to cope with an interesting and continuously evolving set of opportunities and problems resulting from the focus on each individual customer (Prahalad and Krishnan, p. 29). The greater the complexity of the environment faced by an organization, the greater the decentralization of its decision-making should be. This assumes, of course, that qualified and dedicated people exist in sufficient numbers at lower levels of the organization (Gordon, 1991, p. 570). On-boarding or hiring the right people become the focus of the organization's culture at every level. We begin to view all human capital as *Knowledge Workers*, capable of making decisions and acting on them as required. The organization of the future will be a part of the new *Cerebral Economy* in which human capital is highly skilled and educated and they seek opportunities to put their knowledge to work in creative and interesting ways.

The structure of an *Open Organization* is a complex adaptive system that meets the emerging needs of smaller culturally diverse, *Happiness* optimized organizations of the future. With a decentralized complex adaptive system, the challenge becomes how we create stability while being flexible enough to adapt and change to new environmental conditions. What we know is that when complex systems of any kind (swarms of bees, businesses, and economies) are at the edge of chaos, the place where there is neither too little structure nor too much, they produce complex adaptive behaviors (Allee, 2003, p. 232). The ecosystem of an *Open Organization* requires perfect balance in its structure. It is in this fine balance where the organization is most alive, creative, and adaptable (Allee, p. 232). This balance can be easily disrupted when someone within the organization strays from the laws that govern the equilibrium of the organization. In an adaptive system, such an intrusion will call for the organizational system to attack or push (off-boarding) out the offender to regain critical balance.

All systems have some kind of boundary. These boundaries might be visible or implied. Despite the nomenclature of *Openness*, an *Open Organization* displays purposeful barriers and boundaries. Without boundaries, an organization will slip into chaos. Boundaries are designed to impose limits on the organization and they spell out what may not be done (Kesler and Schuster, 2009, p. 21). GitHub is an example of an *Open Organization* with clear purposeful boundaries. GitHub freely shares about 90 percent of their business model with those outside of its structure. However, because they are a for-profit organization, there are certain trade secrets that cause the system to remain closed. There are certain times when information becomes "need to know." Boundaries like this help to distinguish between the system and its environment (Cummings and Worley, p. 86). Most traditional organizations operate within a closed system which is relatively rigid and impenetrable, whereas an *Open Organization* has far more permeable borders (Cummings and Worley, p. 86). In a closed system, the traditional organization hordes information at the upper levels of management and rarely shares needed information, unless it becomes mission critical for the workers to know. While there still remain certain "need to know" scenarios within the *Open Organization*, information is typically shared widely and openly within the organization.

The most distinguishable attribute of an *Open Organization* is the lack of layers of administrators and bureaucratic levels that divide the more traditional organization into self-competing fiefdoms (Titchy, 2002, p. 43). Entering into an *Open Organization* is quite obvious because of the visually stark contrast you will find from a traditional organizational setting. GitHub has *Open* spaces, couches, tables, and clusters of chairs that make the place feel more like the recreation hall at your state university rather than a multimillion dollar organization. It just feels and looks different in an *Open Organization*. Open bars stocked with alcohol, fully stocked kitchens, music, video games, and more are standard fixtures in many *Open* environments. Not only does it look and feel much different than a more traditional organizational setting, they are more efficient as well.

On the other hand, organizations with bureaucratic layers, known as closed systems, are notorious for wasting time and emotional energy as they deal with bloated corporate staffs, protecting the interests of their own units, and positioning themselves for the next step up the corporate ladder (Titchy, p. 43). A more traditional organization finds itself competing between human capital and office space rather than focusing on its more important asset, its people. The danger of a closed system comes from self-competing internal jockeying of the staff that causes them to lose sight of what is important and thereby keeping the organization from competing successfully in a fast-paced global marketplace (Tichy, p. 43). This self-competing internal jockeying comes from our need to self-preserve in what is seen as a hostile environment. This self-preservation also manifests itself in other interesting ways. In a closed system, the hiring manager may be more compelled to hire individuals with less experience or education so they do not feel threatened by the new hire. In an *Open Organization*, individuals are hired to be the smartest people in the room.

In a decentralized *Open System* such as *Open Organizations*, there is no clear leader, structure, or central location (Brafman and Beckstrom, p. 19). The benefit of a decentralized system is found in its agility under pressure. When a decentralized system is attacked it becomes more decentralized and more difficult to stop (Brafman and Beckstrom, p. 21). As noted in Chapter 1, the decentralized system is not necessarily better at making decisions and is more able to respond quickly to changing conditions because members have access to knowledge and can make decisions (Brafman and Beckstrom, p. 39). Centralized organizations have been the norm simply because of our tribe mentality that emotionally connects them through a common leader and/ or idea (Foster, 2011c). However, it is argued that *Open Organizations* have a better chance of surviving and more effectively adapting to the culture, current business climate, increasing competitiveness, and attacks in general because it is autonomous and is more agile in its ability to react to changing conditions (Brafman and Beckstrom, pp. 48–49). Non-traditional organizations are considered more flexible (Galbraith, 2002, p. 13). Regardless of the design, these non-traditional structures will become our contemporary traditional styles of organizational design.

These days, more corporate leaders are encouraging their members to break the norms and to embrace more non-traditional approaches to their work. Some organizations are encouraging their workers to break off into entrepreneurial, startup-like teams: giving a section of the office, in effect, to serve as the hub for these *Intrapreneurs* (Bhanot, 2013). *Intrapreneur* is an emerging buzzword that describes the concept of the *Open Organization* from the perspective of an established traditional organization that is beginning to embrace a more flexible workspace. *Intrapreneurs* are supposed to be dynamic employees from the inside out (Bhanot). While the idea of the *Intrapreneur* may not be a new one, it certainly is gaining more attention as leaders seek to facilitate more collaborative performance from their workforce.

Leaders who are able to facilitate collaboration can improve performance through the global community (Branch, 2012). However, there is a danger in group collaboration that global leaders must consider. When a team builds a strong bond and places a higher priority on cohesion rather than on effective problem solving and peak performance, there runs the danger of developing *Groupthink* (Foster, 2011a). *Groupthink* is characterized as a group that puts unanimous agreement above all other considerations (Hackman and Johnson, p. 214). Collaboration must include the ability to consider all the alternatives, reexamine each course of action, gather additional information, weigh out risks of each choice, work out contingency plans, and discuss important ethical issues (Hackman and Johnson, p. 214). One could argue that *Groupthink* is more likely to be developed in organizations where the leader exerts dominant behaviors rather than facilitate collaboration and synergy (Stagich, 2001, p. 19). Collaboration requires some level of competitiveness. When we introduce competition, success depends more on intrinsic, self-sustaining principles of synergy and how well we facilitate it to achieve said goals (Stagich, p. 21). Leaders prone to more dominant behaviors must learn to let go of their preconceived notions of how people operate and essentially have faith that individuals will act appropriately to get the job done (Foster, 2011c). Collaboration requires the global leader to understand the given skills of their followers and get out of their way to allow them to do what they do best. It is through this empowerment that a global leader will likely achieve greater performance from their teams.

An *Open Organization* can take on several organizational structures, such as an *Affinity Network, Boundaryless, Flat,* and *Matrix*:

Affinity Networks are groups of people who are drawn together based on one or more shared personal attributes and their activities are highly relationship-oriented and typically include networking, mentoring, and representing a collective voice in both organizational and external community affairs (Rothwell and Sullivan, 2005, p. 564). *Affinity Networks* are all around us. We find them as networking groups, clubs, religious institutions, and even individuals coming together to raise money and awareness for charities. *Affinity Networks* are the most basic level of an *Open Organization* we can find and are the most naturally occurring.

The *Boundaryless* organization is more permeable and flexible between vertical and horizontal organizational silos, not to mention connections with external stakeholders and bridges across geographic divides (Hesselbein and Goldsmith, p. 167). *Boundaryless* organizations are less easily identified because there appears to be no distinct boundaries or distinct members of the organization. Wikipedia is a good example of a *Boundaryless* organization in that most anyone can contribute as many times as they wish. These contributions are made across multiple barriers and cultural silos to achieve an *Open* encyclopedia.

The *Flat* organization is high on horizontal differentiations and low on vertical differentiations, or rather, there are fewer middle managers to coordinate between the top executives and the lower levels in the organization (Burton, et al., pp. 71–72). W.L. Gore is an example of a *Flat* organization with only three layers. *Flat* organizations still contain many of the hallmarks of a traditional hierarchy, except the distance between top decision-maker and workers is minimized and the upper-level leadership is more likely to empower mid- and lower-level workers to get the job done.

The *Matrix Organization* is a "grid-like" structure that allows a company to address multiple business dimensions using multiple command structures (Sy and D'Anninzio, 2005, p. 40). The *Matrix Organization* still maintains a certain level of rigidity as found in the more traditional organization structure. *Matrix Organization* structures are comprised of multiple business dimensions and are not only focused on product and function, but also deal with geographic differences (Sy and D'Anninzio, p. 40). Dell, Inc. is a *Matrix Organization*. It has multiple business dimensions (consumer, enterprise, and government) and must deal with many geographic differences. The *Matrix Organization* allows companies to leverage vast resources while staying small and task-oriented (Sy and D'Anninzio, p. 40). In visiting the Nashville Dell offices, you will find several floors of a call center. Each floor is configured in rows with a team leader at the end of each row. While workers have specified jobs, they are also given the freedom to wander about the complex and to visit other teams to get their work done. An employee working in the consumer division can visit the enterprise division to help a consumer who is setting up a small business. This cross-pollination within the organization is designed to meet the needs of the client by permitting the workers from within to cross organizational silos to get their work done. They do not need to follow a chain of command but are permitted to go straight to the source of their need without having to check in with their supervisor at every turn.

Scalable

An *Open Organization* must be *Scalable*. *Scalable* refers to the extent to which a system, component, or process is able to expand and contract with the needs of the organization (LINFO, 2007). *Scalability* describes how easy it is to expand the organization's business model and grow revenues significantly without equally increasing fixed costs (Liu, 2013). Because an *Open Organization* is an agile flexible system, the organization must be able to expand and contract with market conditions. An *Open Organization* should be able to grow in size and number without altering the structure of the organization's *Governance, First Principles*, or level of *Openness* which had previously made the organization the success it has become. When an *Open Organization* experiences growth, it should seek to maintain equilibrium and stay true to its roots of *Openness*. Without *Scalability* an *Open System* would naturally progress toward a closed system. *Scalability* coupled with the organization's *Governance* and *First Principles* are the fulcrum from which equilibrium is maintained.

Creating a *Scalable* organization doesn't come easy and figuring out ways to streamline, to improve the process, to grow the company as you grow your employees is a constant struggle for an *Open Organization*, requiring continual evaluation (Holman, 2011f). *Scalability* requires constant monitoring and adjustment by everyone within the system. As the organization grows, the workflow may not always work the same for 1,000 employees as it did for a few hundred. What must remain are the core values and ideas of the organization. Once you figure out your core values, you will likely need to adapt and refine them over time as your organization grows. Maintaining *Scalability* is required by everyone, not just a select few within the organization. While the founder/CEO might play a part in evangelizing the organization's *First Principles*, it is up to the entire organization to adjust processes and systems as the organization grows.

Creating a *Scalable* organization requires constant evaluation and definition of who you are as an organization. *Scaling* correctly requires the organization to constantly maintain the values and beliefs. These values and beliefs are originally developed by the founders and instilled in the staff as the organization grows. Essential to the idea of *Scalability* is in hiring people who not only possess the appropriate skillset for the job but also have a personality that meshes with the companies culture (DaSilva, 2013).

Culture

People have a desire to be accepted by their peers, have friendships, be part of a group, and be loved. In the organization, these needs influence the desire for good relationships with co-workers, participation in a work team, and a positive relationship with supervisors (Daft, 2002, p. 280). However, overcoming cultural barriers creates challenges in nearly any business environment.

Operating an *Open Organization* within a global context adds new layers and challenges related to languages, customs, values, traditions, and laws. Challenging these barriers will certainly create friction and can affect our ability to listen and understand the viewpoints on those we lead. Lack of understanding creates frustration, mistakes, and deters trust and relationship building between the leader and their followers. Learning local customs and language is helpful; however there is no easy fix to these barriers. Creating greater understanding through language is the mechanism that helps people organize their perceptions and shape their worldviews (Hackman and Johnson, p. 297). A global leader's ability to connect people and build successful teams in a cross-cultural environment is a crucial competency with the *Organization 3.0* era (Johnson, 2012). In dealing with cross-cultural communication we must acknowledge that communication encompasses not only words and actions, but also all types of non-verbal communication and patterns of interaction in society at large (Eisenberg and Goodall, 2004, p. 139). Building a cross-cultural relationship requires an ability to process or decode information from our environment as well as learning to encode by effectively conveying messages and taking the most appropriate actions to overcome problems (Northouse, p. 165). The ideal scenario for any cross-cultural organization would be the creation of synergy by which decision-makers draw on the diversity of the group to produce a new, better than expected solution (Hackman and Johnson, p. 305).

In considering cross-cultural patterns within an organization, power–distance is an important attribute to consider in the development of a cross-cultural communication strategy within an *Open Organization*. Power–distance is the extent to which the less powerful members of institutions and organizations within a culture expect and accept that power is distributed unequally (Tamas, 2007). All societies are unequal and within High power–distance cultures, the inequality is considered to be a natural part of their world while in contrast, Low power–distance cultures are uncomfortable with differences in wealth, status, power, and privilege (Hackman and Johnson, p. 302). Power–distance, specifically High power–distance cultures, can become a barrier to the successful operation of an *Open Organization* as they do not accept the equal distribution of power. An *Open Organization* requires little power–distance between leaders and followers. The greater the distance between a leader and their followers, the closer the supervision of the follower's activities and the less *Open* an organization becomes (Hackman and Johnson, p. 302). Followers in High power–distance countries expect managers to give direction and feel uncomfortable when asked to participate in decision-making (Hackman and Johnson, p. 302). This creates a challenge in an *Open*

Organization where followers are expected to make their own decisions with little input from leadership. Organizations operating in Low power–distance countries are less centralized and distribute rewards more equally (Hackman and Johnson, p. 302). Low power–distance cultures, by nature, have an easier time developing and operating within the context of an *Open System*.

There is a danger in hiring only like-minded workers. When we consider homogeneity, we must focus on skillset first, and then culture (DaSilva). An *Open Organization* culture is about work/life balance, commitment to excellence, and a shared passion you have in the work that you do (DaSilva). Culture is that thing that organizations must protect as the organization *Scales* up and down with the market conditions. People come and go, it is the core values of the organization that must withstand the test of time.

Optimizing for *Happiness*

When was the last time you played? Why is it that we stop having recess when we reach a certain age? What we are discovering is that we have to learn to play again … to have fun and unfetter our creative imaginations. It is for these very reasons that *Happiness* is emerging as a crucial element of how innovatively an organization will compete in their future work environment. *Happiness* is not just a theory. A recent study of Americans showed that nearly 45 percent said that having work they enjoy is their greatest professional priority (Brooks, 2013).

The idea of optimizing for *Happiness* is completely counter to the traditional organizational structures which say you are here to do a job and not to have fun. *Happiness* encompasses many elements and speaks to the

> *30 percent of the 100 million American workers who work full-time are actively engaged in their work.*
>
> *Gallup Polling*

followers in different ways. While it seems counterintuitive to our training, playing at work—recess if you will—has a profound impact on the organization's human capital. *Happiness* is very much important to how we engage the Millennial generation. But optimizing your organization for *Happiness* is not just a Millennial issue. *Happiness* increases productivity, stimulates creativity, and makes employees more willing to take risks (Kreamer, 2013). Evidence appears to indicate that employees that like what they are doing and where they are doing it are far more productive and most likely to stay loyal to their organization. What we are really talking about is the way we motivate human capital to work. *Happiness* is about tapping into an individual's intrinsic motivators. Intrinsic motivators are those things that make us love what we do and therefore we find ways to do them well (Morrison, 2013). Happy employees are productive employees. If this fun and *Happiness* is authentic; if everyone in the business has a role to play in the overall culture; and fun is owned and fostered by all people in the business, *Happiness* can deliver amazing results (Simson, 2013). It is for these reasons that we should begin to create organizations optimized for *Happiness*.

According to Gallup's 2013 State of American Workplace Report, only 30 percent of the 100 million American workers who work full time are actively engaged in their work (Southward, 2013). This is staggering considering that unhappy workers cost billions in lost productivity every year (Simson). As workers disengage from their work, organizations must find new and compelling ways to create a culture of engagement and *Happiness*. Organizations that do not find effective ways to engage their workforce will experience lost productivity to the tune of $450 billion to $550 billion annually (Southward). Organizations are finding that they must create a culture optimized for *Happiness*. Engaged employees are more profitable, more customer-focused, safer, more likely to stick around and have 20 percent higher profits (Simson). With a diminishing workforce, organizations can no longer afford to operate with a 30 percent engagement rate.

Optimizing for *Happiness* means that the organization is more focused on creating *Happiness* in its human capital than in creating wealth for its shareholders. This is counterintuitive to the classic business structures of the past two centuries. Under the classic model of business, the purpose of business is to optimize the investment of the shareholders and to create wealth. The *Open Organization* begins to recognize that focusing on wealth alone is no longer sustainable. Focusing on the *Happiness* of the organization's human capital translates into greater creativity, innovation, and profitability.

Happiness resonates at many different levels. What we are beginning to understand is that when people feel cared for and their contributions matter they become more engaged in the creative process (Rothwell and Sullivan, p. 655). When they feel respected and are asked to contribute, it is amazing how much more creative people become (Rothwell and Sullivan, p. 655). But *Happiness* is much more than creativity and the generation of novel ideas. *Happiness* is measured by how much fun an individual is having doing their work. An idea of an *Open Organization* is to create a workplace where people can have fun and want to work (P2P Foundation, 2011a).

For some, *Happiness* is generated when they are permitted to work on or *hack* on side projects. *Hacking* is a relatively new term which is typically associated with the activity of breaking into a secure computer for the purpose of exploiting the computer and/or information. *Hacking on the side* refers to the activity of working on a side project that may or may not have anything to do with the work that an employee typically engages in. GitHub allows its employees to *hack* on a side project that may or may not become a market-viable product. Some of the *hacking* done at GitHub is much more like playing. One of the cool toys at GitHub is a 3D printer, which allows users to create interesting items on the printer.

Happiness is really just about four things: perceived control, perceived progress, connectedness (number and depth of your relationship), and vision/meaning (being part of something bigger than yourself) (Hsieh, 2010, pp. 232–233). *Happiness* creates a positive mood and increases the level of flexible decision-making and analytical precision (Kreamer). As we learned with GitHub, optimizing for *Happiness* covers many areas of human capital engagement. One such area is linked to work hours. The *Open Organization Model* abandons the notion of clocking hours and redirects itself to accomplishing objectives. Rigid schedules and time constraints no longer work within the global marketplace and affect the employee and their level of *Happiness* (Pozin, 2013). It is argued that setting specific work hours deemphasizes the work objectives and ties their success to their work hours rather than their ability to meet their goals and objectives. In the era of the *Open Organization* productivity is not tied to the presence of an employee (Pozin). Employee presence does not necessarily equal a more productive employee. GitHub has over 200 employees spread across the globe and multiple time zones. Work is expected to be completed regardless of geographic location. With the advent of high-speed Internet connection, email, video conferencing, and an emerging global marketplace, presence is no longer a measurement of successful human capital.

GitHub not only illustrates for us the abandonment of work hours, but also the embrace of the work-anywhere office. In the world of an *Open Organization*, the office becomes as flexible as the employee's imagination. Organizations in the 1990s began to understand that remote jobbing was a serious way of eliminating commuting time and thus increasing productivity. However, remote or flexible work locations are not for everyone. Some employees may prefer social interaction that working at the organization's physical location can provide (Gordon, 1991, p. 634).

The *Open Organization* seeks to employ individuals who are passionate about their work. One way to engage them is to let them do their work in the ways they see fit (Pozin). The main reason for this is that individuals rarely are able to fit their tasks into a 9 to 5 schedule, therefore forcing them to focus on the number of hours they must clock rather than on meeting their goals (Pozin). As with GitHub, an *Open Organization* allows employees to determine where they work and for how long. Putting an employee on the clock compels clock-watching and induces the need for the employee to exit as soon as the clock strikes 5pm. (Pozin). Changing the way we address the organization's standard work hours will require a cultural shift, but a shift that is known to reap benefits of increased flexibility and autonomy (Pozin). *Happiness* is not about appeasement, but about engaging human capital in the most logically way possible, through their intrinsic needs.

Decision-Making

It is impossible for leadership of any organization to be everywhere all the time. What we are discovering is that complex agile systems require individuals who are willing to take risks and make decisions. This requires leadership that is willing to embrace and bestow explicit decision-making power to the members of the organization. Decisions within an *Open Organization* are decentralized and made via *Adhocracy*. Warren Bennis coined *Adhocracy* to characterize organizations that are temporary by design and are best suited to the performance of complex and uncertain tasks in a turbulent environment (Morgan, p. 50). *Adhocracies, Affinity Networks, Virtual Teams*, crowdsourcing, and other *Egalitarian* methods are emerging in the workspace today. Organizational agility is tied to the organization's ability to draw individuals together to perform tasks for a given purpose. In some cases, once a project is completed, individuals will regroup in other teams devoted to other projects (Morgan, p. 50–51).

While *Adhocracies* are most common in innovative electronics and high-tech firms, the idea of *Open* is not for the tech field alone (Morgan, p. 51). At its core, the *Open Organization* seeks to normalize *Adhocracy* in many differing silos of business and industry. In its most basic form it sometimes emerges as a differentiated unit of a larger organization: for example, an ad hoc task group or project team performing a limited assignment or contributing to the strategic planning and development of the organization as a whole. It is also frequently used in research and development (Morgan, p. 51). The *Open Organization*, through *Adhocracy*, uses a variety of ad hoc or temporary liaison devices (tasks forces, integrating roles, project teams, and crowdsourcing) along with a flexible structure that can respond to a complex, changing environment (Gordon, 1991, pp. 527–528). The *Open Organization* capitalizes on the skills, abilities, and personal attributes of available human capital. Their activities are highly relationship-oriented and in all cases there is a high level of transparency and accountability amongst the members of the *Open System*.

The central attribute in decision-making within The *Open Organization* is the level of autonomy given to the members of the system. Autonomy has to be bestowed upon the members through empowerment by the organization's leadership. Because of this empowerment, the *Open Organization* breaks free the bonds of the traditional top-down organization through autonomy thereby increasing the levels of empowerment within the workforce. Autonomy indicates the degree to which a job provides freedom and discretion in scheduling the work and determining work methods (Cummings and Worley, p. 106). In the most general of context, autonomy refers to the amount of independence, freedom, and discretion given to employees to schedule and perform tasks (Cummings and Worley, p. 346). When we examine GitHub, we find a high degree of autonomy in that employees can choose when they go to work, how they complete their work, and on which projects they focus their attention. What we find within an *Open Organization*, and in the case of GitHub specifically, is that employees are more likely to experience responsibility for their work outcomes when high amounts of autonomy exist (Cummings and Worley, p. 346). An *Open Organization* connects super-smart, super-talented individuals in a free-wheeling, innovative environment with no bosses, no middle management, and no bureaucracy; just highly motivated peers coming together to create awesome (Valve, 2013). Decision-making connects with the knowledge of the working. Hiring very smart people and then releasing them to do some really awesome things is the essence of the *Open Organization*.

> *It's amazing what creative people can come up with when there's nobody there telling them what to do.*
>
> *Valve Corporation*

For the classically trained manager, extoling higher levels of autonomy on their employees may seem foreign and counterintuitive to their command-and-control, top-down training. Despite the discomfort, employees are growing to expect more autonomy in doing their jobs and more participation in making decisions related to their jobs (Yun, et al., 2006, p. 381). The more complex the business environment becomes, the less a leader can expect to accomplish all that needs to be done on their own. No longer can a manager afford to micromanage their followers. Leaders must find new and innovative ways to empower their workforce to meet the demands before them. In this new era, the leaders of an *Open Organization* view their members as highly motivated, creative, intelligent, and talented individuals who come together to collaborate on projects and to achieve objectives. These talented members care more about having control over their flexibility and when they believe they have some level of control, or options, in setting priorities and organizational support, they are happier, more loyal, and more productive (Benko and Weisberg, 2007, p. 88). Happier, more loyal employees make better decision-makers.

The very definition of an *Open Organization* calls for collaboration throughout the organization and its decision-making process. An *Open Organization* presupposes the presence of a high level of trust, honesty, *Openness*, and respect. To effectively collaborate requires a consensus on the part of subordinates to work together toward a given goal. Such consensus has three components: (1) each group member has the opportunity to present his/her perspective; (2) the group systematically structures and evaluates multiple options; and (3) everyone commits to implementing the group's preferred course of action (Keidel, 1995, p. 89). Consensus however is not the same as unanimous consent. Consensus means moving ahead by "no objection" (Cleveland, p. 224). If no one in the group speaks up, then it is implied that there is agreement within the group. Consensus decision-making follows several guidelines (Awad and Ghaziri, 2010, p. 211):

1. Differences of opinions are viewed as helpful not harmful.

2. Make sure everyone is heard from and feels listened to.

3. Approach a decision on the basis of logic and common sense.

4. Listen to what is being proposed and understand its reasoning.

5. Avoid changing one's mind simply to reach agreement, especially when running short on time.

6. Avoid pushing for an agreement by calling for a majority vote.

7. Do not assume that someone must win and someone must lose.

Within the *Open Organization*, collaboration has two equally important strengths: it brings multiple perspectives and resources to bear on an issue or decision or problem, and it virtually guarantees that the group or team will be committed to implementation (Keidel, pp. 89–90). However, it is difficult to bring together many differing perspectives and to create change without a high degree of trust. Trust is a central issue in human relationships and without it you cannot get things done (Kouzes and Posner, 2002, p. 244). To achieve greater collaboration, individuals must set aside their egos and trust one another and share their expertise willingly (Ferrazzi, 2012). Collaboration becomes a selfless act of giving and growing within the context of the *Open Organization*.

Decision-making in an *Open Organization* is about workers coming together to collaborate and solve complex problems. This effort gives rise to a sense of group IQ—the sum total of the abilities, skills, and savvy of all those included in the group (Awad and Ghaziri, p. 345). Members of the *Open Organization* are typically hired for their knowledge and abilities. Thus, a high group IQ (and highly productive team) in social harmony demonstrated when the team brings in a pool of talent (*Knowledge Workers*) and skills (verbal skills, creativity, empathy), has an effective leader, establishes order and discipline in the way the group approaches problems, and provides emotional support through the process (Awad and Ghaziri, p. 345). While high group IQ is important to the overall success of the organization, the group cannot lose sight of the fact that tension in the decision-making process is important to maintaining the highest degree of *Openness*.

One of the greatest perils of a collaborative environment can be the tendency toward *Groupthink*, when "concurrence seeking" becomes so dominant in group dynamics that it overrides realistic appraisals of alternative courses of action (Schoemaker, 2002, p. 163). *Groupthink* evolves in teams that must build a strong bond with each other to carry out tasks so that they may potentially place a higher priority on cohesion rather than on effective problem solving and peak performance (Hackman and Johnson, p. 214). Groups that suffer from such a syndrome fail to consider all the alternatives, reexamine a course of action when it doesn't seem to be working, gather additional information, weigh the risks of their choices, work out contingency plans, or discuss important ethical issues (Hackman and Johnson, p. 214). Members of an *Open Source* organization should be encouraged to be critical evaluators and even assign individual members the role of *Devil's Advocate* to argue against prevailing opinion (Hackman and Johnson, p. 215). Avoiding *Groupthink* is one of the keys to success of an *Open Organization*. Teams should divide into subgroups on a regular basis and then negotiate any differences to develop a consensus. Once a group consensus is reached the members should be given as many chances to express doubts about the solution as needed (Hackman and Johnson, p. 215).

The decision-making process may include tension between one or more *Knowledge Workers* as they work through the best possible solution. Conflict in a group can serve as a catalyst for a group member to step in and take responsibility for resolving the situation (Kuczmarski and Kuczmarski, 1995, p. 196). It is this tension that maintains the natural order or balance of things within the *Open Organization*. GitHub is transparent in their admission that they have a lot of conflict in the process of collaborating on projects. Diversity within a team can be a source of creativity as well as contribute to a healthy level of conflict that leads to better decision-making (Daft, 2004, p. 367). Conflict itself helps prevent *Groupthink*. But conflict can also come in the form of an individual who abuses their freedom, underperforms, or is constantly at odds with their colleagues.

While an *Open Organization* operates within the confines of complexity and sometimes conflict, there are certain rules of engagement for the process of conflict resolution. Because decision-making is shared with all members of the team, the fate of an employee will then rest in the hands of the team. The team may resolve to censure an employee through the extraordinary process of exclusion. Exclusion is the result of an individual or group who repeatedly does not fulfill their commitments and are thereby excluded from current and/or future tasks by the group or organization as a whole (P2P Foundation, 2011a). If an individual underperforms on a regular basis, the members of the organization can elect to release the individual from employment (off-boarding). Exclusion is not taken lightly within the organization.

Equifinality

The *Open Organization* embraces the idea of *Equifinality* or the concept that there may be many different ways of arriving at a given solution (Morgan, p. 41). This differs from the traditional hierarchical closed system which is managed through fixed structures and process patterns of achieving a specified goal (Morgan, p. 41). In fact, *Taylorism* itself was an idea that workflow should be approached scientifically and that the most effective way to complete a task is through a well-designed process. An *Open Organization* takes a different view of workflows and human capital. The organization must be flexible to allow the achievement of specific results from different starting points with different resources in different ways (Morgan, p. 41). The *Open Organization* requires we step outside of the classical view of leadership and organizational efficiencies with an open-mind to new possibilities.

Equifinality embraces Bertalanffy's principle that an organization can attain the same goal from different starting points and by a variety of paths and methodologies (Burke, p. 48). Systems and contingency theories suggest that there is no universal best way to design an organization (Cummings and Worley, p. 87). When individuals are permitted to enter into the organizational decision-making process from different angles, it creates what I will call a three-dimensional approach to problem solving thereby permitting the organization to view a problem from a 360 degree view. A closed system, on the other hand requires individuals to view, approach, and solve a problem from the view of one given vantage point and timeframe.

Equifinality explains why there is no one-size-fits-all approach to lead or manage an organization and no one right way to guide organizational change (Authenticity Consulting, n.d. (b), p. 144). The concept of *Equifinality* empowers the members of an organization to approach problems with creativity and to find new and innovative solutions. *Equifinality* is one of the secret ingredients to an *Open Organizational* structure.

The *Matrix*

In Chapter 4 we introduced the structure and complexity of the *Open Organization*. The idea of the *Open Organization* is described in many different ways such as: *Flat, Agile, Managerless, Leaderless,* and *Matrix*. We would be remised in writing about the concept of *Open* without addressing the *Matrix* and its contribution to the *Open Organization* structural concept. By its simplest definition, the *Matrix* is a grid-like organization structure that allows a company to address multiple business dimensions using, multiple command structures (Sy and D'Anninzio, p. 40). The *Matrix Organization* emerged from the aerospace industry in the 1960s and is comprised of multiple business dimensions (Sy and D'Anninzio, p. 40). The term *Matrix Organization* was coined to capture a visual impression or organizations that systematically attempt to combine the kind of functional or departmental structure of organization found in bureaucracy with a project–team structure (Morgan, p. 51).

Matrix-based organizational structures are attempts to combine the advantages of the functional structure (emphasizing the vertical) and the product/service structure (emphasizing the horizontal) (Beitler, 2006, p. 110). *Matrix Organizations* appear to be the natural progression from a more rigid hierarchy to a more *Open* concept of organizational structure. Organizations such as Dell, W.L. Gore and Semco are all illustration of a *Matrix Organization*.

A primary challenge in operating in *Matrix Organizations* is aligning goals among many different dimensions. Dimensions can refer to functions, products, customers or geographic regions, among others (Sy and D'Anninzio, p. 42).

While there are multiple advantages for *Matrix* structures, this structure makes specialized, functional knowledge, and skills available to all projects and promotes the flexible use of organizational talent (Beitler, p. 110). *Matrix Organizations*, while maintaining a structured appearance, permit individuals from one location within the organization, regardless of position, to interact with other members elsewhere in the organization regardless of their positions within the *Matrix*. *Matrix* and other team-based organizations provide a means of breaking down the barriers between specialisms and allowing members from different functional backgrounds to fuse their skills and abilities in an attack on common problems (Morgan, p. 51–52). A *Matrix* is a collaborative form of organization that structurally improves coordination by balancing the power between competing aspects of the organization, installing systems, and developing roles designed to achieve multiple objectives simultaneously through dual systems, roles, controls, and rewards (Nadler and Tushman, p. 99–100).

The *Matrix* structure is best when environmental change is high and when goals reflect a dual requirement, such as for both product and functional goals (Daft, 2001, p. 47). Making the *Matrix* work requires ensuring that the roles of the project and functional managers are clear (Gordon, 1991b, p. 524). *Matrix Organizations* also facilitate innovation—both new-to-the-world and line extensions—by encouraging collaboration at the intersections of brand, geography, and function (Galioto, et al., 2006, p. 2). A high-functioning *Matrix Organization* enables an enterprise perspective on performance, trends, and investment priorities while highlighting select growth opportunities around the world—opportunities that might have been previously overlooked (Galioto, et al., p. 3). *Matrix Organizations* facilitate innovation, enable disciplined execution, and help companies negotiate the inevitable trade-offs that attend managing a highly complex, multifaceted global business (Galioto, et al., p. 8).

The *Matrix* is but one expression of an *Open Organization* structure or model. Other structures might be expressed as *Lattice, Star, Web, Rational,* or even *Natural Systems.*

Matrix Guardian

One of the arguments against an *Open Organization* focuses on the importance of measuring performance. Classically trained leaders and shareholders look toward performance measurements or metrics such as return on investment (ROI), market share, and profitability. These remain important elements of any enterprise. Because of the *Flat*, self-led focus of an *Open Organization*, there still needs to be a mechanism for tracking the performance metrics of the organization. Without these performance metrics, organizations will find it difficult to spot problems and take the necessary steps to fix them (Sy and D'Anninzio, p. 45). Therefore an *Open Organization* can engage a *Matrix Guardian* to monitor key attributes of organizational health. This can be the role of one or more individuals within the *Open* structure. A *Matrix Guardian* works to ensure that each of the teams is established, roles and boundaries are clarified, and lateral connections are fostered and supported (Kates and Galbraith, 2007, p. 125). A *Matrix Guardian* can be an individual or group of individuals who monitor and then report their findings through the organization's *Knowledge Commons*.

The *Matrix Guardian's* role is to help the organization develop and maintain the *Governance* and *First Principles* of the organization. The *Matrix Guardian* engages all of the members of the organization to help craft the essential elements and guidelines under which everyone will agree to operate. The *Matrix Guardian* does not act authoritatively but is the binding agent that brings all parties together to collectively agree on how things will be done.

Meritocracy

More than ever a great deal of attention is given in the press to the *Managerless, Leaderless, Agile, Flat, Flexible, Open Organizational* structure. Whatever we call it, the landscape of organization structure is changing. The days of top-down, formal, rigid structures are numbered for many and the era of *Meritocracy* has arrived. Websters (Meritocracy, 2001) defines a *Meritocracy* as a group of people whose progress is based on ability and talent rather than on class privilege or wealth.

My thesis for some time has been that the way we do business, the way we treat human capital is broken. The people doing the work know better how to do their jobs than the leaders dictating the way the work is to be done. The *Open Organization* values and provides public feedback, both positive and negative, on contributions and contributors (Yeaton, 2012). When we begin to listen to our employees, a new dynamic enters. Structures are weakened and human capital is strengthened through empowerment. In this process, recognition of one's contributions can be in the form of individual comments and feedback; while some organizations have created an infrastructure for the organization to provide recognition of achievements (Yeaton). The *Open Organization* lives and breathes because of the *Open* flow of information.

In the case of an *Open Organization* or *Meritocracy*, members are rewarded based on their own intrinsic motivators and therefore their contributions to the organization. Some are rewarded by completing something cool and some by being part of something bigger than themselves.

Holacracy

In late 2013 Zappos made news when it announced that it was evolving into a *Holacracy*. The term *Holacracy* is derived from the Greek word *Holon*, which means a whole that's part of a greater whole (Groth, 2014). *Holacratic* organizations are clustered in circles where workers are members of several circles depending on what they are working on at a given time (Ross, 2014). *Holacracies* operate in the same manner as any other *Flat, Open System*. Decision authority is still distributed throughout the organization, with everyone focused on the core purpose and strategy (Ross). In the end Zappos will have done away with any formal structure, titles, and managers. *Holacracies* presume that leaders will cede some level of power in their organization in order for the structure to work.

Holacracies are based off the structural idea of cities. In cities people are self-organizing and Zappos is attempting to recreate the same efficiencies as they grow. The thinking, according to John Brunch of Zappos, is that when cities double in size, innovation and productivity per resident grows by 15 percent (Ross). When an organization doubles in size, innovation and productivity per employee actually goes down (Ross). At full implementation in December 2014 it is expected that there will be around 400 circles and employees will have any number of roles within those circles (Groth). A *Holacracy* is just another method of *Open*. The advantages of this and other *Open Systems* is that its members get to work in a radically transparent, politically-free, quickly-evolving purpose-driven organization. A *Holacracy* is about creating a structure in which people have flexibility to pursue what they are passionate about (Groth). Like most *Open Organizational* structures, *Holacracies* were immediately dismissed as another spin on self-directed, managerless work team models of the 1980s. *Open Systems* such as the *Holacracy* continue to challenge the conventional management hierarchy as they do not fit into our general understanding of how organizations should operate.

The structure and rules of a *Holacracy* are very specific and are broken into five general areas (HolacracyOne, 2013):

1. **Energizing Roles:** A Energizing Role is Holacracy's core building block for organizational structure. Energizing Roles covers the basic authorities and duties conveyed to a partner filling a role.

2. **Circle Structure:** A circle contains and integrates many roles. The Circle Structure describes how a circle is structured, and how the roles within it are assigned, elected, or formed into further sub-circles.

3. **Governance Process:** A circle's Governance Process is used to define its roles and policies. The Governance Process defines this process and the ground rules for proposing changes or objecting to proposals.

4. **Operational Process:** The members of a circle rely on each other to help get their operational work done. The Operational Process covers the duties of circle members with respect to supporting one another, and how tactical meetings work.

5. **Adoption Matters:** Adoption Matters deals with the transition from pre-*Holacracy* to operating under this Constitution, and provides rules when adopting *Holacracy* within a board structure with a group of representatives in lieu of a single Lead Link.

Open Systems such as a *Holacracy* are difficult to describe because they are not what we traditionally understand a corporate hierarchy to be. Traditionally, when we think about corporate hierarchy, we are thinking about a management system where the power is held by a person who will typically delegate from the "top" (Bowers). In an *Open Organization* there is no management hierarchy and we describe it as *Flat* or *Agile* and the power is held by roles, not people, and those roles are empowered through the organization's *Governance* process and not from a boss (Bowers). Understanding an *Open System* requires that we begin to throw out traditional understandings of what an organizational structure is and how it might act. What we know is that it is very difficult for many to wrap their minds around the concepts of *Open*. The *Open Organization* like anything takes practice and requires discipline to achieve the desired state of operational effectiveness.

Chapter 5

First Principles

Perhaps one of the most interesting elements of an *Open Organization* comes from the concept of *First Principles*. An *Open Organization* offers a sense of community and the application of *First Principles* is the test of whether the organization talks or acts like the community it espouses to be (Brafman and Beckstrom, pp. 94–95). An *Open Organization* is *Egalitarian*; meaning that everyone is treated equally and are included equally in the process of developing the organization's *First Principles*. Without absolute inclusion of all members of the organization, *First Principles* become nothing more than edicts from on-high. Inclusivity in processes means that everyone belongs and differing viewpoints are not only encouraged but needed for the system to work effectively (Daft, 2002, p. 261). In an *Open Organization* there is free and unfettered access to information and knowledge throughout the entire organization.

First Principles have their roots in the fields of mathematics and philosophy. They are the core values that tell the members of the organization what is important in the organization and what deserves their attention (Cummings and Worley, p. 503). These principles are tied to the organization's culture or set of values, guiding beliefs, and ways of thinking that are shared by members of the organization and are taught to new members (Daft, 2004, p. 601). *First Principles* are the embodiment of the values and culture the founders and members believe to be true. An organization develops a value system/ culture based on their actions and behaviors and thus requires explicit and clear principles (ISACA, 2003). These values must be set by the organization's leadership in terms of the organization's mission, goals, attitudes toward stakeholders, business tactics, internal controls, risk, ethics, sustainability, and the degree of social conscience (ISACA). These values should then permeate the *Open Organization* and are constantly evidenced in behaviors, attitudes, priorities, annual reports, public relations, ad campaigns, and slogans, in the products and just about everywhere else (ISACA).

First Principles are much more than the organization's mission statement or goal. *First Principles*, the organization's ultimate irrefutable truths, are about constantly asking fundamental questions and then measuring the answer against the organization's defined *First Principles*. In essence the *First Principles* of an *Open Organization* are about the things that can be generalized and looked at time and time again, regardless of when you do something (Sculley, 2011). The *First Principles* offer a framework for the organization and its aim is to represent a set of values and practices for the organization to engage (P2P Foundation, 2008).

GitHub defines their culture on *First Principles* such as goals, purpose, and the overall focus of the organization. They are constantly testing their actions against their *First Principles*. Everything they do can be linked back to those shared beliefs. *First Principles* are deeply imbedded in their culture. If there is any question as to whether the organization should proceed in a particular direction, it is tested against their *First Principles*. These *First Principles* act as the rules for conflict, decision-making, and the overall direction of the organization. GitHub is very much an *Egalitarian* organization and these *First Principles* are observed by everyone in the company. There are no exceptions to this rule. For many *Open Organizations*, *First Principles* are one of the few constraints that are placed on the entire organization from its inception.

First Principles are about creating and sustaining organizational culture through core values. For example, at iAcquire, a digital marketing agency founded in 2009 with over 100 employees, their core values or *First Principles* are defined in the form of an acronym CRAFT (DaSilva):

- **Creativity:** Creativity and out-of-the-box thinking fosters innovation. iAcquire selects and develops team members who challenge the status quo.

- **Responsibility:** We honor our clients and take it upon ourselves to always deliver results.

- **Acumen:** Talent and expertise with every engagement as a strategic partner to clients.

- **Fortitude:** We stand up for our beliefs in the face of challenge or adversity. We use times of challenge as a platform for growth.

- **Transparency:** We believe in being honest and *Open* with our clients, partners, and employees.

It is important to note that *First Principles* are not the same as goals. While goals are designed to help keep an organization focused on a stated achievement, *First Principles* can be described as the fulcrum from which the organizational ecosystem finds balance. Goals will typically change over time while an organization's *First Principles* are meant to remain, for the most part, static. *First Principles* are the prevailing approach of an *Open Organization* and are the soul and core Guiding Principles of the organization. An organization's *First Principles* are the foundation on which everything else stands. It is the default question that everyone must ask as often as needed. For example, Steve Jobs's *First Principles* were: "no compromises; the hardest decisions is what you leave out, not what you put in; the user experience is the most important part of the product experience" (Sculley). *First Principles* find their way into every conversation and decision made in an *Open Organization*. GitHub's *First Principles* ask simply, "What are we trying to do and what is our core reason for doing it?" These fundamental questions should be asked as often as needed.

Zappos offers another example of *First Principles*. Their *First Principles* are summed up in 10 Family Core Values which are (Zappos, 2012): (1) Deliver Wow through service, (2) Embrace and drive change, (3) Create fun and a little weirdness, (4) Be adventurous, creative, and open-minded, (5) Pursue growth and learning, (6) Build *Open* and honest relationships with communication, (7) Build a positive team and family spirit, (8) Do more with less, (9) Be passionate and determined, and (10) Be humble. These core values or *First Principles* at Zappos are attributed to their reason for hitting their goals. In fact, they define these as part of their competitive advantage (Hsieh, p. 137).

Zappos Core Values

Deliver Wow through service,

Embrace and drive change,

Create fun and a little weirdness,

Be adventurous, creative, and open-minded,

Pursue growth and learning,

Build Open *and honest relationships with communication,*

Build a positive team and family spirit,

Do more with less,

Be passionate and determined, and

Be humble

First Principles are essentially a mechanism for the social structure of the organization in which they begin to affect behavior only as they enter into decisions about how to behave (Scott, 1998, p. 17, 50). *First Principles* are a set of emotional rules of the *Open Organization* that are not violated by members. Members who violate them are likely to be censured by the group. These principles are as important today as they were on day one. We could argue that, like Steve Jobs, these *First Principles* are sacred to the organization and the direction in which it moves. *First Principles* are the litmus test to ensure that the members of the organization are abiding by the organization's irrefutable truths. *First Principles* stand for the fundamental assumptions on which the organization's procedures are thought to be based (First Principles, 2013). In essence they become core assumptions that serve as a foundation for more complex ideas in which we build our beliefs and preferences (DeGraff, 2011).

First Principles are designed to guide an organization toward a specific course of thought and action when confronted with complex and ambiguous situations (DeGraff). They are used to keep the organization on task and on path. *First Principles* should inform and even drive what we think and what we do (DeGraff). Google is known to have *First Principles* which state "Don't be evil." Like Steve Jobs, Zappos, and Google, it is through these *First Principles* that we begin to recognize our opportunities to develop pathways for growth and that they hold true for both organizations and individuals, differing only in scope and scale but not in the nature of the process (DeGraff). *First Principles* are not meant to limit the scope and scale of reach by the organization. They can be built upon and expanded as the organization progresses. One of the *First Principles* of Steve Jobs was that Apple would make "insanely great" products (Lashinsky, 2012, p. 90).

While the use of *First Principles* is an emerging concept that is certainly adoptable by non-*Open Organizations*, it is a critical tipping point that delineates an organization as *Open*. Organizations that adopt and faithfully live by *First Principles* become the anchor from which an organization truly manifests itself as an *Open Organization*. Developing *First Principles* requires vision and absolute adoption throughout the organization. An *Open Organization* should develop a set of *First Principles* that are (Wideman, 2003):

1.   universal to all areas of the organization;

2.   capable of straight forward expression in one or two sentences;

3.   self-evident to others; and

4.   carry a concise label reflecting its content.

Developing *First Principles* takes time and effort from everyone in the organization. Defining an organization's *First Principles* is important to the running of a successful *Open Organization* because if you don't define what you believe in, someone else will do it for you (Sugar, 2010). Without a set of *First Principles* an *Open Organization* becomes nothing more than an incubator of chaos. These *First Principles* become the tension point that keeps the system balanced and aligned. For an organization's *First Principles* to be effective, they must be used daily. They must become part of the operational culture of the organization and referred to as often as needed. *First Principles* may evolve over time and certainly organizations can add to their list as needed and through the general consensus of the members of the organization.

Deciding what principles will guide your organization is important to its success. Once you have developed your set of *First Principles* getting them to work for your organization requires you to (Broudy, 2009):

- **Get clear on what's really important to you.** Your personal philosophy is so deeply ingrained, that it's often hard to specify, so take some time, think about it, and write it down. Ask everyone in the organization for their input. Find the commonalities and then share the results with the team.

- **Walk your talk all the time.** You absolutely cannot violate your own "Guiding Principles" or they become meaningless. If you find this difficult, there's a bigger problem.

- **Make them public.** Post these principles on the wall, on the trucks, in your advertising, and so on. Not only post them everywhere but talk about them all the time.

- **Enforce them.** If you're aware of a violation, make sure the employee gets a reminder, then a warning, and then consider termination (and do NOT accept the "I do my job, what's the big deal" whine).

- **Only hire people who share your values.** Don't think they'll fall in step later.

First Principles are very much the fulcrum of the *Open Organization*. Without them, the organization will struggle to find and keep its balance. It is essential that everyone (including leadership from every level) adhere to the confines of the organization's *First Principles*. These principles should never be seen as negative constraints that keep an organization from its fullest state of creativity and efficiency. Rather, these principles should be seen as the absolute Guiding Principles that keep the organization in a state of creativity and absolute efficiencies. These are the principles that remind us every day what we are here for and why we are doing what we are doing. *First Principles* should always be seen as the illumination of our path through which our organization finds sure footing.

> Open Organizations *are not lawless frontiers but very much rules-driven and purposeful.*

To be effective, our *First Principles* should address "who we are" and "who we want to be" as individuals and as an organization. They should be designed to inspire commitment from everyone, so you will want to get input from everyone involved in your organization (Piscopo, 2012). Your *First Principles* should convey in concise terms, in easy-to-understand everyday language, how your organization defines itself: its values, attitude toward customers, vision, and measure of success (Piscopo). The key to *First Principles* is in its simplicity and its continual reference by everyone in the organization. *First Principles* must be ingrained into the very fabric of the organization's daily activities.

First Principles are so deeply embedded as part of the organizational culture that they are talked about all the time. An organization with *First Principles* becomes evangelists of their principles. They talk about them with friends, with clients, with the media, with everyone that will listen. An *Open Organization* will be best known for their principles because they are not only talking about them all the time, but actually modeling them out in the open.

Governance

Some classically trained leaders may believe that an *Open Organization* is a leaderless, chaotic, aimless organization, void of rules, direction or goals. *Open Organizations* are not lawless frontiers but very much rules-driven and purposeful. The *Open Organization* is a specific system with very specific rules embedded into a written "constitution" or *Governance* (Compagne, 2014). These very specific rules define the type of *Open System* and the level to which employees are empowered within that system.

As organizations empower employees to increase innovation, efficiency, and competitiveness through an *Open Organization*, the need for *Governance* and compliance solutions increases exponentially (Black Duck Software, 2012). For an *Open Organization* to operate effectively, it must have a published written *Charter* or *Governance* which sets out how it chooses to implement, given its particular circumstances, the processes (and therefore values) which make it an *Open Organization* (P2P Foundation, 2008). Organizational *Governance* is essential to manage transactions, information, and the knowledge necessary to initiate and sustain economic and social activities within and sometimes outside of the *Open Organizational System* (IT Governance Institute, 2013). These activities increasingly rely on globally cooperating entities to support, sustain, and grow the business and find success (IT Governance Institute). In Chapter 4, we mentioned that an *Open Organization* must be *Scalable*. *Scalability* must be an essential component of any organizational *Governance* in order to maintain a high degree of *Openness*.

The *Governance* of an *Open Organization* is similar in idea to standard operating procedures (SOP) of the traditional organization. However they are much more general in nature and less cumbersome. In some sectors the *Governance* is also known as the *Charter* or the Constitution of the organization. GitHub, like many other *Open Organizations*, has a *Governance* outlining the rules of engagement for individuals to participate in particular tasks. In some cases, working groups within an *Open Organization* may also have written *Governance* which must be compatible with the organization's *Governance* (P2P Foundation, 2008). Whether the organization or a workgroup's *Governance*, it must define the methods of implementation and measureable goals for its chosen task(s) and must be approved by the organization as a whole (P2P Foundation, 2008). An organization's *Governance* is much like a *Covenant* or promises, bargains, and contracts which reflect a real trade-off and transfer of power and responsibility from leaders to their followers (Li, p. 109). A key part of an organization's *Governance* is accountability, spelling out what happens if someone doesn't keep their side of the bargain (Li, pp. 109–110).

It is important that we separate corporate governance, the meeting of legal requirements of governance embodied in legislation and corporate *Charters* (board rules and bylaws), from what we term as the operating *Governance* of the *Open Organization* (Kesler and Schuster, p. 17). Board Rules, bylaws and other *Covenants* are designed as legal structures to protect publically traded organizations. The *Governance* of an *Open Organization* ensures the organization is aligned with the company's *First Principles* and objectives (Vescuso, 2011). The *Governance* has to do with how decisions are made within the *Open*

Organization's community (Goldman and Gabriel, p. 10). A *Governance* outlines how decisions are made and by whom and does not necessarily imply some sort of hierarchy, voting procedures, or strict process (Goldman and Gabriel, p. 233–234). With effective *Governance*, individuals within an *Open Organization* can gain control over the complexities and mitigate the organizational risks (Hewlett-Packard Development Company, 2007, p. 3). The *Governance* is the outline of the rules of engagement for all members of the organization.

Twitter offers one of the best examples of *Open Source Governance* or *Code of Conduct*. It outlines the behavioral expectations of those who participate in the organization's product/service development and offerings. It expressly governs how they behave in the *Open* setting (Twitter, 2013). Members of the organization are expected to honor this code. Twitter's *Code of Conduct* or *Governance* requires everyone to (Twitter):

1. **Be *Open*.** They invite anybody, from any company, to participate in any aspect of their projects. Twitter's community is *Open*, and any responsibility can be carried by any contributor who demonstrates the required capacity and competence.

2. **Be empathetic.** They work together to resolve conflict, assume good intentions, and do their best to act in an empathetic fashion. They don't allow frustration to turn into a personal attack. A community where people feel uncomfortable or threatened is not a productive one.

3. **Be collective.** Collaboration reduces redundancy and improves the quality of our work. Members prefer to work transparently and involve interested parties as early as possible. Wherever possible, they work closely with upstream projects and others in the free software community to coordinate efforts.

4. **Be pragmatic.** Nobody knows everything! Asking questions early avoids many problems later, so questions are encouraged, though they may be directed to the appropriate forum. Those who are asked should be responsive and thankful.

5. **Step down considerably.** Members of every project come and go. When somebody leaves or disengages from the project they should tell people they are leaving and take the proper steps to ensure that others can pick up where they left off.

While Twitter's *Code of Conduct* is not exhaustive or complete, it serves to distill common understanding of a collaborative, shared environment, and goals and members are expected to follow it in spirit as much as in the letter (Twitter). An *Open Organization's Governance* is not meant to be exhaustive but more of a template of operational standards.

The *Governance* of an *Open Organization* should not restrict individuals from working on projects other than those directly assigned to them by management as this will discourage individuals from participating and thereby begins to create a closed system (Aitken, et al., p. 3). An *Open Organization* assumes that there is great freedom within the organization. The *Governance* should reflect the way that decisions are allocated and is the process that is intentionally designed or by happenstance to empower individuals (Kesler and Schuster, p. 18). The management of an *Open Organization* should be holistic and systemic in the day-to-day cross-functional operations of the organization (Hearst, 2011). There are five features of an *Open Organization Governance* (O'Mahony, p. 144): (1) Independence, (2) Pluralism, (3) Representation, (4) Decentralized decision-making, and (5) Autonomous participation.

Independence requires that decision-making at the lowest levels is unencumbered from any single external controlling influence (O'Mahony, p. 11). The *Governance* must outline the level of independence under which the members operate. Pluralism means that individuals from different backgrounds are together in a social context but continue to have their different traditions and interests (Pluralism, p. 1490). Pluralism is the mechanism in an *Open Organization* that helps it compete more competitively in a globalized economy. Representation means that the *Governance* creates a mechanism through which all members of the organization are represented. The organization's *Governance* must embrace decentralized decision-making and outline the rules of engagement for it. And finally, the *Governance* will define the level of autonomous participation available to the members of the organization.

Governance is the system and process by which power is managed (Kesler and Schuster, p. 17). A *Governance* structure is "the explicit or implicit contractual framework within which a transaction is located" and is viewed as a mechanism that instills order where potential conflict threatens the opportunities to realize mutual gains; and is thus essential for the *Open Organizations* due to complexities that characterize inter-organizational relationships (Feller, et al., 2009, p. 300).

An organization's *Governance* contains certain promises that dictate how things will operate within the confines of the *Open Organization* (Li, p. 109). These covenants outline certain organizational belief systems, project engagement, and organizational boundaries. An element of *Governance* is the accountability which includes what happens if a member doesn't act responsibly within the *Open Organizational* structure (Li, p. 109). The organizational *Governance* can be broken into four levels of control (Kesler and Schuster, p. 19): (1) belief systems, used to inspire and direct the search for new opportunities; (2) boundary systems, used to set limits on opportunity-seeking behavior; (3) diagnostic control systems, used to monitor and reward achievement (merits) of specified goals; and (4) interactive control systems, used to stimulate organizational learning and the emergence of new ideas and strategies.

The *Governance* of an *Open Organization*, like the policies of traditional organizations, does not remain unchanged over time. Most companies, regardless of structure, will go through several revisions as they gain experience and then find it useful to establish periodic reviews and fine-tune their policies as needed (Olson, 2012). The nature of an *Open Organization* is constant change. As an organization grows, it evolves and the organization's *Governance* may also change over time.

By arguing for *Governance* we are not necessarily implying some sort of hierarchy or procedure, but more the expression of sharing ideas, responsibilities and decisions. In the case of an *Open Organization*, members are rewarded based on their own intrinsic motivators. Some are rewarded by completing something cool and some by being part of something bigger than themselves. *Governance* should not be a list of restrictions and don'ts insomuch as it is a methodology for flow and control of information within and sometimes outside of the organization. An *Open Organization* removes silos or divisions of business and creates one merged mass of an organization.

A *Governance* Model

An *Open Organization Governance* is the way an organization controls the use of resources within their products and services, supply chains, and business management activities, and the associated business and legal processes (Black Duck Software, 2013). An organization's *Governance* is the system of management used to ensure compliance, and is a closed-loop process that monitors and reports on the state of a system and whether it is achieving its goals (Black Duck Software, 2012). The *Governance*, working together with the organization's *First Principles* are essential elements to keeping the organization in check. The *Governance* and *First Principles* act as the organizational referees. Everyone in the organization must be committed to the preservation of both in order to preserve the purity and integrity of the *Open Organizational* structure.

Creating an *Open Organizational Governance* is not a trivial matter and requires multiple areas of responsibility, points-of-view of each member and is reconciled if it is to be successful (Black Duck Software, 2012). A key element of an organization's *Governance* is in the understanding it creates of how a project operates, what to expect, and most importantly, how members of the organization can get involved with the process (GitHub, 2012). Because an *Open Organization* is a *Meritocracy*—(which means literally, govern of merit), made up of consensus-based community projects, anyone with an interest in the project can join, contribute to, and participate in the decision-making process through the provision within the *Open Organization Governance* (GitHub). Most organizational *Governances* are not lengthy. In fact, they are best noted for their level of simplicity and brevity. The *Governance* should not only be as short as possible, but also available in the organization's *Knowledge Commons* for everyone to access at any time or place.

There are four specific steps to creating effective *Governance* for your *Open Organization*:

The first step is to identify the key stakeholders in the organization (Black Duck Software, 2012). Stakeholders are anyone that is affected by the *Governance*. In some organizations they might include clients, outside vendors, and even contract labor.

Second, there will need to be an organization-wide commitment from all stakeholders for the development of the *Governance* (Black Duck Software, 2012). This is certainly the single most important factor to the success of going *Open* (Black Duck Software, 2012).

Third, draft the *Governance* through a series of interactive meetings with the participation of the relevant stakeholders in the organization (Black Duck Software, 2012). This is where the trade-offs inherent in any policy development must be discussed and resolved in a way that best meets the organization's needs (Black Duck Software, 2012). Some common trade-offs include (Black Duck Software, 2012):

- controlling risk vs. productivity;

- broad, simple rules vs. specific, more complex rules;

- self-checking vs. independent checking;

- use of judgment calls vs. detailed prescriptions.

The fourth step in this process is the review of the draft *Governance*. The document must be circulated among the stakeholders for review and approval (Black Duck Software, 2012). Most organizations should be able to develop a final version of their *Governance* in two or three revisions (Black Duck Software, 2013).

   The *Governance* outlines the roles and responsibility of each member of the organization, the contribution process, and the decision-making process. The following is a template based on the GitHub *Governance Model* (GitHub):

ORGANIZATIONAL FOCUS

Here the organization outlines their *First Principles* and defines the type of *Governance* that will be instituted with the organization. GitHub defines their organization as a *Meritocracy* and explains what that means in context to the organization's culture and operation.

ROLES AND RESPONSIBILITIES

In this section, the roles and responsibilities of the member of the organizational community are outlined. Here, the roles of the customer and employees are described. This section might outline the customer as a "user of product or service." In the case of many *Open Organizations*, the customer is very much integrated into the decision-making process. We would also find the rules of engagement for a *Matrix Guardian*, the CEO and/or founder and other individuals as deemed necessary. Roles and responsibilities do not really fit the idea of an *Open Organization*. Ownership and being responsible are proactive concepts that imply an active attitude from members of the organization (de Bree and de Weil). Roles and responsibilities should flow naturally as a response from the members of the organization. Roles are typically more entrepreneurial and adaptable within an *Open Organization*. The *Open Organization* may be led by what is referred to as a benevolent dictator and managed by the community (NuGet, 2013). While the community actively contributes to the day-to-day workflow, the general strategic line is drawn by the benevolent dictator (NuGet). The role of the benevolent dictator is less about dictatorship and more about diplomacy (Gardler and Hanganu, 2013). Like with any leader, the benevolent dictator is about developing influence over others to achieve some stated goal. The *Governance* must encourage continuous search activities and create information networks to scan and report critical changes, and make it the practice to widely share information and insights (Kesler and Schuster, p. 20).

CONTRIBUTORS

Whether a customer or employee, participants are considered "contributors" within the organization. Anyone in the organization can become a contributor and there is no expectation of commitment to a project. The organization might outline how someone can become a contributor and the process by which contributions are received within the *Knowledge Commons*. In the confines of a *Meritocracy*, as contributors gain experience and familiarity with projects, their profile, and commitment to, the community increases. High-profile contributors are seen as "committers."

COMMITTERS

A "committer" is someone who has been recognized by their colleagues as showing their commitment to the continued development of projects through ongoing engagement with the community. Being a "committer" does not mean that they have more authority than a contributor, but that they have demonstrated a consistent level of contribution to the objectives of the organization. They have shown a willingness and ability to participate in the project as a team player and have provided valuable contributions to the project over a period of time and number of completed projects obtained.

The *Governance* will outline how a "committer" is nominated and what activities they may participate in beyond the role of contributor. In the spirit of *Openness*, achieving the notation of committer does not create hierarchy insomuch as it creates recognition of achievement. This is an earned privilege that can be removed in extreme circumstances. Any number of employees can be defined as "committers." A committer who shows an above-average level of contribution to the organization can be nominated to become a "reviewer."

REVIEWERS

A reviewer, also known as a project administrator, has the additional responsibility within an *Open Organization* of overseeing the work of the committers. This ensures the smooth running of organizational objectives. Reviewers are expected to review contributions, participate in strategic planning, approve changes to the *Governance Model*, and manage the copyrights within the project outputs (GitHub). Because an *Open Organization* is powered by accountability, the contributions of a "reviewer" are reviewed by other "reviewers." They do not have significant authority over other members of the community, although it is the "reviewers" that vote on new "committers" and they make decisions when community consensus cannot be reached.

CONTRIBUTION PROCESS

Within an *Open Organization*, anyone can make contributions, regardless of their skills. Under the contribution process an organization may outline standards for contributing to the decision-making process, project completion, and the day-to-day functionality of the organization.

DECISION-MAKING PROCESS

In Chapter 4 we noted that *Open Organizations* seek to normalize the concept of *Adhocracy*. The *Governance* outlines the rules of engagement for the organization's *Adhocracy* decision-making process. It might define the levels and kinds of decisions to be made by the members of the organization. Some *Open Organizations* might operate under the policy of a *Lazy Consensus* which allows the majority of decisions to be made without resorting to a formal vote. In fact, the decision-making process of an *Open Organization* should include: proposal, discussion, vote and decisions. Whatever the format, an *Open Organization* is a community-based structure in which the community operates as a participatory democracy where each employee has a say and influence in the operations of the organization (de Bree and de Weil). In an *Open Organizational* setting, anyone in the organization can make a proposal for consideration by the members of the organization. The *Governance* should outline how to initiate the discussion of new ideas and where that discussion should take place within the organization's *Knowledge Commons*. The *Governance* will outline the process of review, discussion, and approval of the proposed idea. The great benefit of an *Open Organization* is that most of the members have a shared vision and there is often little discussion needed to reach a consensus.

Lazy Consensus is an important concept within an *Open Organization* as it allows large groups of people to efficiently reach consensus, as someone with no objections to a proposal need not spend time stating their position, and others need not spend time reading such emails. In order for *Lazy Consensus* to be effective, it is necessary to allow time (up to 72 hours) before assuming that there are no objections to the proposal. This ensures that everyone is given enough time to read, digest, and respond to the proposal.

VOTING

There are certain cases where a *Lazy Consensus* is not an appropriate course of action for the organization. Issues such as strategic direction or legal standing must rely on the mechanics of a formal vote. The organizational *Governance* should outline how a formal vote is called, administered, and certified. In the case of GitHub, their votes are cast via email. If they do not respond to the email, it is considered an abstention from the vote. The key to voting within the *Open Organization* is that every member of the organization has a vote.

The default of an *Open Organization* should be to make every effort to allow the majority of decisions to be taken through *Lazy Consensus* unless an objection is raised. Voting is the mechanism used by the *Open Organization* to ensure a more fully transparent decision-making process.

Executive Override

Executive intervention in decisions should be few and far between. For many leaders, the most difficult aspect of leading an *Open Organization* is in determining when to step in at the appearance that something might be going wrong. This should be clearly outlined in the *Governance* of the organization. A leader must gauge each decision made by the group and, when its looks as if the decisions of the group are going to go the wrong way, they must know when to step in and take some of the control back (Ousterhout). If the organization is truly *Open*, most issues take care of themselves without executive intervention. In case of disagreement, the benevolent dictator will resolve disputes within the community and to ensure that the project is able to progress in a coordinated way (NuGet). The danger in a leader stepping into the middle of a group decision-making process, especially one that they've not been participating in through the *Knowledge Commons*, is that the leader begins to defeat the idea of *Openness* by opting for decisions outside the control of the group members.

Too many interventions by leadership begins to override the *Egalitarian* spirit of the *Open Organization* and thereby creates anger amongst the members and creates questions such as, *"Why did you ask our opinion and then ignore it?"* Or *"Why did you make the decision secretly?"* (Ousterhout). When a leader overrides the group without discussion, they will eventually put the spirit of *Openness* at risk and diminish the desire to for anyone to participate in the process of *Openness*. The best option is to permit the decision process to continue as planned because typically a leader will eventually find that their fears were unfounded or that the group was able to come around once all of the information was available to them (Ousterhout). Before the leader makes a decision to counter the plans of the group, the leader must carefully think through whether or not the group is right or even whether an issue is important enough to justify an override. If an override of a group consensus must take place it is best to do it as publicly as possible explaining the reasons for the intervention and apologizing for the override of the group's decision, and promise that you won't do this very often. The override will probably create some frustration, but it's better to handle it publicly rather than secretly (Ousterhout).

Other overrides in the organization's *Governance* could manifest in the form of slack *Governance*. Breakdowns in the organization's *Governance* make executives appear incompetent; will bring question to their integrity; and their commitment to due process (ISACA). Because the leaders of the organization should also be the *Matrix Guardian*, they must be vigilant in their protection of the organization's *Governance*, *First Principles*, and the needs of the members of the organization. Breaking this solemn vow degrades the foundation of *Openness*.

Implementation

The final step in developing organizational *Governance* for an *Open Organization* is the implementation which is achieved through a series of processes. These processes must contain adequate checks and balances to insure the organization's *Governance* is consistently followed (Black Duck Software, 2013). A key element of implementation is training for all participants in the *Open Organization* system. The implementation process will require greater dialogue, debate, and sharing of power and influence amongst the members of the organization.

The *Governance*, like *First Principles*, is essential to the long-term survival of an *Open Organization*. The power of the organizational *Governance* is held in the level of participation permitted by the members. An *Open Organization* will not survive if the members do not have the freedom to contribute on their own terms (O'Mahony, p. 148). This is where the leaders must let go of power, get out of the way, and let the magic happen. The *Open Organization* is different from traditional structures in that it focuses on transactions rather than on commodities or services and shifts attention away from technical production concerns to the *Governance* (Scott, p. 112). Part of what will attract individuals to work in an *Open Organizational* setting is the opportunity to contribute, learn, solve problems, and improve their skills (O'Mahony, p. 148). The *Open Organization* will attract those who thrive in the zone of curiosity. The organizational *Governance* should empower members to contribute on the basis on their own interests, motivations, and abilities (O'Mahony, p. 148). Implementation is about understanding the organization, its culture, and the intrinsic motivators of the members at large. It is possible that not all of the members of the organization will want to go along with the implementation process. Not everyone is ready for an *Open Organization* and that is ok. However, for those who will see the genius behind the *Open Organization*, we will see strides in creativity, innovation, efficiencies, and *Happiness*.

Chapter 6

Communication

There cannot be an effective organization without the flow of information. The flow of information requires a transaction to take place between those who have the information and those who need the information. The *Open Organization* requires the free flow of information at all

The fastest growing and most agile companies are built on a platform of Openness ...

Black Duck Software

times. What we have learned is that some of the fastest growing and most agile organizations are built on a platform of *Openness* (Black Duck Software, 2012). Effective communication keeps an organization aligned and focused through a philosophy and a culture of ample interaction (ISACA). Communication requires a commitment to transparency and clarity in messaging. Misunderstanding and unproductive conflict is a direct product of poor communication. In fact, most problems within a system can be traced back to the process of communication or lack thereof. Communication within an *Open Organization* requires a commitment by all to nurture different perspectives, thoughts and solutions.

Communication is complex and has many facets. Psychologist Albert Mehrabian (1971) noted that communication can be broken down into three essential parts: words (7 percent), tone of voice (38 percent) and body language (55 percent). In this digital age, how we communicate becomes even more imperative in that, if we are to believe Mehrabian's study, it is not what we say but how we say it that creates effective communication. In this digital age, employers must continue to find ways to leverage changing technology to allow their companies to prosper (Southward). This means that organizations must embrace new ways of facilitating human interaction in their dispersed, techno-linked workforce. When organizations engage their human capital through effective communication, they begin to create a level of *Openness* that addresses and vets concerns rather than disciplining those who communicate such concerns (ISACA). In the *Open Organization*, good communication includes establishing a standardized lexicon and implies a well-planned information access and delivery structure (ISACA). Such standards and lexicon helps alleviate some of the challenges presented in communicating in a digital world.

As we learned with GitHub, an organization requires good communication to best achieve *Open* decision-making. Within the traditional top-down hierarchical system, the communication flows from the top-down to the followers. In a hierarchical system, communication is often in the form of directives and very little feedback is filtered back to the top from the bottom layers. In an *Open Organization*, like GitHub, communication occurs directly between all of the organizational members (Brafman and Beckstrom, p. 53). One of the most important ingredients for success of any *Open Organization* is its ongoing feedback, or communication, among all the members of the organization (Authenticity Consulting, n.d. (a), p. 141). In an *Open Organization* this communication must flow across all of the organizational, geographical, and time zone boundaries. Communication within an *Open Organization* is focused on the conversation and the curiosity of finding answers above and beyond any defense of turf or ego.

Often, during training sessions I like to illustrate the importance of communication in the process of sharing information. I typically ask a volunteer to assist me. Once I secure a volunteer, I tell them that they will need to put together a simple puzzle in five minutes or less. I hold up a small plastic bag with a puzzle in it. The volunteer will agree to help me put it together. This is when I provide just a little more information. The volunteer is then told that they will have to put the puzzle together with a blindfold on over their eyes and with no outside help. The volunteer typically will look surprised and some might even protest that it is not possible to do so while blindfolded. Obviously, the blindfolded volunteer is not able to complete the task without additional assistance.

Communication within any organization is about the free flow of information. The free flow of information is essential for workers to get their work done. Without it, you might as well have a bunch of blindfolded employees bumping around trying to get their work done. An *Open Organization* seeks to remove the blindfolds from their eyes and gives them every opportunity to achieve success. Without freedom to communicate and share information an organization cannot find its natural state of efficiency and success.

Communication in an *Open Organization* is very much a multilateral exchange of ideas. Information flows to and from clients, vendors, and the members within the organization. If an organization obtains feedback on how well its output is being received it can respond to its customers or clients more effectively in the future (Burke, p. 47). Communication however is not about reacting to feedback, but also exchanging ideas in the hopes of preventing future negative feedback. When the feedback is negative; then, corrective action can be planned and taken (Burke, p. 47).

Communication in the context of an *Open Organization* is about sharing all types of information throughout the company, especially across functional and hierarchical levels (Daft, 2002, p. 320). The sharing of information is more powerful than hording information. This runs counter to the traditional flow of information in which information is held close and shared sparingly. Many times, information flows from supervisors on what they believe to be an "as needed basis." People through the organization need a clear direction and an understanding of how they can contribute (Daft, 2002, p. 320). The power of communicating in an *Open Organization* is that all the information a worker would need to get their job done is provided in advance and is free to be used as needed. This free flow of information permits members of the organization to be more agile, make better decisions, and to be more efficient in their workflow.

Information

Communication at its most basic element is nothing more than the transfer of information from one space to another. Communication can be seen as a tool that people use for the transfer of information to accomplish their objectives (Eisenberg and Goodall, p. 23). Information is derived from the word, inform, which means "to give shape to." Information means shaping the data to arrive at a meaning in the eyes of the perceiver (Awad and Ghaziri, p. 69). In my blindfold example, the volunteer could not complete the puzzle because they lacked the right amount of information (vision) to get the job done. The volunteer was unable to arrive at a meaning because they could not see the puzzle.

An *Open Organization* requires unfettered and timely transfer of all information for members to do their job. Unfettered would indicate that all information within the organization is located in one place and accessible to all members at any time for the purpose of achieving goals. If information is not freely accessible by everyone in your organization, your employees are no better off than my blindfolded volunteer trying to put together a simple puzzle without assistance. This level of transparent data opens the possibilities for an individual's self-managing because all the information they need to monitor their work and make wise decisions is available to them (Hamel, 2011, p. 55).

In an *Open Organization*, members need transparent cross-company information to calculate how their decisions will help achieve the overall goals and *First Principles* of the organization (Hamel, 2011, p. 55). An *Open Organization* reveres information as a corporate asset owned by all. Information sharing provides ownership across organizational boundaries and diminishes fiefdoms because no one individual owns any of the information within the context of the organization. For example, Whole Foods, which is structured through self-managed units, provides performance and financial data—including compensation and bonuses –to everyone in the organization (Choi, 2013, p. 52). This helps the members think about the organization holistically as there are no information silos within an *Open Organization* (Hamel, 2011, p. 55).

The essence of the *Open Organization* is its ability to share information openly and transparently with all its members. However, *Open* does not necessarily mean that all information is available at all times. There are certain scenarios where information is still on an as-needed basis. For example, in 2012, GitHub secured venture capital of $100 million. Tom Preston-Werner said that during the time of negotiations with the venture capitalists only he and a small handful of members knew about the discussions. As with any organization, this level of transaction requires a certain level of confidentiality to maintain the integrity of the deal. Tom indicated that this was a very difficult process because up until this point most everything that happened in the organization was shared with all members. Tom knew that by not sharing the information he had to carefully explain the case for why this information had to be held confidential until it was time for the announcement.

Open communication does not mean that the organization shares its trade secrets outside of the organizational barriers. Every organization has a specific concern about confidential information getting out, be it product features, client information, intellectual property, or employee gossip (Li, pp. 115–116). Confidentiality means that members of the organization will not disclose confidential company information to anyone who is not authorized to receive it. In my observation of GitHub I saw firsthand how they work to protect certain trade secrets, asking anyone who is not a member of the organization to step outside the office while certain key information is being discussed.

Aside from an event like negotiating for large sums of venture capital or even taking a company public, information should flow openly between members of the organization. This open flow of information permits feedback from those who know best how the organization is operating. If an organization obtains feedback on how well its output is being received it can respond more effectively in the future (Burke, p. 47). The *Openness* of this information also helps members of the organization to voice their concerns and to offer feedback based on their own knowledge and experiences. In the end, sharing information helps the organization make more informed decisions. It is important to note that feedback can be both positive and negative in the confines of an *Open Organization*. This is especially true when the feedback is negative; then, corrective action can be taken to change some elements within the input–throughput–output and feedback set of events (Burke, p. 47).

Dialogue

In my observations of GitHub I realized that everything they do is about dialogue (conversations). Because they are a dispersed workforce, most all of their daily communication takes place in chat, *Knowledge Commons*, and on wiki boards. The way they get things done is through dialogue about everything. When they are dialoguing about a problem, they are much more focused on the discussion than necessarily the solution. That is not to say that solutions are not created, but the process of getting to the solution is much more important that the solution itself.

Dialogue is about engaging individuals through curiosity. Curiosity is about developing an understanding of how something functions and what possible solutions are available to the organization. Curiosity is about thinking, learning, and understanding. This whole concept puts the traditional organization on end. Most organizations are about the bottom line; the quickest way to the solution. Curiosity is an essential component of learning. In an *Open Organization*, the goal is to find the best solution and there is no emphasis on timing.

Dialogue is about creating a more effective collaborate community. To collaborate is to decide jointly through the process of consensus (Keidel, p. 89). Dialogue brings multiple perspectives and resources to bear on an issue, decision, or a problem, and it virtually guarantees that the members of the organization will be committed to implementation of necessary changes or solutions (Keidel, p. 89). Dialogue is a critical competency for achieving and sustaining high performance in the organization (Kouzes and Posner, p. 242).

Listening

Open communication requires the sharing of all types of information throughout the company and runs counter to the traditional top-down flow of selective information from supervisors to subordinates (Daft, 2002, p. 320). Sharing of information is not only the giving of information but also the receiving. Listening plays a key role in how we share information amongst our colleagues. Listening is just as important as the sharing of ideas. The simple act of listening to what other people have to say and appreciating their unique points of view demonstrates your respect for others and their ideas (Kouzes and Posner, p. 249). Without the ability to receive information, the effectiveness of the *Open System* diminishes. The *Open Organization* requires members to secure the skillset of both sending and receiving information in an effective and efficient manner.

People from all walks of life want to be heard and understood. Successful organizations know that the way you build trust and understanding is through listening to those around you who are engaged in the process. Leaders are discovering that people listen more attentively to those who listen to them (Kouzes and Posner, p. 249). Listening means respecting the opinions of others, recognizing their needs, avoiding distractions, paying close attention to their main points of concern, and taking action on their complaints or suggestions (Eisenberg and Goodall, p. 237). Listening requires that we identify our own bias and filtering. Listening is the act of actively engaging in the process of understanding the transmitter of the message. Listening is the active connection of one person to another in an effort to interpret wants, needs, and feelings. Careful listening within *Open Organizations* will aide in the effective communication of ideas, solutions, and disagreements.

Conflict

As we noted in Chapter 4, when two or more are gathered in a collaborative setting conflict is sure to be present. Conflict is a normal part of group interactions and personal relationships (Kuczmarski and Kuczmarski, pp. 195–196). In traditional organizations, conflict is a dirty word that is avoided at all costs. Traditional organizations spend a great deal of time and resources in training individuals to avoid conflict. It is believed that during interpersonal conflict, we are least likely to pause, analyze the situation, and evaluate the principles that might prove most relevant (DeVito, 1988, p. 232). In the context of an *Open*

Organization, we are not talking about the conflict that should be avoided. We are not speaking of personality conflicts. What we mean by conflict is the process of tension that enhances the creative process. There is nothing personal about conflict in a creative environment.

GitHub is known internally to have had some epic conflicts between individuals. It is through this conflict that we find the catalyst for creativity. In the traditional organizational setting, conflict occurs among members largely because people in different positions of power pursue different interests (Eisenberb and Goodall, p. 287). While *Open Organizations* remove the culture of power and flatten the hierarchy, conflicts can still arise. In the context of an *Open Organization* conflict is seen as part of the creative process and helps defeat *Groupthink*. This kind of conflict gives license to the members to speak their minds and to share honestly their thoughts and feelings on a given subject without recourse. Conflict in an *Open Organization* is not about abuse or neglect, but about creating "Awesome." Conflicts, when handled correctly, are about sharpening the creativity of everyone involved in the process.

What we have found in empirical research is that when ideas aren't fully formed, criticism and constructive conflict are vital to testing and strengthening the value of those ideas (Burkus, 2013, p. 152). Without healthy conflict there are no challenges to the status quo. Without conflict we end up doing what we've always done without questioning why we are doing it. Without conflict the organization is nothing more than *Groupthink* with a cult leader telling us what to say. Conflict is the necessary lifeblood of an *Open Organization's* culture and survivability. Conflict can mean that there is a high level of competition to develop and test ideas and to wade through the wide variation in knowledge and perspectives (Burkus, 2013, p. 152). When healthy conflict is present, the *Open Organization* is operating within its optimal status. With healthy conflict the organization is able to be more creative, more innovative than their competition.

Peer Review

An *Open Organization* is about having a participatory culture. Communication is an important part of this culture of participation. An *Open Organization* is about peer interaction and review. *Open Organizations* rely predominantly on information provided by co-workers who have the most knowledge about the work being done (Choi, p. 52). Peer review is about human connections and being accountable to everyone in the organization. Such peer reviews or accountability create a cohesive, high-functioning team in which no one has the option of handing off tough calls and everyone must be able to justify their performance (Hamel, 2011, p. 56).

There is a social risk in doing something your colleagues think is stupid (Hamel, 2011, p. 56). Because of this social risk, members are more vigilant about measuring what they say and how they say it. Most of the communication takes place in chat and wikis so members have to use concise wording before acting. No one is allowed to fire off a response in anger, but is expected to offer well thought through arguments to the problems being presented. Peer review is an important part of the accountability process that keeps the organization focused on their *First Principles*. Organizations that put a priority on autonomy, trust, and empowerment such as peer review, build a strong culture (Choi, p. 52).

Chapter 7

Knowledge Commons

The flow of information is vital to any organization's form and function. Information is power and how we share that information is critical to its effectiveness. An *Open Organization* is different from a closed structure in that it recognizes the *Intellectual Capital* of

All men by nature desire Knowledge.

Aristotle

its members. *Intellectual Capital* or *Intellectual Property* (*IP*) is the sum of the organization's knowledge, experience, understanding, relationships, processes, innovations, and discoveries (Daft, 2004, p. 297). *Open* and free flow of information is best defined as the function of a *Knowledge Commons*. A *Knowledge Commons* is much like removing the blindfolds from individuals so that they can do their work. A *commons* is a general term that refers to a resource shared by a group of individuals such as the family refrigerator, sidewalks, playgrounds, libraries, the atmosphere, and the Internet (Hess and Ostrom, 2007, pp. 4–5). A *Knowledge Commons* is therefore the shared knowledge and resources within the confines of an *Open Organization* and accessible by all members of the organization.

Aristotle once said that "all men by nature desire knowledge" and Sir Francis Bacon is credited with saying "knowledge is power." Knowledge refers to all intelligible ideas, information, and data in whatever form in which it is expressed or obtained within the organization (Hess and Ostrom, p. 7). Arguably the first known *Knowledge Commons* was a library in Alexandria Egypt where as many as 700,000 scrolls, the equivalent of more than 100,000 modern printed books, filled the shelves and was open to scholars from all cultures (The Library of Alexandria, n.d.).

From the perspective of an *Open Organization*, knowledge is cumulative and the knowledge produced by the organization must be recorded and maintained in publically accessible archives, or *commons*, so that individuals within the organization can benefit from it (P2P Foundation, 2010). Like a library, access to information within the *commons* must be available to everyone. The key attribute of a *Knowledge Commons* is not only its accessibility to the members within the organization, but the contribution of all members and the preservation of this infinite amount of knowledge (Hess and Ostrom, p. 8). A *Knowledge Commons* should be organized and presented in a way that minimizes the difficulty of learning from it and allows knowledge to circulate where it is needed, providing the maximum benefit to the organization (P2P Foundation, 2010). The result of a *Knowledge Commons* is the public ownership of the knowledge within the *Open Organization*. The power of a *Knowledge Commons* is the archival attributes of knowledge. Information is captured for all to see for the life of the *Knowledge Commons*. This accessibility is available for use in future decision-making as it provides a catalog of what was said and done and by whom.

Perhaps the best example of a *Knowledge Commons* is Wikipedia. Wikis, as they are called, exemplify the spirit of *Knowledge Commons* in that most activities are uncoordinated—people individually pursue their own interests and connection (Li and Bernoff, 2008, p. 24). Wikis (derived from the Hawaiian word for quick) are sites that support multiple contributors with a shared responsibility for creating and maintaining content, typically focused around text and pictures (Li and Bernoff, p. 24). Successful *Open Organizations*, such as GitHub, use Wikis to capture ideas, to debate, and to create solutions to problems. Wikis are a powerful example of *Knowledge Commons* in use in an *Open Organizational* setting. Wikis provide a creative space for individuals to develop their critical thinking skills and to enhance the innovative process of the organization.

An *Open Organization* requires the use of a *Knowledge Commons* because its human capital is most likely dispersed. GitHub has over 200 employees spread across the globe, with only about 40 of them physically in the office at a given time. This means that GitHub, like other *Open Organizations*, must adopt technology to capture ideas, workflow, and dialogue about the projects in process. In the case of GitHub, the *Knowledge Commons* is also used to archive the *Beer:30* sessions and other communications, *First Principles*, and even the organization's *Governance*.

Knowledge Workers

The greatest attribute of a *Knowledge Commons* are the individuals or *Knowledge Workers* that reside within them. In fact, we are now in what we call a *Cerebral Economy*. The *Cerebral Economy* contains *Knowledge Workers* who have substantial expertise, often beyond that of their so-called leaders, and they expect to be free to make decisions in their own areas of competence (Bennis and Nanus, 2003, pp. 213–214). *Knowledge Workers* are individuals who transform business and personal experience into knowledge through capturing, assessing, applying, sharing, and disseminating it within the organization to solve specific problems that create value (Awad and Ghaziri, p. 455). A *Knowledge Worker* will exercise considerable influence over their own work, setting their own schedules and such; decisions are shaped far less by leadership authority than by collaboration, shared values, and mutual respect (Bennis and Nanus, p. 214). Without *Knowledge Workers*, there would be no one to compile the knowledge required for the *Open Organization* to operate effectively. The *Knowledge Worker* of the future will require the freedom and the flexibility to do their job that only an *Open Organization* can provide.

Knowledge Workers* are generally not looking for a clearly marked career path. Individuals who seek clearly defined paths of advancement will be clearly disappointed in their role within an *Open Organization*. Within an *Open Organization*, solutions are situational and require flexibility to find solutions. Too much structure within an *Open Organization* will lock the organization in an endless loop of doing what they've always done and blaming others when the solutions fail. *Knowledge Workers* thrive in the element of ambiguity and chaos. It is in this place that they are most able to produce results.

Knowledge System

A *Knowledge Commons* is a system consisting of the values, norms, content, technology, and individuals and it addresses such issues as what constitutes authentic knowledge, what form it should take, how it should be distributed, who should have access to it, how access should be provided, how it should be preserved, and who is responsible for developing the required methodologies and technologies sustaining the *Knowledge System* (Birdsall and Shearer, 2007, p. 44).

A *Knowledge System* is a secure online platform for collaboration, open communication, and innovation within the organizational system. The purpose of a *Knowledge System* is to foster a performance culture and is the holy grail of decision-making effectiveness; creating an environment in which people naturally take responsibility for cross-boundary communication and cooperation. The *Knowledge System* of an *Open Organization* is a technological system used by its members to archive, search, retrieve, and modify information. A *Knowledge System* must be decentralized, distributed, local, organic, flexible, and collaborative (Birdsall and Shearer, p. 46).

A *Knowledge System* seeks to diminish misaligned goals, unclear roles and responsibilities, ambiguous authority, lack of *governance* and silo-focused employees that may plague more traditional organizations. A *Knowledge System* responds to these challenges by creating a structure for communicating goals, roles, and responsibilities which create a format for empowerment and authority among employees, training them to step outside of their silos and to participate openly in the organization.

The central element of a *Knowledge System* is to create continuous feedback and responses which result in better understanding and efficiencies. A *Knowledge System* opens the door for better communication and more feedback. When the system and subsystems have enough feedback, the results can produce more clearly directed planning, intelligent design, useful products, and necessary services.

Virtual Organizations

With advancements in technology and a greater shift toward a globalized economy, we are seeing more organizations begin to adopt virtualized offices. These *Virtual Organizations* rely on *Cloud Computing* technology to link their human capital to the organization's *Knowledge System*. *Cloud Computing* is the storing and accessing of applications and data often through the Internet and a web browser rather than running installed software on a personal computer or office server (Cloud Computing, n.d.). This means that information is available just about anywhere an Internet connection is available. Creating a *Virtual Organization* is about finding ways to leverage technology to create human connectedness amongst a dispersed workforce.

A *Virtual Organization* means that we take things that we currently do within the confines of a physical office and we shift them online or rather into a virtual platform. Originally billed as remote offices and tele-commuting, the idea of a virtual office setting is nothing new. A virtual office can be literally anywhere the user can gain access to the Internet (Eisenberg and Goodall, p. 334). A *Virtual Organization* is designed to link an Internet-dependent dispersed workforce together as *Virtual Teams*.

The essential features of a *Virtual Organization* are identification with shared concerns or issues and temporal and geographical separations of members of the community (Stanford, pp. 314–315). While GitHub does have a brick and mortar office space, only a handful of the over 200 employees actually work from the company headquarters on a daily basis. GitHub utilizes a *Knowledge Commons* to connect their human capital together from around the world and every time zone. The employees of GitHub are members of a *Virtual Team* which is made up of geographically dispersed members who are linked primarily through technology and whose members use email, voice mail, video conferencing, Internet and Intranet technologies, and various types of collaboration software to perform their work rather than meeting face-to-face (Daft, 2002, p. 359).

Virtual Teams, like those at GitHub, are sometimes called distributed teams and may be temporary cross-functional teams pulled together to work on a specific problem, or they may be long-term or permanent self-directed teams (Daft, 2002, p. 360). The use of *Virtual Teams* taps into a particular kind of culture and decision-making practice unlike those found in the more traditional organizational structures of the past. A *Virtual Team* may include suppliers, customers, and even competitors to pull together the best minds to complete a specific project and may change fairly quickly, depending on the task to be performed (Daft, 2002, p. 360).

As organizations continue to embrace globalization, the use of *Virtual Teams* is likely to grow as companies seek to harness knowledge and respond faster to increased global competition (Daft, 2002, p. 363). The expanding use of a *Knowledge Commons* and *Virtual Teams* will likely increase as a byproduct of demographic shifts in the globalized workforce. As the rate of available full-time workers decreases, organizations will be pressed to find ways to compete within the new realities of limited human capital. The *Virtualization* of their organization along with an optimization toward the use of consultants will position the organization of the future to compete in the new market space.

While many organizations are moving toward a virtual setting, workers still require meaningful face-to-face engagement. The more time we spend communicating with others by way of machines, the more important face-to-face experiences become (Johansen, 2007, p. 175). As economies and industries become more globally distributed and we engage with colleagues from remote geographic locations the more isolated we will become. One of the challenges of an *Open Organization* is to continue to engage its human capital in meaningful connections and face-to-face experiences. GitHub does a great job of connecting its members with each other—whether through their *Knowledge Commons* and chat tools or their *Beer:30* events each Friday afternoon. The lifeblood of an *Open Organization* is community and organizations like GitHub make it a priority to develop community through structures like *Beer:30*. Smaller organizations that do not have the technology to stream a live meeting can still use products such as Skype, Face Time, and Google Hangouts to help them stay in touch with the organizational members.

Cloud Computing

Cloud Computing is the term we use to describe remote access of information through the Internet. *Cloud Computing* is central to the *Open Organization* because it connects a dispersed workforce with information and processes required to achieve a given task. By the year 2017, it is estimated that 52 percent of organizations in the United States will standardize on some form of *Open* infrastructure through *Cloud Computing* (Babcock, 2013). *Cloud Computing* is about accessing information quickly and using it in the collaborative effort. With the widespread use of smartphones and tablet computers, access to the *Cloud* has become common in our modern lexicon.

Cloud Computing is commonly marketed to consumers and businesses as backup and storage solutions. But online storage is not the only feature of the *Cloud*. More and more, corporate applications like Salesforce.com (customer relations management), Yammer (internal messaging), and Social text (knowledge sharing) are no longer software, but *Cloud* Internet services accessible with a login from any Internet-connected device (Bernoff and Schadler, 2010, p. 15). *Cloud Computing* gives organizations powerful tools and remote access to data with limited hardware requirements as datacenters are remote and accessed through the Internet. This reduces the overhead costs of a global organization.

A Gartner Survey indicated the *Cloud Application Services* market (Software as a Service—SAAS) to be 33 percent of the entire *Cloud* market and is projected to be a $160 billion market by 2016. A *Cloud* application such as a *Knowledge Commons* is a growing industry. Because a *Knowledge Commons* is scalable, nearly any size organization can benefit from its use. There are currently over 150,000 known organizations already utilizing some form of *Knowledge Commons*. Most *Knowledge Commons* available via *Cloud Application Services* or SAAS, are currently nothing more than a *Customer Relations System* (CRS) or a project management tool. Technologies like smartphones and tablet computers are pushing the envelope of the mobile office with APPS (applications) that connect the *Knowledge Worker* to the office anywhere in the world. The *Knowledge Commons* of the future will evolve into solutions that provide chat, archives, Wikis, video conferencing, collaborative tools, and more, all on the go and in varying environments.

While *Cloud Computing* allows workers access to websites and web services via the Internet, we do find that *Cloud Services* can create security risks, network congestion, and possibly decrease productivity (Bernoff and Schadler, p. 129). While security and productivity issues are important to consider, the benefits of *Cloud Computing* are numerous. Workers may identify sites that are valuable sources of information; find cheaper resources to solve computing problems or develop *Cloud Services* that will serve customers more effectively (Bernoff and Schadler, p. 129). *Cloud Computing* provides powerful tools and immediate insight to the organization's *Cloud Workers*.

Chapter 8
Leading the *Open Organization*

Traditional leadership relies on formal lines of authority which relates to power and is a force for achieving desired outcomes through formal hierarchies and reporting relationships (Daft, 2004,

> *If the leader of an* Open Organization *does their job right, leading is much easier compared to more traditional styles of leadership.*

p. 494). However, in the non-traditional *Open Organization*, authority is not vested in organizational positions. In a traditional organization authority flows down the vertical hierarchy and exists along formal lines in a chain of command (Daft, 2004, p. 494). In the *Open Organization* authority flows throughout the organization and is given equally to all members. The idea of an *Open Organization* appears to make some traditionally trained leaders nervous because the idea of being *Open* is counterintuitive to what they know and understand of organizational structures.

An *Open Organization* is considered a distributed organization. Meaning there are technically no managers and no one to tell people what to do. *Open Organizations*, like GitHub, will vehemently avoid the actions of telling people what to do. Leading the *Open Organization* requires a shift in mindset from telling people what to do and requires the art of empowerment and leading by example.

The power of an *Open Organization* is that everyone, not just a few lucky or special individuals, can be a leader as leading is about contributing to collective cognition and enabling shared sense making (Barbour, 2012, p. 42). However we must be clear that self-leadership does not abrogate a leader's responsibilities; as no leader can delegate responsibility only authority (Hesselbein and Goldsmith, p. 311). In the case of GitHub, Tom Preston-Werner still holds the final say in the organization. But to be clear, his "final say" is governed by the organization's *First Principles* and *Governance*.

Tom very much lives out the idea of empowerment in his organization and offers a true freedom for members to get their jobs done as they see fit. But like Tom, the leader of an *Open Organization* is, and will always be, responsible for everything their organization and its members do or fail to do (Hesselbein and Goldsmith, p. 311). If the leader of an *Open Organization* does their job right, leading is much easier compared to more traditional styles of leadership. The most important role of the leader of an *Open Organization* is to empower employees and set the direction of the organization. Empowering followers gives the leader more time to work on things that are important to the overall success of the organization, rather than getting bogged down in the daily minutia.

Leadership requires facilitating a broader architecture that creates balance between the innovators and the implementers of the organization. W.L. Gore divides their workers into rainmakers and implementers. The rainmakers come up with the wild ideas while the implementers make them happen (Safian, 2012). Rainmakers can drive implementers crazy and implementers will gravitate toward control, so organizations must be able to handle a good dose of chaos to keep the two in balance.

Leaderless

Flat, Agile or otherwise, *Open Organizations* are often called leaderless organizations. In Chapter 4 we established that such labeling creates great uneasiness among the classically trained leaders. Organizations of the future are deliberately getting rid of leaders and managers who boss people around to build the kind of culture that pushes forward creativity and collaboration with everyone leading rather than following (Chen, 2013). GitHub offers the example of emerging organizations that avoid the notion of leaders and managers.

Demographic trends are proving that organizations must flatten their hierarchies and do more with less human capital. Most managers are classically trained to run an organization via the command-and-control hierarchy. However, management will be forced to evolve into something greater than a single position of status. Organizations are not moving to leaderless in an effort to dump leaders insomuch as they are trending toward self-leadership models where everyone contributes from their own strength and skillset. Everyone has a say in the strategy and direction of the organization as a whole. For many it appears counterproductive to let everyone loose to do whatever they want (Chen). This is where organizations must begin to rely on strong *First Principles* and *Governance*.

My first thoughts on a leaderless organization takes me back to the classic book *The Lord of The Flies*, in which a group of kids find themselves stranded on an island with no adult supervision and no sense of who should be in charge. What ensues in the novel is utter chaos! Unlike *The Lord of the Flies*, an *Open Organization* does not mean it is a lawless free-for-all; it is a structure in which people manage themselves and each other (Chen). In fact, we are about to see the greatest shift in organizational leadership since Fredrick Taylor adopted the *Scientific Management Approach* to production in the 1890s. This shift comes from the way we approach leadership from the ground up. We must begin to acknowledge the correlation between effective leadership and how much autonomy is given to the followers.

A leader who does not trust their followers appears to have the most trouble with these changes. Leaders who tend to micromanage their human capital will have the most to overcome. Leaders must let go and learn the art of empowering their followers. The power behind the *Open Organization* is that people already tend to self-manage when everyone else can see what they're doing. *Open* allows other people to jump in when they notice something is going amiss and everyone learns when someone makes a mistake or does something brilliant. Organizations must begin to hire *Knowledge Workers* whom are highly skilled and able to work independently and within teams where needed. No longer can an organization hire individuals to do one job based on title and job description. Organizations must hire individuals to be problem solvers and decision-makers.

Managers of classical hierarchies will tend to strangle agility, bogging the organization down in the process of decision-making. Many classically trained managers seek to define the organization based on the flow of information based on an organizational chart. However, the organization chart of the future will look completely different if not absent altogether. The organization chart explains in detail the channels of decision-making and communication within an organization. Organizational charts are nothing more than a nineteenth century design for command-and-control which is most often focused on the leader(s) at the pinnacle or top of the organization chart. Even in a matrix organizational chart there is a top and bottom. No matter how flashy or descriptive, the organization chart's days may be numbered.

First—organization charts represent a structure that is subject to bottle-necks in decision-making and limits the organization's agility. If you want to see where the problems are in an organization, you may not need to look any further than the organization chart (if you can find it). If you were to take an earnest survey of any organization you might find that the structure presented slows down decision-making and impacts the overall agility of the organization. In contrast to the average company today, the twenty-first century organization will require greater flexibility as its access to full-time human capital diminishes. An organization will not improve under twenty-first century conditions if its structure remains rigid and cumbersome.

For many leaders the organization chart is a safety blanket that provides them with absolutely no real coverage. Asking simple questions such as, "How long does it take for a decision to be made?" "Does your front line have to ask their manager for approval for everything?" or "Are you hiring based on an outdated slot on your org chart or are you hiring the best and empowering them to do their jobs?" will all offer insight into the problems present in the current organizational structure.

As we have established in previous chapters, this is not how systems work in the natural world. Organizations are flattening, embracing self-leadership and a more *Open Approach* to the process of business. Organizations must find organic approaches to dealing with change and innovation. The organization of the future must be unfettered to make decisions. Leaders must redefine their roles in relation to organizational effectiveness. The organization of the twenty-first century must be more agile than ever before. Organizational design is essential to how the organization deals with the challenges it now faces.

Leaderless is not about focusing on your product or service but on your company's people, processes, and technology, which are the real drivers of success (Chen). When we throw out the organization chart we begin to focus on drivers of success rather than the structure. Leaderless organizations work by building, evolving, and finessing a working configuration of the right people, processes, and technologies—relaxing certain traditional controls but making sure to harness the autonomy to useful effect (Chen). In contrast, traditional structures lock organizations into channels of thinking that limit their natural ability to change as conditions require. In the end the *Open Organization* is not really leaderless, but an organization of self-leaders. A leaderless organization is really about deemphasizing the role of leader and elevating all of the organization's members to the role of decision-maker and active stakeholders of the organization's direction and success.

Catalyst

The role of a leader, such as the founder or CEO, within an *Open Organizational* context can best be defined as a *Catalyst*. A *Catalyst Leader* gets a decentralized organization going and then cedes control to its members (Brafman and Beckstrom, p. 92). Typically the *Catalyst Leader* is the founder of the organization. An attribute of a *Catalyst Leader* is their explicit trust in the members of the organization. In the context of a *Catalyst Leader*, their role is as an inspirational figure who spurs others to action (Brafman and Beckstrom, p. 93). The *Catalyst Leader* is seen as the one who casts the vision and direction of the organization including the organization's *First Principles* and *Governance*. A *Catalyst Leader* may also engage members on policy matters and help settle disputes, but beyond that they people within the organization incredible amounts of freedom to do their jobs (Brafman and Beckstrom, p. 112). The *Catalyst Leader* is constantly looking for ways to elevate individuals. They are actively seeking ways to help others and empower them. It takes a special kind of leader to acknowledge that their goal is to become obsolete within the organization.

Open Leadership

The *Open Organization* relies heavily on *Open Leadership* which means ceding control to others via technologies and other means to reduce transaction costs and enable collective action (Barbour, p. 42). The idea of *Open Leadership* mirrors that of the *Open Organization* in that leadership is shared amongst the members of the organization. An *Open Leader* has a balanced blend of personal confidence, intellectual humility, and open-mindedness (Taylor and LaBarre, 2006, p. 110). The leader has strong self-esteem and an ability to engage human capital at a higher level of efficiency than their traditional counterparts. The *Open Leader* does not operate as a command-and-control micromanager. Elevating transparency, the *Open Leader* does not operate in hiding and will do their best to keep decisions and actions out in the open, explaining the basis on which decisions were made (Rider, 2006, p. 62). An *Open Leader* assumes employees have a high level of control over situations within the organization, meaning the extent to which members contribute directly by their own actions or indirectly by actualizing the resources of others to the innovative improvement of a situation (Bodo, pp. 11–12). When possible, the *Open Leader* will assume the possibility that the organization's human capital is more than capable of achieving success and that nothing is done in secret.

An *Open Leader* not only believes that their employees will show initiative, engagement, and independence, but encourage it every chance they can (Bodo, pp. 11–12). It is this belief that empowers the members to do their jobs with excellence. Within *Open Leadership*, each member of the organization is managed differently and they have their own abilities, talents, preferences, and way of thinking (Bodo, p. 12). The *Open Leader* recognizes the strengths of each member and releases them to act within their areas of expertise. An *Open Leader* will regard their leadership as a constant dialogue between themselves and their followers and attempts to transfer knowledge to their followers (Bodo, pp. 12–13). Because we as humans want to be heard and understood, the power of interacting and listening to followers is essential to who an *Open Leader* is and should be.

Empowerment

An *Open Organization* cannot be considered *Open* if empowerment of human capital is not present. Leading an *Open Organization* requires an explicit amount of empowerment of the organization's human capital. Empowerment provides the followers with meaningful, self-fulfilling jobs and organizations that are responsive to their needs (Kuczmarski and Kuczmarski, p. 21). Empowerment is the engagement of self-management and leadership within the confines of the organization's structure. Empowerment cannot be present without a high level of self-confidence from leadership at all levels.

The *Open Organization* concept relies heavily on the leader distributing power among their followers. While this may appear counterintuitive to the classically trained leader, what we find is that a leader will gain more power by empowering others (Hackman and Johnson, pp. 143–146). There are five major reasons why a leader should share power. In an organizational setting, distributing power increases job satisfaction and performance of employees; fosters greater cooperation among members; distributed power means collective survival; effective leadership helps personal growth and learning; and sharing power prevents abuse of power (Hackman and Johnson, p. 143–146). Self-managed teams exhibit increased performance and peer pressure is a strong motivating force as employees are willing to please people who mean something to them (University of Iowa, 2012). Empowerment also decreases the psychological distance between leader and followers and helps build stronger, more cohesive teams.

Empowerment is more than just giving authority to members of the organization. Empowerment is about acknowledging the skills, abilities, and trust the leader has in their human capital. Empowerment also means helping followers to believe in their own abilities or what psychologists call *Efficacy Expectation* (Hackman and Johnson, p. 150). Belief in self is powerful. Followers who believe that they have the personal power are more likely to take initiatives, set and achieve higher goals, and to persist in the face of difficult circumstances (Hackman and Johnson, p. 150). In the case of GitHub, you sense that there is a great deal of ownership of products and services because there is an explicit empowerment within the organization.

An example of empowerment at GitHub came in the form of a solution for a software bug that disrupted a particular client's workflow. Not only did a member of GitHub take the initiative to fix the bug, they refunded the company an entire year of support payments for their trouble. The refund was in the six figures and was not only a powerful example of empowerment but also excellence in customer service. When Tom Preston-Werner was asked about his feelings over refunding such a large amount of money, he said that he didn't even know about the incident but was happy the employee took the initiative and was proud of their decision. Tom's response exemplifies the absolute trust he has in those he has empowered. Organizations that are bottom-line, revenue-driven would have never permitted an employee to make this level of decision-making without the input of several layers of management. GitHub works because they make their customers happy—not just with refunds where necessary—but with excellent products backed up with superior customer service. This level of service is hard to achieve in a strict hierarchical setting. What could have been a customer service disaster turned into a public relations win for GitHub. While the cost to the company was in the six figures, the loss of just one client and bad press would have cost the company far more than the refunded contract amount. In the end, the GitHubber made the right decision and their powerful example has created a very happy customer base.

Members of an *Open Organization* are not just interested in reaching out to customers but are ready to create solutions that will transform the organization's business model (Bernoff and Schadler, p. 7). The truest essence of empowerment is through the members of the organization who are now permitted to think and act for themselves—to think about solutions to problems and to anticipate future wants and needs of the clients. It is difficult for a top-down command-and-control organization to permit employees to act in such free patterns of decision-making. For an organization to achieve *Openness* they must empower the members to solve problems (Bernoff and Schadler, p. 7).

Empowering the organization's human capital does not mean that they are waiting for something to break, but are constantly seeking new and inventive ways to meet the client's current and future needs. For this to happen, leaders must let go of the reins and allow human capital to come up with solutions on their own. This would mean that leadership's new job, aside from casting the vision, is to support and empower employees in their effort to create new and lasting solutions (Bernoff and Schadler, p. 7).

Empowerment provides members of the organization with strong motivation because it meets the higher needs of individuals by releasing potential and motivation within employees through increased responsibility and an expectation that people will strive to do their very best (Daft, 2002, p. 296). Tom Preston-Werner at GitHub is clear that he does not abdicate his role as CEO, but maintains the right to the final word on things. In fact he, like all leaders of *Open Organizations*, does not actually give power to his members but shares his power with them. An *Open Organization* is more powerful because everyone has a share of the power and, in turn, the employees use more of themselves to do their jobs (Daft, 2002, p. 296). Because leaders are limited in their amount of time, energy, knowledge, and scope of authority, empowering employees enlists the aid of many to cope with uncertainty beyond the leader's own limits (Yun, et al., p. 375). Power sharing becomes a magnifying effect in that two are better than one and three are better than two. Followers have flexibility to engage their own ability more fully to help the organization enhance competitiveness; today's employees increasingly view their jobs as a means of personal fulfillment, not just a paycheck and, as a result, people increasingly expect control and influence over their own jobs and over the decisions that are related to their own jobs (Yun, et al., p. 375).

The empowering leader emphasizes follower self-influence, rather than providing followers with orders and commands. An empowering leader is one who leads others to influence themselves to achieve high performance, not one who leaves others to do whatever they want to do (Yun, et al., p. 378). GitHub achieves this through the creation of "mini-managers" who take responsibility for making their own decisions. In reviewing the practices of GitHub no evidence was found of command-and-control. What was found was a great deal of discussion around ideas with the chance for members to participate in the dialogue until there was a consensus on the desired solution to a problem.

Transparency

Transparency has long been an important management topic: how much, with whom, and about what should be shared within the organization. Transparency is built into an *Open Organization* through empowerment and the use of a *Knowledge Commons*. Transparency is the essence of an *Open Organization's* ecosystem. Everyone within an *Open Organization* can complete their assignments easily and with as much accuracy as possible, giving them an understanding of what matters and provides information, and what boosts buy-in and energy from the organization's members (Griffith, 2012, p. 26). We find that when there is no transparency in a decision-making process, the decisions appear arbitrary and possibly even self-serving (Griffith, p. 26). *Open Organizations* like GitHub work hard to make sure that decisions are public so that there is little chance for them to be seen as arbitrary. When things are done in hiding, they create distrust. When they are done in the open, they create outlets for understanding and acceptance.

Transparency brings information to the organization and allows for everyone to embrace the reality of each circumstance before them (Safian). Transparency requires an organization whose leaders are growing in maturity to share complex issues with its broader population. Leaders such as, W.L. Gore's CEO, feel it is important that the broader population of the company see the stress and appreciates the challenges that their leadership may face (Safian). This kind of transparency builds a stronger level of trust with the workers. There is no sugar coating the challenges facing the organization. This level of transparency coupled with explicit communication helps the members of the organization to get behind the push to find solutions to the problems faced. Within more traditional organizations we find the polar opposite, as leaders feel the need to insulate the employees from the challenges and thereby creating a disconnected workforce. Workers, especially the younger generation, are exposed to so much information and do not expect it to be filtered (Safian). When you filter information you create a workforce that is helpless to affect positive and useful change in the organization. Sharing information becomes central to the effectiveness of the *Open Organization*.

When members of an *Open Organization* regularly publish their work in a *Knowledge Commons*, everyone in the organization benefits because this information is now considered part of the organization's public ownership of knowledge (P2P Foundation, 2011a). When there is public ownership of knowledge, others are able to contribute in the process of decisions and solutions. Permitting this level of transparency allows others to recognize interdependencies between you and other groups because they can see what you are doing and people can identify possible consequences of your work and hold individuals accountable for the work they do (P2P Foundation, 2010). Transparency provides a more thorough view of what is going on from all angles within the organization. Transparency helps individuals—if they can see what others are doing they can understand how their work relates to it (P2P Foundation, 2010). When we are able to see the how our work connects with others, we are able to be more effective in the work we do. When your work, your communication, and ideas are displayed transparently in a *Knowledge Commons*, members of the organization know where you stand, why you make the decisions you make, and how you operate on a day-to-day basis.

Accountability

In an *Open Organization* everyone, including the leadership, is accountable to everyone else. Accountability helps to regulate or constrain behaviors so that things will work but this constraining function can also hinder your ability to drive adoption of your innovation if it requires people to act in ways that conflict with prevailing accountabilities (Krippendorff, 2008, p. 86). Accountability is measured against the organization's *First Principles* and *Governance*. Accountability works because the members know that their actions are judged by others in the organization. In studying GitHub it was found that accountability is a powerful tool that helps members think clearly before posting a response to a problem on the *Knowledge Commons*. This means that knowing you are being held accountable helps self-regulate responses. Accountability in these instances helps the participating members to create clarity of thought before responding. This would mean that there is less "firing from the hip" and more concise thought process going into an idea.

Accountability creates higher levels of cohesiveness within self-managing teams and thereby encourages increased performance (Science Daily, 2012, p. 63). Cohesiveness expresses how well individuals work together. As is the case with GitHub, cohesiveness can include higher levels of disagreement and healthy doses of peer pressure. In fact, peer pressure is a strong motivating force within an *Open Organization* and a worker's willingness to please people who mean something to them is often a stronger motivating force than any financial rewards management might throw their way (Science Daily, p. 63). Properly maintained accountability creates healthy levels of peer pressure which creates a need for members of the organization to please others around them. Studies have noted that peer pressure is an important social force, as workers don't want to disappoint their team members, so appealing to the team spirit is more effective even than money as a motivating tool (Science Daily, p. 63). We all have a desire to be accepted and liked. This need to be "liked" is so strong that peer pressure from team members is more effective in prompting strong performance from workers (Science Daily, p. 63).

Team cohesiveness and accountability permits discussions that will help transform ideas into realities but also help individuals search for possible effects of their actions and to adapt their work to prevent adverse results (P2P Foundation, 2011 a). Accountability creates a more holistic approach to decision-making in that those who hold pieces of the knowledge collectively create a more thorough view of the results of one action over another. In an *Open Organization*, accountability means that those who are affected by a decision can participate in making that decision and sets limits by allowing those who are affected by a decision to overrule those who are working on it, even to cancel a project if a major problem arises (P2P Foundation, 2011a). This is a powerful element of the *Open Organization* concept in that decisions are made and monitored by all who affected by them. This creates care in decision-making that is not likely achievable in a more traditional command-and-control, top-down hierarchical organization.

Metrics of Success

The *Open Organization* does not abandon metrics of success. Regardless of structure, all organizations must have some way of measuring their level of success in the marketplace. Traditional hierarchical organizations have performance appraisals and sales commissions as part of their awards system. In an *Open Organization*, metrics of success rely on cultural attributes such as employee satisfaction, *Happiness*, participation, and overall integration of the organization's *First Principles*. Each organization develops their own metrics of success as part of their *Governance*.

Some organizations, such as GitHub, have a form of *Gamification*, in which contributors are recognized for the amount of code they develop over a period of time. *Gamification* is the study of building game-like logic and workflow into products, services, and environments (Bacon, 2012). An *Open Organization* engages workers in the process and rewards them with intrinsic motivators for their contributions. The criterion for *Gamification* is primarily hinged around the idea that accomplishments should be based upon "new experiences" and the "acquisition of new skills" (Bacon). *Gamification* is a layer in the optimization for *Happiness*. Merit awards or "trophies" are awarded as recognition for achievements. Some of these awards are automated while others may be manually awarded by members of the organization.

PART III
The Twenty-First Century Organization

Chapter 9
Cultural Literacy

We live in a time of unprecedented globalism. Businesses, people, and economies are tied together in ways we could not have imagined 40 years ago. Organizations must now compete within a global landscape where clients and even the workforce are culturally diverse and geographically dispersed. Organizations are

When we know how someone thinks we are able to better lead them in a context that they will understand.

networked and interlaced around the globe through the Internet and mobile technologies. Crossing and operating within cultural boundaries must become a skill of the leaders and followers of the future. Organizations of the future must become culturally literate if they are to successfully compete under these emerging paradigms.

In Chapter 1 we introduced the era of *Organization 3.0* in which organizations increasingly find themselves comprised of individuals from differing cultural origins. How we engage culture is truly based on the way we see others. In dealing with cultural differences we must begin to consider our own worldview or presuppositions which we hold about the basic makeup of the world around us (Sire, p. 16). Understanding a worldview forces us to ask fundamental questions such as "What is our worldview and biases of other cultures?" Considering one's worldview helps us to understand the challenges multinational companies have in their integration of activities that take place in different countries (Galbraith, 2000, p. 3). Understanding an individual's worldview or cultural influence should be an essential element in the success of an *Open Organization.*

In Chapter 4 we discussed how decision-making is achieved in an *Open Organization.* We begin to understand that decisions are a complex matter derived from personal understanding and experiences. Decision-making styles are very much influenced by culture and culture is the perceptual filter or lens which in turn establishes people's decisions (Mintzberg, et al., p. 269). Perceptual filters and lenses are directly related to the culture to which one belongs. Because we understand thought to be culturally based and constructed, members of a culture not only think about different things they simply think differently (Zweifel, 2003, pp. 14–15). Understanding how people think within the context of their culture is a powerful tool leaders must employ within the *Open Organization*. When we know how someone thinks we are able to better lead them in a context that they will understand. Breakdowns in communication, decision-making, and a resistance to change appear linked to a shared commitment to beliefs which encourages consistency in an organization's behaviors, and thereby discourages change in strategy (Mintzberg, et al., p. 269). Arguably, it boils down to how a person's worldview may influence the organization. Considering a dispersed workforce in a global economy, we begin to see the challenges emerging for the leaders of the future.

Much can be said for the individual who attempts to understand and seek greater familiarity with a given culture. This creates emotional connections with followers that are best achieved through sincere interest in their language, customs, food, and other cultural attributes as well as skillfully listening and responding to needs. Considering the cultural attribute of time, we note that time is more fluid in Latin cultures which do not place the same importance on punctuality as their American counterparts.

Arriving early within a Latin culture is considered rude. When leaders begin to understand difference in cultural attributes, they are better able to assimilate into the culture and are less likely to offend. Leaders begin to sharpen their global literacies when they are able to embrace these differences. Understanding these global literacies will better assist in our ability to lead with a worldview and a fresh global approach to our work (Rosen, et al., 2000, p. 58).

While English remains the global language of business, we must still deal with differing languages that create barriers to effective leadership within the global context. As we found in Chapter 6, communication is central to the concept of an *Open Organization*. How information flows within the system is important to the global success of the organization. It therefore becomes imperative that leaders of global organizations begin to understand the impact their approach to communication and relationships has on differing cultures (Prichard, 2012). When we begin to engage human capital within the context of their culture, we produce greater success within the context of optimized *Happiness*.

There has long been certain barriers in cross-cultural communication. They exist when individuals are not able to effectively communicate wants, needs, and desires to one another. A global leader must be able to effectively communicate and build the organization's vision despite these challenges (Marquardt and Berger, 2000, p. 31). This becomes a greater challenge when the organization, such as an *Open Organization*, is dispersed across many cultures and is linked together through technology. When individuals do not share a common language, it becomes difficult to get people to comprehend the vision or direction of the organization (Marquardt and Berger, p. 31). While not speaking in a common language creates its own challenges, the ability to listen for verbal and social cues in a foreign language becomes a greater challenge. When an individual does not understand what is being communicated a barrier is present.

Global leaders understand language is not just about communication between individuals but is the very reflection of the culture in which the organization operates (Zweifel, p. 25). Holding a common language aids in the development of lasting friendships and trust within the context of differing cultures. Unfortunately our natural impulse is to homogenize everything rather than relish diversity and learn from it (Marquardt and Berger, p. 50). In business we tend to homogenize in an effort to keep everyone on the same page. In the case of a dispersed, global organization there becomes a pressure to set standards that are designed to keep everyone in the communication loop. English, for example, is considered the language of business with more than one billion people in over 100 countries speaking it as either a first or second language (Marquardt and Berger, p. 4). More specifically, English has become the global language of media and carries certain cultural and social values (Marquardt and Berger, p. 4). Breaking down barriers is about human relationships and how they are developed through understanding of languages and culture.

While English may still be the universal language of business, not everyone speaks it fluently. With the advent of more sophisticated technology, we one day may be able to type or speak our language of choice into our computers and it would then be translated into the receiver's language with little effort. Until such time, cross-cultural communication will remain a challenge. It can be extremely difficult for differing cultures to interpret information conveyed in a foreign language, either written or verbal, as colloquial expressions and subtle meanings within the given language can present certain barriers to effective communication (Eisenberg and Goodall, p. 211). Literature reveals cultures as human (symbolic) creations which create varying assumptions, expectations, and rules for interaction (Hackman and Johnson, p. 297). Each culture creates its own communication patterns of verbal and non-verbal codes used to convey meanings in face-to-face encounters (Hackman and Johnson, p. 297).

Perhaps the reason less material is translated as a whole is due to the enormity of the challenge of effectively knowing the nuances of two or more languages at a level needed to effectively convey the original message.

Cross-cultural communications is critical not just in the business world, but with governments and people alike (Johnson). Language is the mechanism that helps people organize their perceptions and shape their worldviews (Hackman and Johnson, p. 297). A global leader's ability to connect people and build successful teams in a cross-cultural environment is a crucial competency (Johnson). Building a cross-cultural relationship requires an ability to process or decode information from their environment as well as learning to encode by effectively conveying messages and taking the most appropriate actions to overcome problems (Northouse, p. 165). In dealing with cross-cultural communication we must acknowledge that communication encompasses not only words and actions, but also all types of non-verbal communication and patterns of interaction in society at large (Eisenberg and Goodall, p. 139). The ideal scenario for any cross-cultural organization would be the creation of synergy by which decision-makers draw on the diversity of the group to produce a new, better than expected solution (Hackman and Johnson, p. 305).

High- and Low-Context Cultures

In dealing with culture in an *Open Organization*, we must begin to understand the context by which individuals process information. In the 1970s, Edward Hall developed the concept of High- and Low-Context cultures as a way of describing the methodology by which individuals interact within a given cultural setting. Hall defined High-Context cultures as: covert and implicit; messages are internalized; strong use of non-verbal coding; reserved reactions to messages; distinct in-groups and out-groups; strong interpersonal bonds amongst members; high commitment among members and time is *Open* and flexible (Katz, 2006).

High-Context cultures assume that the people we speak to understand the context of our message and the implied ideas of our message (Foster, 2012). In High-Context cultures, such as China and Japan, individuals receive information about the meaning of a messages based on the setting in which the message is communicated (Katz). The challenge of a High-Context culture is in the fact that ideas are not spelled out nor defined in detail (Katz). In High-Context environments individuals who share common implied meanings prefer communicating in more indirect or covert ways through non-verbal communication and meanings (Katz). In contrast a Low-Context culture would consider High-Context cultures to be somewhat passive aggressive in their communication styles (Katz).

Low-Context cultures such as Great Britain and Germany use their words to embed greater meaning and their messages are more direct when speaking (Katz). Hall defined these Low-Context cultures as: overt and explicit; messages are plainly coded; message detail is direct and verbalized; message receivers' reactions are on the surface; flexible in-groups and out-groups; interpersonal relationships are more fragile; commitment is low; and time is highly organized (Katz).

Within a Low-Context culture, individuals are willing to work alone and with others they don't know as long as the process and procedures have been well defined (Peters, 2011). In an *Open Organization*, projects are optimized best for Low-Context cultures (Peters). Conversely, High-Context cultures have a more difficult time participating in an *Open* context with people they've never met and have no previous relationship with (Peters). Building an *Open Organization* requires understanding of both High- and Low-Context cultures to best meet the needs of all members of the organization.

High-Context communication assumes that the people we speak to are wise to the context in which our message is set and ideas are not spelled out in detail (Babel, n.d.). Group members make the assumption that they share common meanings and prefer indirect or covert messaging that relies heavily on non-verbal codes and understanding (Hackman and Johnson, p. 300). We could argue that in some cases an *Open Organization* may act like a High-Context environment in that individuals are thought to understand the context by which they receive information.

Power–Distance

Within an *Open Organization*, Hofstede's power–distance is also an important attribute to consider in the development of a cross-cultural communication strategies. Power–distance is the extent to which the less powerful members of institutions and organizations expect and accept that power is distributed unequally (Tamas). Hofstede argues that all societies are unequal and within High power–distance cultures the inequality is considered to be a natural part of their world. In contrast, Low power–distance cultures are uncomfortable with differences in wealth, status, power, and privilege (Hackman and

Johnson, p. 302). Power–distance, specifically High power–distance cultures, can become a barrier to the successful operation of an *Open Organization* as they do not accept the equal distribution of power.

Management and national boundaries are no longer congruent. The scope of management can no longer be politically defined (Zweifel, p. 2). The norm since 1648 has been the nation-state; however since the Second World War we have seen a transformation of our global identity (Zweifel, p. 8). Understanding the impact of globalization is helpful to the cross-cultural leader. Lack of understanding will create serious difficulties for leaders when dealing with followers who prefer different communication styles (Hackman and Johnson, p. 301).

An *Open Organization* requires little power–distance between leaders and followers. The greater the distance between a leader and their followers, the closer the supervision of the follower's activities and the less *Open* an organization becomes (Hackman and Johnson, p. 302). Followers in High power–distance countries expect managers to give direction and feel uncomfortable when asked to participate in decision-making (Hackman and Johnson, p. 302). This too creates a challenge in an *Open Organization* where followers are expected to make their own decisions with little input from leadership. Coercive, authoritarian leadership is more common in High power–distance countries; democratic leadership is more often the norm in Low power–distance cultures (Hackman and Johnson, p. 302). Organizations operating in Low power–distance countries are less centralized and distribute rewards more equally (Hackman and Johnson, p. 302). Low power–distance cultures, by nature, have an easier time developing and operating within the context of an *Open System*.

An *Open Organization Approach* requires a healthy attitude among both leaders and followers. This attitude will require the suspension of fears related to risk and rewards (Simoes-Brown, p. 51). Within an *Open Organization*, the approach to decision-making appears counterintuitive or even contradictory to an individual's *upbringing* and, despite the individual's background, consensus is actually much easier to achieve than they might think (Ousterhout). An *Open Organization* will require not only the vulnerability of the followers but also the leader. From a leadership perspective this requires understanding of the culture from which they operate (Foster, 2012).

Improving Cultural Communication

As noted in Chapter 6, communication skills are essential to the operation of an *Open Organization*. Improving these skills requires an understanding of the mechanics of communications. In 1967, research by Mehrabian and Ferris inferred that communication is 7 percent verbal (words), 38 percent vocal (para-verbal), and 55 percent facial/body language (non-verbal) (Lapakko, 1997, p. 63). The non-verbal dimensions of intercultural communication are both important and culturally specific (Eisenberg and Goodall, p. 261). It becomes clear that understanding cultural nuance is essential to success in any culture. The greater challenge is in understanding what those nuances are and how to effectively utilize them in a cross-cultural setting.

Within the discipline of communication, literature reveals general axioms, such as *we cannot not communicate* or *meanings are in people, not in words* (Lapakko, p. 63). When combined with Hofstede's characteristics of High- and Low-Context cultures, we begin to understand the deeper implications of the Mehrabian and Ferris axiom of communication. Both High- and Low-Context cultures hold different delivery and receptions of verbal and non-verbal messages. Considering the Mehrabian and Ferris research, High-Context cultures rely heavily on facial/body language to interpret messages while Low-Context cultures are more likely to utilize all coefficients of the communications process.

Understanding the differences in High- and Low-Context cultures is only part of the process leaders must achieve. Add to these mechanics an understanding of Polychronic and Monochronic communication processes and you've added an additional layer of complexity to the messages being communicated. For example: Monochronic cultures presume that a Polychronic culture is disinterested in the message being sent because they are often multitasking during message delivery (Foster, 2012). Likewise a Polychronic culture might believe a Monochronic culture to be strict in their approach to communication (Foster, 2012). Additional considerations would be in how the culture approaches appointments and time. While some may find chronic lateness to be acceptable, other cultures might perceive this as rude. Understanding these deeper nuances as the sum of the communication process is important to interpreting the messages being presented (Foster, 2012).

Given these complexities, we cannot simply define communication as the act of conveying information through the combined effect of simultaneous verbal, vocal, and facial attitude. Listening skills are essential to good communication, but we must consider how the interpretations of such conveyed information is achieved. When we consider the non-verbal dimensions of intercultural communication we must confront the differing cultural behaviors. These cultural nuances become essential to the overall success of the leader from within the culture they operate (Foster, 2012).

Curiosity and the insatiable desire to learn will lead one to not only embrace their experiences, but also make sense of them (Black, et al., p. 61). Such curiosity is at the heart of the *Open Organizational* structure. Central to the *Open Organization's* spirit is the pursuit of learning at every opportunity. It is through learning we are able to better make sense of the so-called ever-changing kaleidoscopic images viewed through our paradigms as cultural bias and acquisition (Black, et al., p. 61). While not perfect, the pursuit of learning through curiosity is what makes an *Open Organization* more culturally adept. We are all humans on one planet and with such complexity we must learn to observe, deliberate, and ponder to best master our approach to people (Black, et al., p. 58). The human condition appears to be sublimated to our ability to desire and achieve relationships with others. It is through this relationship that we build understanding, mutual respect and trust (Foster, 2012).

Improving communication skills also requires an understanding of generational bias. Avoiding such bias is important to the success of an *Open Organization*. Cultures change over time and older cohorts within a given culture may not be the same as the younger cohorts within that culture (Hackman and Johnson, p. 298). Therefore, it is reasonable to argue that when listening and sharing ideas within a culture we must take into account these demographics. Older generations typically wonder how effective younger generations are in the workplace because the younger generation is constantly connecting through social networks (Lancaster and Stillman, 2010, p. 198). The Boomer generation is more likely, at least in the West, to wonder whether or not the younger generations are pulling their weight (Lancaster and Stillman, p. 198). Not every member within a cultural group will act and respond the same way (Hackman and Johnson, p. 298).

When we recognize that cultural activities outside the market create customized products relevant to the culture (Branch, 2012) we create innovation and cultural market viability. Millennials want to be innovators and have mastered the ever-evolving array of technology (Lancaster and Stillman, p. 102). While it is argued that changes within a given culture are difficult because cultures are organized around deeply rooted assumptions and values, we must relish diversity and learn from each other so that these cultural differences thrive and coexist (Hackman and Johnson, p. 243; Marquardt and Berger, 2000, p. 50).

Conflict Resolution

Finally, we learned in Chapter 6 that conflict is an important element in the structure of an *Open Organization*. Understanding how conflicts arise is essential to operating within an *Open System*. There are ways we can be more culturally sensitive in handling resolution of conflicts (Elmer, 1993, p. 46). The goal of conflict resolution within a given culture is to understand that everyone has a vested interest and those who gain awareness and understanding of such interest can creatively manage the situation as to protect the dignity of those involved (Elmer, p. 59). Conflict resolution requires an understanding of values and an ability to communicate within a given culture.

Understanding values helps the communicator understand why a culture will attempt to preserve itself when threatened (Foster, 2012). Cultural barriers in language restricts the communicator's ability to listen, understand, and approach the culture with sensitivity to those who operate within the culture (Foster, 2012). Such disconnect might hinder any emotional connection with those within the culture (Black, et al., p. 120). While Westerners prefer and default to a more direct approach to communication without taking it personally, shame-based cultures prefer more indirect approaches to conflict. Individuals are not singled out and problems are seen as a communal affair (Elmer, p. 46). Language in North America supports directness and holds some distinct advantages, yet such communication style may alienate those originating from a more indirect culture (Elmer, p. 46). Some may see directness in communication as crude, harsh, uncultured, and certainly disrespectful if not cruel (Elmer, p. 50). Global leaders grow to understand that forcing someone to change from their cultural experience means the leader is avoiding their own awkwardness of changing and thus expecting someone to be more like them (Elmer, p. 53). Global leadership understands that each individual has a vested interest and how they protect the dignity of those within the culture builds *Openness* and trust in the relationship the leader has with his followers (Elmer, p. 59).

To interpret the culture and its impact on conflict we must begin to understand inquisitiveness of self is at the core of effective global leadership (Black, et al., p. 27). To best bridge the gap of conflict it becomes important to consider one's own cultural literacy. We must start with our own core values and beliefs and then be able to clearly communicate them to our followers (Rosen, et al., p. 191). Yet, understanding one's own core values is only the start. We must understand the culture from which we operate. Westerners will often misinterpret cultural responses specifically in the area of cultural indirectness.

Literature argues that personal transformation is needed in doing business across cultures (McCall and Hollenbeck, 2002, p. 215). Transformation begins with leaders who are able to manage their mindset as it relates to: themselves (the reflective mindset); organizations (the analytical mindset); context (the worldly mindset); relationships (the collaborative mindset); change (the action mindset) (Stanford, p. 225).

Conflicts are inevitable. Conflicts are most likely to occur when a person or a group feels that their social, psychological, emotional, physical, or other space is threatened (Stanford, p. 235). We must transcend our own cultural defaults and look beyond the horizon to other ways of thinking to begin to understand cultural conflicts. The application of adaptation and an ability to separate the person from the problem is essential to a leader's overall effectiveness in cross-cultural communication and conflict resolution (Lanier, 2012; Foster, 2012).

For some conflict is to be avoided at all costs. This permits conflict to go unresolved or shifts the responsibility on others for solving the problem. It does not allow these individuals to preserve important goals, values and ideas—nor does it allow them to preserve relationships (Fletcher, 2012; Elmer, p. 36). From a Westerners point of view, the idea that avoiding conflict somehow causes it to go away most often creates the dynamic in which the individual ends up with weak or superficial relationships and little to no influence on important decisions (Elmer, p. 36). However, strategic withdrawal can be a wise choice when emotions are running high and if the confrontation may cause someone to act unwisely or lose control (Elmer, p. 39). Conflict avoidance is also wise when the potential consequences of confrontation are too serious (Elmer, p. 39). Avoiding conflict can be a sign of wisdom and maturity in some cases and in others it may signal an unwillingness to discuss important issues or a refusal to take a stand on a given decision (Elmer, p. 39).

While some seek to avoid conflict, others seek compromise. Compromising seeks to set a middle ground between two parties (Fletcher). However, many simply give in to accommodate or smooth over the differences (Elmer, p. 39). Smoothing over these differences through accommodation may or may not actually resolve the conflict. Some may see most issues as negotiable and differences not worth fighting about (Elmer, p. 39). Those who are more apt to accommodate are most often willing to forfeit personal goals and values and can be taken advantage of since they are most likely unable to say no (Elmer, p. 39). Contrary to the Western view of conflict resolution, our Asian counterparts are more likely to work to prevent conflicts or avoid them altogether (Fletcher). While conflict avoidance is typically preferred, some recognize the benefits of conflict and its role in generating different ideas and perspectives as well as facilitating the sharing of information (Eisenberg and Goodall, p. 288). Therefore, some degree of conflict is essential to achieving higher levels of productivity and effective communication (Eisenberg and Goodall, p. 288).

In dealing with conflict, leaders should develop a *cultural hermeneutic* that assist the leader and organization to function successfully within a given culture (Branch, 2011). The essence of a *cultural hermeneutic* should be to develop processes whereby the source of conflict is understood and where possible avoided. To develop a *cultural hermeneutic* we must first understand the nature of conflict in what is defined as the interaction of interdependent people who perceive opposition of goals, aims, and values, and who see the other parties as potentially interfering with the realization of these goals (Eisenberg and Goodall, p. 288). Literature argues that conflicts should be understood as a portion of a broader network of interdependencies that produce an increasingly wider impact within the culture (Eisenberg and Goodall, p. 169). Language is used to frame and work through the context of conflict and is invaluable in assisting individuals understanding of dealing with disputes (Eisenberg and Goodall, p. 169). It can be argued that developing a *cultural hermeneutic* should include an understanding of cultural context and language as well as the impact of conflict within the culture and its use as a lubricant to information sharing and productivity.

Understanding the nature of conflict is important to its management. Understanding the nature of conflict is critical to developing and maintaining lasting relationships (Gudykunst and Kim, 2003, p. 296). Literature reveals several sources of conflict. First, they occur when people misinterpret behaviors (Gudykunst and Kim, p. 296). This misinterpretation comes from the way we view our surroundings through our own cultural lenses and filters. Second, conflict arises from perceptions of incompatibility, such as personalities or group characteristics (Gundykunst and Kim, 2003, p. 296). When there appears an affront to one's culture, members of that culture will defend it in what James Sire called *cultural relativism* or the need to preserve the culture from threat of change (Foster, 2012). Culture influences the way we think about conflicts and our preferences for managing them (Gundykunst and Kim, p. 297).

Conflict arises from either instrumental or expressive sources (Gundykunst and Kim, p. 297). *Expressive conflicts* arise from a desire to release tension, usually generated from hostile feelings and *Instrumental conflicts* stem from a difference in goals or practices (Gundykunst and Kim, p. 297). Finally, conflict arises when people disagree on the cause of their own or other people's behavior (Gundykunst and Kim, p. 296). All incidents of conflict have the same thing in common: *polarized communication*. *Polarized communication* is when the communicator has an inability to believe or seriously consider one's view as wrong and the other's opinion as truth (Gundykunst and Kim, p. 295). Understanding culture and its values aids the communicator in dealing with conflict resolution (Foster, 2012). Dealing with cross-cultural conflict implies that one must deal with certain preferences for conflict styles based on cultural individualism–collectivism and power–distance (Gundykunst and Kim, p. 303).

The goal of an organization is to influence individuals to work effectively together to meet goals and objectives (Stanford, p. 223). Group members may know what they are to achieve but may stall on making decisions, problem solving, handling conflicts, communication, and boundary management (Stanford, p. 223). The matter of conflict is largely attributed to an individual's attitude and is likely to occur when an individual or group feels that their social, psychological, emotional, physical, or other space is threatened (Stanford, p. 235). Cultural communication involves the negotiation of cultural codes through communal conversation which are communicative processes through which individuals negotiate how they will conduct their lives (Gudykunst and Kim, p. 89). While cultural conflicts differ from culture to culture, their commonality is *polarized communication*. Given that patterns of thought are culturally constructed, an inability to believe or seriously consider one's view as wrong and the other's opinion as truth can be debilitating (Zweifel, pp. 14–15; Gundykunst and Kim, p. 295). Such polarization exists when individuals look out for their own interests and have little concern for others' interests (Gundykunst and Kim, p. 295). Polarization requires an understanding of *cultural relativism* which attempts to bring meaning to behaviors in the context of their culture (Gundykunst and Kim, p. 138). The path to resolving cultural conflicts in communication appears to rely heavily on our ability to connect, understand, and empathize with our cultural counterparts.

Several conflict styles are used to manage conflicts: factual–inductive, axiomatic–deductive, and affective–intuitive. The factual–inductive style, typical of the United States, focuses on facts and inductively moves toward a conclusion (Gudykunst and Kim, p. 299). These align with the Universalist culture which prescribes consistent standards irrespective of cultural norms (Lanier). The axiomatic–deductive style relies on general principals and deduces implications for specific situations (Gudykunst and Kim, p. 299). The affective–intuitive style is based on the use of emotional or affective messages

(Gudykunst and Kim, p. 299). Axiomatic–deductive and affective–intuitive styles are synonymous with countries like the Soviet Union (Gudykunst and Kim, p. 299) and are aligned with the Universalist or collectivist cultures (Lanier).

Conflict can be managed, if not averted altogether, through a familiarity of the culture (Lanier). Literature predicts cultural differences are based on five styles: integrating style, compromising style, dominating style, obliging style, and avoiding style (Gudykunst and Kim, p. 300). The integrating style focuses on managing conflict out of high concern for self and others (Gudykunst and Kim, p. 299). The compromising style focuses on moderate concern for self and moderate concern for others (Gudykunst and Kim, p. 300). The dominating style represents a high concern for self and a low concern for others and is typically used to control or dominate (Gudykunst and Kim, 2003, p. 300). An obliging style presents a low concern for self and a high concern for others and is present when we give in to others to avoid conflict (Gudykunst and Kim, 2003, p. 300). Finally, the avoiding style involves low concern for self and others and the topic of conflict is avoided by all at all times (Gudykunst and Kim, 2003, p. 300).

As contemporary Western organizations tend to be task-oriented, conflict becomes inevitable in a cross-cultural setting (Kelly, 2012). Such conflicts are directed toward anyone who aligns themselves with said group (Elmer, p. 58). Elmer (1993) offers the following guidelines for involvement of multiple groups (p. 58–59):

1. Know the groups with whom you intend to work. What has been the history of their relationships? What is the present status of their relationships and are there any underlying issues with explosive potential?

2. Assuming satisfaction, can you work with both groups, lay the foundation by meeting with leadership from both groups at the same time and avoid perceptions of favoritism?

3. Keep time and budget commitments equally divided between the two groups.

4. Maintain regular and joint meetings with the leadership, being sensitive to subtle, indirect messages that may suggest one party is feeling disgruntled about something.

While conflict avoidance is typically preferred, some recognize the benefits of conflict and its role in generating different ideas and perspectives as well as facilitating the sharing of information (Eisenberg and Goodall, p. 288). Therefore, some degree of conflict is essential to achieving higher levels of productivity and effective communication (Eisenberg and Goodall, p. 288). The key to conflict resolution becomes a matter of both understanding the nature of conflict and the management or lack of management thereof.

As organizations become more globally integrated and attempt to develop a more *Open* structure, leading from a global context becomes a complex matter rooted in an ability to understand and connect with the culture and its people. Given that *Open Organizations* rely heavily on an ability to share information across all boundaries, organizations must develop ways to connect with individuals within a given culture and improve the quality of their decisions through the development of close relationships and loyalty with followers. Leading in a global context requires understanding of not just the people but the context of their worldview, customs, local conditions, and laws.

Developing an *Open Organization* requires leaders to develop humility, inquisitiveness, and the earnest desire to build honest connections with those who serve the organization in foreign places. At the end of the day, the successful global leader is more interested in building rapport long before they consider the bottom line. Developing a rapport with their followers, leaders are best able to limit the power–distance and to operate within the trust required for all members of an *Open Organization*.

Developing trust requires interpretation of culture. How we view and interpret the culture is based predominantly on how we see the culture through our own cultural lenses. Cultures are defined by the filters and lenses on which we base our decisions. Considering the lenses by which we view the world we can begin to consider the worldview of others. It becomes essential for global leaders to adjust their filters and lenses to include other cultural attributes. Because thought is understood to be culturally-based, we begin to view members of the culture differently and notice that they do not think the same way we do. When global leaders begin to adjust these filters they find that language is not just about communicating with individuals but becomes the very reflection of the culture from which they operate.

At its most basic level, becoming a cultural leader is about human relationships and less about economics, finance, and productivity. To best develop an *Open Organization*, global leaders must apply certain competencies to their approach to global expansion. Becoming a competent global leader requires vigilant study and understanding of culture and its many attributes. These complexities of geography, language, customs, values, traditions, laws, ethics, and national psychology are interpreted through varying lenses of cultural bias and the leader's ability to understand and connect with the cultures in which they operate. Further competencies include an understanding of whether a culture is considered High- or Low-Context. A greater challenge is formed when the global leader must operate within both an *Open Organization* and a High-Context cultural setting. An *Open System*, by its very nature, is best suited to Low-Context cultures. An *Open Organization*, through its operating *Charter*, is designed to encourage members to operate within their given cultural context and across cultural boundaries for the purpose of meeting a given goal or objective.

The secret formula to leading an *Open Organization* would appear to begin and end with the leader's ability to connect and build trust with those in which they may have to influence. Building trust, while a complex matter, is achievable in most all instances. Trust begins with an understanding of power–distances and the defining of the culture as either High- or Low-Context.

When we begin to develop our intellectual and emotional competencies for cultures we open endless possibilities for connection and expansion into markets and cultures which would not have been possible decades ago. It becomes clear that understanding cultural nuances is essential to success in any culture. The greater challenge is in understanding what those nuances are and how to effectively utilize them. To compete globally within an *Open System*, leaders must learn to effectively adapt to the cultures they operate within. Doing so builds trust and a lasting loyalty. Adaptation occurs through a leader's curiosity and desire to not only learn but embrace the culture.

Leading an *Open Organization* requires an ability to balance between the High-Context and Low-Context cultural settings. *Open Organizations* operating within a High-Context setting challenge the leader to avoid attempting to force their followers toward a more Low-Context setting. An *Open Organization* is designed to celebrate the skills of individuals as well as the culture context from which they come. An *Open Organization* focuses on the strengths of the followers within the system. Strengths include language and cultural cues from which they would normally operate. The success of an *Open Organization* relies heavily on the ability of the leader to clearly communicate the objectives of the organization and to develop an organizational *Charter* which is agreed upon by all members of the *Open System*.

Chapter 10

Embracing *Open* in the New Millennia

Imagine it is the year 2025. You walk into your home office and set your Smart Device (SD) on your desk. The SD, about the size of a silver dollar coin and as thick as a credit card, activates when placed on a flat surface. Sitting down, you lean forward and focus your attention on the holographic screen hovering above the SD. You say, "SD, date and time please." In a clear voice your SD responds, "February 8th, 2025. The time is now 0900. Would you like to hear your appointments and tasks for today?" You briefly think to yourself how far computers have evolved in just a short period of time. In fact, you think, the constant we face is a world quickly changing before our eyes.

For the United States and much of Europe, the world has already begun to change as it relates to the way organizations interact with their employees. The field of employment has been shifting since the market crash early in the century. By the year 2040 it is estimated several emerging social and technological changes will greatly affect the way organizations view employment and human capital in the Westernized world.

Your SD speaks again, "You have an incoming call from Jeff and Dustin." You turn your attention back to the hologram and tell your SD, "display call." The hologram shifts to the images of your colleagues. You met Jeff and Dustin in your doctoral program a few years ago and the three of you formed a successful strategic alliance. Today you are meeting to discuss a proposal the three of you are working on. Your alliance with your colleagues has opened the door for all of you to compete with much larger organizations on projects that you would have otherwise avoided.

The Great Shift

Since the late 1980s, Americans have begun working longer and foregoing their retirement. As a result of this trend we are beginning to see an increase in what we now call the *Graying of the American worker*. We are seeing an increase in job-sharing, consulting, coaching, and even strategist positions growing among the Boomer population as *Generation X* begins taking over the reins of leadership. While the working population of the United States is growing older, fertility rates are also dropping amongst American women which ultimately will create a deficit in human capital available to replace an existing workforce. If that weren't difficult enough on businesses trying to fill positions, legal immigration is on the decline in America creating even greater deficits in available workers. As a result of all these sociodemographic trends, we are beginning to see demand and acceptance of more flexible, freelance, and collaborative opportunities in an increasingly less secure globalized world.

> *Emerging social and technological changes are forcing companies to move toward the use of short-term, temporary and independent contractors and consultants.*

Emerging social and technological changes are forcing companies to move toward the use of short-term, temporary and independent contractors and consultants. With advances in technology and availability of WiFi in nearly every location, employees no longer need to pay to drive to an office setting every day nor will organizations need to continue supporting expensive centralized office space. In fact these advances in technology open the door for workers who are no longer limited by geography thereby permitting them to live anywhere they choose. Smaller offices and fewer employees working in those locations permit businesses to focus on finding and keeping essential employees while outsourcing the remaining positions to independent contractors. With these changes, businesses will be better able to shrink overall expenses and employees will gradually no longer see themselves as being employed by a single company. Employees are now able to work anytime and anywhere they choose as long as they are able to meet their job objectives.

The future of employment appears focused more on an individual's talent. In fact, it is estimated that most jobs of the future will require higher education, advanced skills, and high-tech training. The twenty-first century organization will require an ability to share ideas, knowledge, resources, and skills across organizational, generational, and cultural boundaries from within and outside of the organizational system.

The year 2025 is closer than you may realize. Technological and social changes are moving at an alarming rate and while many may see the opening scenario as fantasy, the trends say otherwise. Collaboration will breed a greater competitive advantage, create influence, and consolidate resources and expertise within a given organization and in a future that requires less human capital to produce a product or service. Now is the time for organizations to begin examining the impact of a shrinking workforce. The *Open Organization* will likely be the formal response to the much anticipated deficit in human capital. Organizations will become flatter and there will be a greater level of shared information, and even evaluations will come from co-workers rather than the traditional top-down leadership review. In fact, we could very well be witnessing the end of much of the hierarchies we've grown accustomed to since the early 1800s.

This shift in organizational structure will take time to adopt yet it is believed that these structures will be the most effective way to obtain a competitive advantage in the future. However, organizations may experience managerial resistance in adopting new organizational structures. Success is reliant on the commitment of the organization's leadership. It is necessary for organizations to address the fears of management and leadership in an effort to overcome delays in adoption.

The days of an abundant workforce are coming to a close. This shift in demographics will require organizations to view their structures far beyond the traditional business school training. Experts claim that there is a lack of *future-readiness* in the United State of employers and employment. Great challenges are ahead of us and the best way to address them is take the long-view and plan ahead for a new economy, new organizational structures, and a mobile diverse workforce like we've never seen before. These changes will require rethinking the view of hierarchies, traditional employment, and what it means to be self-employed. Technology will play a key role in the adoption and success of the organization of the future.

The conference call with your colleagues went well and as their holographic images fade, you sit back and smile. "SD," you say, "Open RFP Alpha457." Your SD responds, "Opened. What would you like to do?" You begin to dictate to your SD and so another day in this new world economy begins. You smile and remember a time when you used to work in a cubicle and you think to yourself, "I've surely come a long way from those early days in the working world."

As the story begins to illustrates, the twenty-first century organization will require an ability to share power, authority, ideas, knowledge, resources, and skills across organizational, generational, and cultural boundaries within and outside of the organizational system for the purpose of achieving desired goals. The world will continue to become smaller as technology advances and organizations grow in diversity of individuals from differing cultures and geographical locales. Organizational decision-making styles will grow in influence from the generational and cultural attributes of the individuals within the organizational system.

The challenge for organizational leadership is to find a design that will address the generational, cultural, industry, geographical, and other environmental factors in which it must compete. What we strive for is an appropriate structure that aligns organizational mission, vision, values, principles, strategies, objectives, tactics, systems, structures, people, processes, cultures, and performance measures in such a way as to deliver consistent effective results (Stanford, p. 8). The best scenario for success would be an organizational model that would integrate the intrinsic motivational needs of the individual while facilitating the expressed needs of the organization. Creating a flexible environment that meets the needs of both is a challenge for the leaders of the future. The organization of the twenty-first century must focus on creativity and innovation as it develops and modifies itself to meet the constantly changing needs of the world. While the use of an *Open System* is not yet a widely accepted organizational model, the *Open Organization* offers competitive market flexibility while meeting the intrinsic motivational needs of its members in a structured work environment that is collaborative, autonomous, transparent, generationally inclusive, and culturally diverse.

As organizations become more globally integrated and move toward flatter, more *Open* structures, leading from a global context becomes a complex matter rooted in an ability to understand and connect with a given culture and its people. Given that *Open Organizations* rely heavily on an ability to share information across all boundaries, they must develop ways to connect individuals within a given culture and improve the quality of their decisions through the development of close relationships and loyalty with their followers. Leading in a global context requires understanding of not just the people but their worldview, customs, local conditions, and laws. Developing an *Open Organization* requires leaders to develop humility, inquisitiveness, and an earnest desire to build honest connections with those who serve the organization in foreign places. A successful global leader must be more interested in building rapport long before they consider their bottom line. Developing a rapport with their followers, leaders are best able to limit the power–distance and operate with the trust required by all members of an *Open Organization*. Trust requires the appropriate interpretation of culture. How we view and interpret the culture is based predominantly on how we see the culture through our own cultural lenses. Cultures are defined by the filters and lenses on which we base our decisions. Considering the lenses by which we view the world we can begin to consider the worldview of others. It becomes essential for global leaders to adjust their filters and lenses to include other cultural attributes. Because our thoughts are understood to be culturally-based, we begin to view members of a given culture differently and notice that they do not think the same way we do.

What is clear is that our continuum does not end with *Organization 3.0* and *Open Systems*. Drivers of change are constantly forcing the evolution of markets and human capital needs. What may emerge as *Organization 4.0* and beyond can only be imaged through the use of scenarios and the systematic process of *Strategic Foresight*. As we become more aware of our surroundings and the human condition, we are sure to continue seeing *Leadership and Organizational Theory* evolve beyond our current understanding. Should these trends continue, we are confident in our imagining of a future with many more multicultural, *Flat, Open Systems* structured leadership and organization styles.

The New Millennia will require organizations to learn to deal with uncertainty and flexibility. The absolute nature of an *Open Organization* is found in its ability to flex as necessary to deal with market forces and to be able to respond without a script, to be able to keep your balance and direction—even when there appears to be no order around (Johansen, p. 164). An *Open Organization* creates flexibility through its *Knowledge Commons* and its networked structure. Leading an *Open Organization* will require an ability to flex, draw connections, and stretch boundaries of what we think of as an organization (Johansen, p. 165). No one person controls an *Open Organization*, but the sum of all parts create value and achieve desired goals.

The organization of the New Millennia will be flexible, *Open Systems* with only a few rules in the form of principles. Fewer rules allow for greater flexibility on the part of the organization (Johansen, p. 168). The *Open Organization* is transferable across industries and silos of thinking. It is a new way of sharing and learning where no one is the single holder of knowledge but we all contain knowledge together to create a sum of all parts more powerful than the individual. When done right, an *Open Organization* can be a formidable opponent to your competition. An *Open Organization* truly does create an excellent environment for agility, innovation, *Happiness*, and success.

The *Graying Workforce*

We talk a great deal about the potential impact of a *Graying Workforce* on the organizations of the future. A 2011 Gallup poll indicated many Americans expected to retire at an average age of 67. Some 39 percent of workers currently plan to retire after age 65, up from 30 percent before the recession in 2007. It is believed this trend is a direct result of financial insecurity by workers who believe they won't have enough money to live comfortably in retirement. The American Association of Retired Persons (AARP) supports this claim as 79 percent of Baby Boomers don't plan to stop working at age 65, thereby creating a *working retirement* (Liu, 2012).

In 2010, the United States had the third highest retirement age: 66, and by the year 2030 the United States is expected to tie Denmark as the two countries with the oldest retirement age. Keeping with these trends, the United States Social Security Administration indicates individuals born after 1960 will reach full retirement age eligibility at 67 with the earliest a person can start receiving Social Security retirement benefits being age 62. The harsh reality is that most Baby Boomers have not saved enough to enter into full-time retirement and therefore must continue working to meet basic expenses and needs (Liu, 2012). It is estimated that by the year 2040 the population for the age cohort of 60–79 is estimated to be 72.81 million and the age cohort of 80–89 another 23.25 million. This indicates a potential 96 million individuals who might have otherwise entered retirement. The younger age cohort of 20–39 has 98 million individuals and age cohort 40–59 an additional 94 million. What remains are 97.84 million individuals either too young or too old to participate in labor. Essentially each age cohort identified above comprises about 25 percent respectively of the total population.

Many see the *Graying Workforce* as a potential hindrance in embracing a more agile, *Open Organizational* structure. Rather than discounting them, there is a great benefit to engaging the *Graying Workforce* within an *Open System*. While it is true that many older workers have been classically trained to lead and manage organizations, they are not unlike the younger workers today. Workers of all ages have intrinsic needs and desires. In 2012, Boomers made up about one-third of the United States workforce, and research indicates there will not be enough younger workers to replace them upon retirement (Reeves, 2005). The benefit of an aging workforce is in the loyalty, wisdom, and knowledge they offer their organization.

Mature workers could also provide significant solutions and cost savings at a time when global competition exerts a force the likes of which has never before been seen (Liu, 2012). The aging global population is likely to have profound and negative effects on global economic growth and living standards (Liu, 2012). As the population increases and mortality rates decline, we are left with a large and aging working population and labor shortages in key industries that will force radical rethinking of recruitment, retention, flexible work schedules, and retirement (Reeves). Baby Boomers aren't going to retire in mass anytime soon (Farrell, 2011). If there is any concern for the future workforce, it will come when the so-called gloom lifts and we see a mass exodus of the aging workforce from their current employers for non-profits, startups, and other opportunities (Farrell). Plainly stated, the aging workforce phenomenon is due to a reluctance of aging workers to quit their jobs as they see working and earning an income as the safest retirement plan available (Farrell).

An aging labor market could potentially equate to increased costs through prolonged funding of retirement accounts; increased healthcare costs due to a larger number of pre-existing conditions within the covered population; and higher wages for more senior employed individuals. An aging workforce may require additional investments in training for emerging technologies that are readily available with a younger, emerging workforce. A negative for the aging workforce may be a younger workforce's willingness to work for less than the aging population of employees. This could make certain jobs more competitive and potentially cause organizations to shake up their aging labor force, replacing them with younger employees as openings are available. For those older employees seeking work, they may be forced to take lower paying positions and in some cases work multiple jobs just to survive. These implications may usher in response from government as they begin to assert their authority to protect the aging population.

As the population grows and mortality rates decrease we find an aging population in need of a variety of services such as healthcare and housing (Harf and Lombardi, 2010, p. 53). Declining birth and death rates mean significantly more services are needed to provide for the aging population, all while fewer individuals are joining the workforce to provide the needed resources to pay for these services (Harf and Lombardi, p. 54). We may see a growing set of regional problems as the young educated leave the so-called *Gray Belt* of the north for the *Sun Belt* of the South, Southwest, and West, leaving few to take care of the disproportionately aging population (Harf and Lombardi, p. 54). The fears of the aging workforce are not without merit. In the United States we are beginning to see political debates over proposals permitting workers to park their Social Security contributions in personal investment accounts as well as healthcare and other social services (Harf and Lombardi, p. 55). Organizations are not without their concerns of an aging workforce: increased falls, increased fatality rates, longer healing times, greater overall severity of injuries and more sever musculoskeletal disorders (Nogan, 2009, p. 4).

An aging workforce can present great challenges to our government, businesses, and society as a whole. However it may not be as big a problem if proactively addressed (Gorham, 2012). The question is to what extent is it considered proactive in our approach to fixing the problem. We know that the *graying* of the Baby Boomer generation is emerging as one of the greatest sociological shifts as a larger portion of the population enters into elderly status all at once (Harf and Lombardi, p. 54). This suggests the problem is not merely due to a decline in fertility rates and increased life expectancy (Gorham) but a shift in one group from middle aged to retirement. A larger block of retiring individuals will strain retirement funds including Social Security as well as healthcare and other social services.

The problem of an aging workforce includes areas of continued competition for a finite number of jobs, continued training, and rising healthcare premiums (Foster, 2012). A more seasoned workforce could find competition with a younger generation of workers and mothers who wish to re-enter the workforce.

While we could blame the economy for these troubles, social norms of the younger generation wishing to enter the workforce in the coming years must be considered. As Boomers leave the workforce, companies are faced with the emerging prospect of recruiting and retaining younger employees to replace an estimated 75 million departing retirees (Twenge, et al., 2010). Evidence shows that many organizations have tried to attract young workers by emphasizing their commitment to the environment or by introducing extensive charitable programs that offer paid time for community service (Twenge, et al.). However, persistent company downsizing is likely a reason for younger workers placing little value on teamwork and company loyalty and seeing their jobs as merely a means to make a living; preferring their leisure time, more vacations, and a desire to be under less pressure at work above any other organizational offerings (Twenge, et al.). We are not likely to see the full impact of this issue in the immediate future as it will take time to unpack the social and global implications of an aging workforce and its replacement generation.

Research indicates a growing population of aging workers. The cause in the decline of workers entering retirement is cited as lack of funds available to live comfortably in full-time retirement status. Workers are foregoing retirement to offset financial losses incurred in the recession of 2007. The way organizations engage the aging workforce is important to their future success. Aging workers are a valuable asset to the organization.

The New Organization

To the casual observer, driving onto Dell's sprawling Nashville, Tennessee campus with its acres of parking lots and buildings mirrors any other corporate office complex in metropolis. However, moving past the formality of the entrance and strict security awaits something entirely different from its window dressings. Some may argue this is the organization of the future. An organization that is defined by the sharing of ideas, knowledge, resources, and skills across organizational, generational, and cultural boundaries within, and in some cases outside, the organizational system for the purpose of achieving the stated goals of the organization and its stakeholders. Dell, by all definitions, is emerging as an *Open* decentralized structure.

Dell stands in stark contrast to the traditional organizational settings. I have personally long believed that we do not need a formal office or a suit and tie to do a good job. As a matter of fact, much of my best work (like this book) has been conducted in casual attire sitting in my favorite local coffee shop. I don't believe that I am alone in my assertion that most people work best when they are comfortable, relaxed, and working in a way that best suits them. Yet, a formal dress code or lack thereof is not enough. Understanding what intrinsically motivates the workforce is essential to their effectiveness and success. Troublesome, however, is the degree to which organizations ignore the intrinsic value of their human capital. What we find is a need for more than just good intentions to empower individuals to do what we want them to do (Handy, p. 110). An *Open Organization* requires the decision-making process to be highly inclusive and it must allow consensus to emerge where it exists.

The best scenario for success would be an organizational model that champions the motivational needs of the individual while facilitating the expressed needs of the organization. Creating a flexible environment that meets the needs of both the organization and its members is a challenge for leaders (Foster, 2011, p. 3). As you enter the internal workings of Dell's

Nashville campus the first thing you will notice is how *alive* the atmosphere becomes. There is almost an excitement which drives you to want to be a part of whatever is going on. Entering, you walk past a snack bar and groupings of couches and comfortable chairs. You may even think you were on a college campus as individuals walk around in shorts, t-shirts, flip-flops, tennis shoes, blue jeans, ball caps, and the like. More striking are the rows of short cubicles and a hierarchy of ten subordinates to every one manager. While there may appear to be a formal structure, there is a great deal of wandering and cross-departmental communication.

Dell undoubtedly understands that to be competitive they must change the way they think. They must understand that those who moderate a traditional structure persist in trying to adapt the world to their organization rather than adapting their organization to the world (Handy, p. 4). Non-traditional organizations, like Dell, break free of the former rigidity and they form different shapes, working habits, age profiles, and differing traditions of authority (Handy, p. 15).

While there is no one-size-fits-all organization, the challenge remains to find an organizational design that fits the culture, industry, and other environmental factors. Organizations that do not anticipate the need to adapt to changing circumstances will likely underperform and ultimately go out of business (Stanford, p. 1). For example, when Dell first opened its Nashville Campus in 2000, the culture was much more formal and the structure was centralized with the corporate headquarters in Texas. The dress code was business casual and individuals were expected to stay at their desks and get work done. There was very little talking or wandering in those days. Fast forward to 2011 and the organization is alive and prospering even in a down economy. Employees are permitted to wander, spend time in the recreation room or fitness center. You might even find someone wearing a wireless headset and setting up to putt a golf ball all the while talking technical jargon with a client. Some employees are permitted to check out laptops and work remotely from home two days a week.

Dell appears to be able to maintain a high morale. Constant *Open* communication with the employees not only makes them feel valued but they know that what they say is important to leadership. Dell appears to go out of their way to support the intrinsic motivations of the employees. Dell understands that an *Open Organization* requires all members to let go of their preconceived notions of how people operate and essentially trust in faith that people will act responsibly (Li, p. 18). We find that the biggest indicator of success of an *Open Organization System* comes from an open-mind and the leader's ability to give control over at the right time and place and to the extent which people need the control to get their job done (Li, p. 8).

While there is no one-size-fits-all approach to organizational design, an organization behaves in the ways it has been designed to behave (Stanford, p. 3). An *Open Organization* requires that everyone in the organization have some control over what is going on (Stanford, p. 28) and requires that all members have an equal voice in the process. This requires a great deal of accountability by all members within an *Open Organization* (Foster, 2011, p. 12). In an *Open System*, the process of being accountable would make it necessary for all members to intervene in the decision-making process when another member does not meet their obligations (Foster, 2011, p. 12).

Like most all organizations today, Dell is dealing with the economic uncertain times we are in. By most observations I've made of organizations in these current conditions, morale is normally low and there is a great deal of stress to meet financial and production goals. Interestingly the mood at Dell is much different. While the business climate is difficult and their growth projections have been downgraded from 10 percent to a modest 3 percent growth, the employees appear confident and motivated to get the job done. Dell has not wavered from its *Open* business model. This is in stark contrast to the many organizations that have met the economic down turn with massive layoffs and a tightening of control over employees. It would seem reasonable to assert that Dell understands that if they are to compete and survive this economic turmoil they must stay the course and not waiver. It is the dedication of the employees that will see them through.

While the *Open Organization* is an emergent area of organizational design, there is great potential when organizations internally share information and leaders equip their followers with resources and empowerment to get the job done. Intrinsic motivation plays an important role in the effectiveness and morale of the individuals within an *Open Organization*. Perhaps an *Open System* is not the best option for all organizations, but the attributes of an *Open System* may cause one to pause and take note of the positive affect it appears to have on both the employees and the bottom line of the organization.

Chapter 11
Should You Go *Open?*

Bookstores and libraries are full of texts espousing the latest and greatest leadership and organizational philosophies. Many organizations may even attempt some of these philosophical flavors of the month. However, just because something sounds like a great idea does not mean it is a "fit" for every organization. To become an *Open Organization* requires a time-consuming transitioning process. Going *Open* requires adopting new mindsets and cultural attributes that may or may not exist at present in the organization. Going *Open* might mean changing direction, philosophy, or even some of your staff. While the concept of an *Open Organization* offers many competitive advantages, it also requires a great deal of organizational culture change for it to achieve a state of effectiveness. The most effective adoption of an *Open Organization* typically appears in the form of startup organizations. This is not to say that an established organization can't go *Open*. What it does mean is that an established organization might need to slowly change over a long period of time in order to most fully and effectively embrace the idea of *Openness*. From the beginning there must be attention focused on business continuity and joint decision-making sessions where the employees take the decisions on themselves (de Bree and de Weil). The leadership handoff as well as the development of the organization's *First Principles* and *Governance* must be well thought through. Going *Open* is not something your organization can simply "try out" as many of the concepts once embraced will be much more difficult to remove from the fabric of the organization.

Going Open might mean changing direction, philosophy, or even some of your staff.

While embracing the idea of *Open* should not be taken lightly, I would ask, "Why should only technology firms reap the benefits of an *Open Organization Model?*" Well-known organizations such as W.L. Gore, Zappos, and even Whole Foods are joining companies like Apple, Valve, GitHub, and WordPress in their pursuit of the power of *Open*. Going *Open* is certainly magical but it is not mystical. Going *Open* is as much a mindset as it is a strategy for organizational structure and leadership. In fact, it requires a kind of organizational culture to succeed at being *Open*. Going *Open* helps minimize layers of bureaucracy and will garner more time for your employees to focus on and refine core products, listen to your customers and develop new product and service offerings (Belosic, 2013). The role of a leader in an *Open Organization* is to incubate a culture that seeks to be *Flat* and *Open*. The *Open Organization* structure allows for employees to offer continual input as they put their best skills to use. When authority is shared with everyone in the organization, everyone is more productive (Belosic). This goes a long way toward helping members of the organization truly feel valued for their contributions. Finally, an *Open Organization* allows for quick decision-making including whether or not someone is a good fit for an *Open Organizational* setting (Belosic).

Beyond the arguments of efficiency and agility, there are more practical reasons to consider going *Open*. The most important reason is that there is a decline in available human capital in the workforce. In fact, studies have concluded that the average size of firms in many industries are shrinking—an indicator of rapidly falling transaction costs due to efficiencies created by the Internet—and the largest private employer in the United States today is not General Motors, IBM, or even Wal-Mart, but the temp agency Manpower Incorporated, which as of 2008 employed 4.4 million people (Howe, p. 111). As individuals retire from organizations, the ability to replace them with skilled *Knowledge Workers* will be strained. Not only are there shifts in the workforce domestically, but we now operate in a globalized economy. While globalization makes it easier for competitors to enter and compete more effectively in the most attractive markets, we will likely continue to intensify as digital technology infrastructures become broader on a global scale (Savitz, 2012).

Embracing the concept of an *Open Organization* will cause organizations to shift their attention from the cost to the value side of doing business. Rather than treating employees as costs items that need to be managed wherever and whenever possible, an *Open Organization* forces leaders to view them as assets capable of delivering ever-increasing value to the marketplace (Savitz). Leaders who treat their followers as assets will find employees who are not only more capable, but also more motivated to contribute to the needs of the organization. When we embrace employees as human capital we move from a game of diminishing returns to an opportunity for increasing returns and there is little, if any, limit to the additional value that people can deliver if given the appropriate tools and skill development (Savitz). People therefore become the center of focus for the organization. An *Open Organization* is not about squeezing individuals into cookie-cutter assigned roles or tasks but changing the business model to help people develop more rapidly and achieve ever higher levels of performance (Savitz). The *Open Organization* will not only redefine how we approach the use of human capital but also redefine how organizations operate. Not only will it change the concept of the 40-hour work week, but also when and how we work, whether in a virtual or a physical office environment. Digital technology still has a role to play, but it is now about how to enhance the performance of people so that they can deliver ever more value (Savitz).

As we have learned, going *Open* does not mean that the organization is structureless or even leaderless. An *Open Organization* is not like an airplane without a pilot, but actually an airplane full of pilots ready to take the controls as needed. While we focus on the organizations as *Open*, there are times when an organization is both *Open* and closed at the same time. In my observation of GitHub, I was asked to leave the organization's *Beer:30* meeting so that they could openly discuss proprietary information. This is similar to the analogy of the human body being both an *Open* and closed system at the same time. *Open* because it interacts with the environment around it and closed because there are parts of the body which we cannot see without opening it up to view it.

It would appear to be much more difficult for a closed organization to embrace the idea of *Openness*. Yet, I would argue that even a closed system can operate in an *Open* format. Perhaps opening the entire enterprise up is not an option, but you can embrace the idea of *Open* within certain boundaries of the organization. Formally structured companies are already beginning to embrace this through the concept of *Open Innovation*. Heavily regulated organizations with a central command-and-control structure may struggle the most with the concept of an *Open Organizational Model*. In the end, *Open* may not be for everyone. However I would argue that if your organization is or potentially will compete with an *Open Organization*, you may want to pay attention as your competition by its nature will be more agile and more willing to take risks than your standard competitor will. This could mean that all the things a closed organization is unwilling to do, the *Open Organization* is eagerly moving headlong into embracing.

Because the concept of an *Open Organization* is rather new within general industry, we don't have many examples to point to. However, Semco is a great example of a firm that has successfully moved from a hierarchical structure to an *Open Organization* structure. This 30-year-old Brazilian conglomerate has continually worked at distributing decision-making authority out to everyone

(Kastelle, 2013). Semco has truly embraced the concept of distributing decision-making power across the organization's structure. A key performance indicator at Semco is how long the CEO can go between making decisions (Kastelle). Semco is an example of the cross-pollination of *Open* from technology into general industry.

Research finds that the *Open Organization* can work anywhere, but the following examples are when *Open* works best (Kastelle): The environment in which the organization operates is changing rapidly, an organization's main point of differentiation is innovation, and the organization maintains a shared purpose. What we find is that organizations with flat structures, such as the *Open Organization*, will outperform those with more traditional hierarchies in most situations (Kastelle). It is for this reason alone that many organizations should begin adopting some, if not all, the traits of an *Open Organization*.

Creating an *Open Organization*

In business, organization implies control and is seen as a socially organized arrangement of individual human interactions for a given purpose. This idea of control carries negative connotations that imply some restrictive measure and/or guidelines about what an individual must or must not do (Yun, et al., p. 27). For many classically trained leaders, the organization is defined as a structure dictated by command-and-control. Change requires engaging the psyche of individuals. Psychologically, the exercise of control produces frustrating yet satisfying consequences (Yun, et al., p. 27). Change in this regard is time consuming and requires a great amount of effort. Change is never easy and changing the way we do business is a complex matter. Creating an *Open Organizational* structure from a traditional organizational model should not be taken lightly. For the development of an *Open Organization* to be successful it must include everyone at the table. From the bottom to the top, everyone must be involved in the transformation. Starting with *First Principles* and the organizational *Governance Model*, you are developing a complex model that will take some time to develop and roll out. It is important to note that when you are creating institutional change you will hit the feelings of chaos at some point, but it is absolutely necessary and it can't be rushed (DeMarco and Lister, 1999, pp. 199–200). The transforming idea is something that people in chaos can grab onto as offering hope to them that the end of the suffering is near (DeMarco and Lister, pp. 199–200).

It is important to understand that an *Open Organization* is a nonlinear structure and there are numerous interconnections and divergent choices that create unintended effects and render the universe unpredictable (Daft, 2004, p. 28). The *Open Organization* lives and breathes and is organic in its nature. Because the world is full of uncertainty, characterized by surprise, rapid change, and confusion, managers can't measure, predict, or control in traditional ways the unfolding drama inside or outside the organization (Daft, 2004, p. 28). Leaders who try to "go it alone" will be rendered useless in the fast-paced organizations of the future. An *Open Organization* helps the organization create agility when dealing with higher levels of surprise, rapid change and confusion because everyone is now involved in the decision-making process. An *Open Organization* suggests that organizations should be viewed more as natural systems than as well-oiled, predictable machines (Daft, 2004, p. 28).

For an organization to embrace the change needed to go *Open*, it needs to change its strategy in order to adapt to the changing business environment. People will readily embrace change when they can visualize a better future. We each need a genuine sense that our destination is desirable. We need to be asked more than told. We need to see and feel the case for change (Moore, 2011, p. 16). Organizations should acknowledge that the markets are more complex, turbulent, unpredictable, and extremely competitive and, to succeed, organizations need to adopt an *Open Organization* mindset (Politis, 2006, p. 203).

Control

The traditional organization is all about command-and-control. Hierarchy is a vertical concept in which the focus is placed on the leaders at the top and not toward to customers. The classically trained leader has been programmed to think and operate this way. Embracing an *Open Organization* structure requires leadership to let go of control and empower those around them. To hold on to control implies some restrictive measures and guidelines about what an individual must or must not do (Negandhi, 1975, p. 27). Control is very much a psychological state in which individuals that are able to exercise some control over their own and others' activities experience satisfaction; those who are not able to exercise control and who are, instead, being controlled by others may be dissatisfied and alienated from their activities (Negandhi, p. 27).

The term "organization" implies control or an ordered arrangement of individual human interactions (Negandhi, p. 27). The term *Open Organization* implies an arrangement of control, led by the members of the system, and requires new approaches to command-and-control. You might have noticed that control was used to describe both states of *Open* and closed organizations. The focus of control is moved from leadership to the organizational community. This explains why the term *Open* implies leaderless chaos and anarchy to some more traditionally trained leaders, but is far from the truth. An *Open Organization* relies heavily on high-functioning cohesive teams. These teams typically take over and own most of the management functions of the organization (Science Daily, p. 63). An *Open Organization* maintains certain levels of control over these teams through its *Governance* and member-led accountability. The organizational *Governance*, like the more traditional hierarchies, maintains a certain amount of conformity as well as the integration of diverse activities to bring about conformance to organizational requirements and achievement of the ultimate purposes of the organization (Negandhi, p. 27).

The greatest challenge for the classically trained manager is traversing the hurdle of leaderless or managerless organizations. In fact, it is an absolute myth that an organization will ever be leaderless. In the case of an *Open Organization*, leadership is owned by all the members of the organization. The people doing the work know better how to do their jobs than the leaders demanding the work from their employees. When we begin to listen to our employees, a new dynamic enters. Structure weakens and human capital is strengthened through empowerment. The argument against self-managed, managerless organizations is rooted in the false assumption of chaos. In fact, research shows that an *Open Organization* is not only more flexible but stronger than its more rigid hierarchical counterpart. If we used terms of physics—the tensile strength of an *Open Organization* is much better than a rigid top-down organization design. Because an *Open Organization* is built on the platform of *First Principles* and a simple but strong set of rules, decisions are made within the community and things just get done.

An *Open Organization* removes silos or divisions of business and creates one merged mass of an organization. Everyone makes decisions and all participate in the direction of the organization. An *Open Organization* creates stakeholders of all members of the organization. Some may believe that there is no such thing as a managerless organization. Those who doubt the validity of a managerless organization miss the key attributes of *Open*. *Open* does not equal chaos. *Open* does however present higher levels of efficiency, *happiness*, creativity, flexibility, and competitiveness. An *Open Organization* will require a leader that is willing to enter into a place of vulnerability. As a leader, the idea of *Open* means that we have more capacity and a great deal of pressure off our shoulders. Going *Open* requires us to focus on the *Happiness* of the workforce before and after the *Happiness* of the shareholders.

Reality dictates that innovative companies all have one thing in common; they are moving toward a flatter structure that lends to the *Open Organization* design and function. Organizations such as Valve, W.L. Gore, Zappos, GitHub, and others are very much *Open Organizations.*

Creating Change

Going *Open* requires a great deal of change for the established organization. The one constant of the twenty-first century organization is change. We face it every day. Redirecting an organization's culture and structure toward *Open* can be, like any other change, difficult. The larger and more dynamically complex the change is, the more difficult the process of changing. In fact, as humans we tend to be adverse to change and, in a world which is increasingly changing at an alarming rate, people can be skeptical and resistant to anything that threatens the status quo of their working lives (Kirke, 2013). While the *Open Organization* is employee-centric and benefits all members of the organization, creating an *Open Organization* becomes a challenge because it goes against most every business school tenant learned to date. If history serves as any indicator, we know that not all change is positive and sometimes it seems that doing things differently does not actually equal doing things better in the long run (Kirke). This level of change requires adaptability to situations as they present themselves. To succeed over time, an organization must somehow institutionalize the ability to change, yet in the process continue to be itself (Hesselbein and Goldsmith, p. 215). The challenge is in the process of continuing to remain true to its founding principles and *Governance.*

Creating an *Open Organization* requires careful consideration of the change process. Change and organizational transformation has to be done carefully, sensitively, and collaboratively to aide everyone in the seamless implementation of change (Kirke). Managing change involves three stages of change (Kirke):

1.   Communicate the rationale behind the need for change.

        The first stage of introducing change is to explain to employees why it is important for the change to occur and the intended benefits. This needs to be handled carefully and communicated to all affected parties. There should also be adequate opportunity for people to voice their concerns and contribute their thoughts, views, and opinions. Missing out on this stage of the process will almost certainly damage the change process before it has even properly begun.

2.   Implement the change in phases.

        Change is usually best received when it is implemented in bite-sized
        chunks. Most change can be broken down into phases that can be
        reviewed along the way. Collaboration is key so, if circumstances
        allow, having a pilot group of employees to test the change before
        it is fully embedded is a good way to ensure that more people "buy
        in" to what is happening and why.

3.   Evaluate, review, and report on change.

        Careful monitoring of the entire change process is essential in order
        to be able to measure its impact and evaluate its success. People
        need to be kept informed about how things are progressing, the
        results that are occurring, and whether the change program has
        met its objectives.

The reason an organization decides to embark on the process of changing
from a traditional-style organization to an *Open Organization* may vary from
organization to organization. No matter the reason for change, helping
employees understand what an *Open Organization* is and the benefits expected
from it are essential to the success of changing. The change process will require
absolute participation of all members of the organization. Perhaps the best
place to begin is with the process of transparency, empowerment, and then the
development of the company's *First Principles* and new *Open Governance*.

Resistance

With any change we may find a certain level of resistance. Resistance is
born from an individual's lack of understanding of what is being asked of
them. Resistance is human nature and should be expected with any kind of
change. In fact, people who become resisters feel threatened. (Titchy, p. 136).
Understanding resistance is important to the overall success of the organization
in an *Open System*. In the organization of the future, only adaptive individuals
and organizations will thrive (Kouzes and Posner, p. 291). We protect the way
things are and see change as a threat to our stability and comfort. Resistance is
the result of individuals who do not have the power to positively change a course
of events, so they will attempt to do so negatively (Titchy, p. 136). Embracing
the idea of an *Open Organization* will undoubtedly create resistance from
your followers. Individuals will resist change if they are feeling manipulated,

pushed into the unknown, or being compelled to take risks without apparent gains (Moore, p. 16). Going *Open* creates a feeling of losing control, because the safety nets and structures we hide behind are suddenly stripped away and we are expected to perform under a new set of rules and standards. Embracing an *Open Organizational* structure and leadership mindset requires time, education, inclusion, and a gradual rollout of processes toward a more *Open* structure.

In Chapter 9, we discussed accountability and the need for a cohesive team. However, certain resistance can occur if a team is not getting along. Thereby the lack of cohesiveness can become a hindrance to an *Open Organization*. When teams are not getting along, their ability to self-manage and perform diminishes. When team members don't much care for each other, team spirit diminishes as a motivating factor and the primary motivating factor for improvement and productivity becomes money (Science Daily, p. 63). Money is a selfish motivating factor at this point. Cohesiveness is limited by the ability of the workers to come together for the good of the team or organization instead of the good of self. Money as a motivator does not increase performance, rather social pressure from peers induces higher levels of performance.

Resistance can also come in the form of organizational policies and the political environment. Organizational policies, practices, and procedures can explicitly or inadvertently present barriers to engaging with *Open Organizations* (Aitken, et al., p. 3). Organizational policies are addressed through the organization's *First Principles* and *Governance*. A political environment is more focused on the "who" rather than the "what" (Senge, 1990, pp. 273–274). This form of resistance comes when the boss proposes an idea and the idea is taken seriously, but if someone else proposes an idea, it is ignored (Senge, pp. 273–274). Office politics or political environments in general indicate clear "winners" and "losers" and typically power is concentrated and is arbitrary (Senge, pp. 273–274). If you are considering creating any kind of change in a politically charged environment, you should expect great resistance. Political environments are focused on command-and-control and are in essence authoritarian in nature. Disrupting a political environment will take time and the absolute participation of leadership and starts with the building of a shared vision and the companies *First Principles* (Senge, p. 274). Without a genuine sense of common vision like *First Principles*, there is nothing to motivate individuals beyond their own self-interests (Senge, p. 274). *Openness* is the key to breaking down political fiefdoms and game playing found within so many organizations today. Together, vision and *Openness* are the antidotes to dealing with a political environment (Senge, p. 274).

Research is beginning to surface related to the idea of *Open Offices* and their impact on individual performance within an organization. It has been suggested that employee satisfaction with their surroundings suffered as they felt the new *Open Space* was disruptive, stressful, and cumbersome, and, instead of feeling closer, co-workers felt distant, dissatisfied, and resentful as productivity fell (Konnikova, 2014). The challenge with converting a standard organization to an *Open Office* plan is simply that not everyone is alike. Not everyone is suited for this kind of environment. In the observations of GitHub we found that they offered a wide variety of workspaces in the office as well as the option to work remotely. The most problematic aspects of the *Open Office*, according to research, are more physical than psychological as in noise (Konnikova). While the concerns of an *Open Office* are legitimate, they are certainly workable in that organizations would simply offer work areas more conducive to the more easily distracted workers.

Some may resist the idea of an *Open Organization* because of their formal training and worldview of leadership and management. They see an *Open Organization* as the coming extinction of leadership. In fact, some may argue that the position of the manager cannot become extinct because a leader is the prerequisite for the existence of teams. What we learn from successful *Open Organizations* such as GitHub is that this is far from the truth. Some hold to the idea that leadership and management is so ingrained in the organization's fabric that it will not disappear. They hold on to this idea as if it were their last dying breath. The reason an *Open Organization* does not require high levels of dedicated hierarchical leadership is because the responsibilities of leading and managing are dispersed amongst the members of the organization. However, some more seasoned leaders outright reject the idea of going *Open* and see it as allowing the vision and direction of a company to change at the whim of a group of equals as a dismal failure.

I was involved in a dialogue with some business colleagues on the matter of *who is responsible for the strategy and its achievement in an organization.* The crux of the conversation was around why strategies fail. I was arguing strongly for the coming of the flatter more agile organization and how we are moving away from the idea of a leader dictating vision, goals, and processes. Many of the classically trained leaders pushed back on the argument for an *Open Organization*. There is no question in my mind that the state of leadership is in transition. We are about to see the greatest shift in organizational leadership since Fredrick Taylor adopted the *Scientific Management Approach* to production in the late nineteenth century.

In fairness to my classically trained colleagues they have many valid arguments. Such as, who owns the business? In the case of an *Open Organization* there is a difference between financial owners and owners of process and culture. There is for this argument, two owners. The person(s) who started the company are those who "legally" own the company. For the classically trained leader, the branding of leaderless or managerless creates the idea that there is no one in charge. This is why terms such as agile, *Flat*, or *Open* are far more descriptive of the actual state of the organization. There is always going to be a founder or CEO. However, in an *Open Organization* this level should be stealth. It is much like an autopilot on an airplane. Someone is required to engaged and disengage the process.

I said that there are two owners. Outside of the founder(s) there is a layer of ownership or stakeholders known as the human capital or workers. In order for an *Open Organization* to truly work, the employees must have a stake in the process. They must be empowered to own something. In the case of an *Open Organization*, they own the culture, the process, the ideas, and the achievement of the end-products. This is not to say that the CEO has no say at all. This is a myth of *Openness*. In fact, GitHub offers us a prime view of how this works. The CEO, Tom, has final say in everything that happens within the organization. If the leader is going to use his or her CEO powers they need to be used sparingly or they risk the unraveling of the autonomy so carefully created. This means that empowerment and accountability are keys to the success of an *Open Organization* from the standpoint of the leaders to followers and followers to their leaders. Bottom line, the leaders need to empower their followers and then get out of their way.

The classically trained leader sees the *Open Organization* as leaderless. While the concept of leaderless is actually a myth, there is still a need to create the idea of rotating employees as the *person-in-charge*. While this makes sense to the classically trained command-and-control leader, it actually defeats the purpose of an *Open Organization* where everyone is supposed to make the decisions. As noted, the CEO will always have the final say in the "goings-on" of the organization. But, if you hire the right people, train them, empower them explicitly, and have a great set of *First Principles* and *Governance* there is no need for a dedicated *person-in-charge*. Arguing for a *person-in-charge* lends to the argument for coordination of the different functions within the organization. After all, how will we know who is to do what? In order for an *Open Organization* to be a success you will need to hire the best, empower them, and get out of their way. They will know what needs to be done and it will get done. With accountability in the hands of everyone there is sufficient peer pressure to make sure things get done.

The problem we older leaders have is in wrapping our brain around this idea of leaderless. There *are* leaders—a CEO and everyone else in the organization. Our reservations are likely based on our idea of the *Great Man Theory* and even *Taylorism* and our belief that workers are inherently lazy. The reality is that if you hire the right people and empower them, they will want to do a great job. Are they leaders? YES! The power of an *Open Organization (Meritocracy)* is not in how often the leader engages the followers insomuch as how little the leader is seen as obtrusive. Leaders should be available for coaching, mentoring, and the work they need to accomplish and not in managing and arranging human capital. The best leaders, as found in the example of Semco, are hardly heard from. That means there are few reasons for the leader to engage. In my mind a real leader is one who empowers individuals to do what they do best.

We know that the *Open Organization* structure works for creative and technology firms, but what about general industry firms? We are beginning to see general industries such as W.L. Gore, with over 10,000 employees, adopting the idea of the *Open Organization*. While not completely flat, they are one of the best examples of an *Open Organization* in general industry today. There is a CEO and a handful of functional heads and then everyone else (Kastelle). Gore employs the idea of self-managed teams including hiring (on-boarding), pay, project assignments, and just about everything in between (Kastelle). One further note about Gore is related to their CEO. The head of the company is elected democratically by their peers. Their current CEO Terri Reilly feels it is better to rely upon a broad base of individuals and leaders who share a common set of values and feel personal ownership for the overall success of the organization (Kastelle). Reilly, like other CEOs whom embrace the concept of *Open*, are finding that their employees are responsible and when empowered they will serve as overseers of the organization better than their top-down-led counterparts.

Much of the resistance to *Open Organizations* appears to center on the idea that they are without form, structure, or rules. In fact, *Open Organizations* are less focused on the form of the organization and more focused on the process and rules of the organization. Regardless of what we call it—*Open, Agile, Flat, Holacracy,* or even *Meritocracy*—the focus remains on the process and rules of the organization over any structural features. The classically trained leader can rest in the fact that an *Open Organization* is likely more structured than their current traditional system. While there is structure to the organization, it is limited to roles and not people.

Independent Work

An *Open Organization* implies that individuals within the organization are working independently. This is not just a boutique management idea but is being driven by emerging trends where approximately 43 million people, or roughly 35 to 40 percent of the private workforce in the United States, are currently doing some kind of independent work; this number is expected to grow to 65–70 million by the year 2023, well ahead of the 1 percent rate at which the labor force is growing (Johnson, 2013). Independent workers are one of the rapidly growing subset in the United States with about 17 million independents working in the economy today. This number is expected to increase to 23 million by 2017 as both large and small corporations, as well as the government, continue to migrate toward a contingent labor force. While these statistics appear to indicate that independent work environments are being forced on employees, of those who went independent in 2012, 57 percent chose to with only 13 percent desiring to go back to a traditional employment model (Johnson, 2013).

Interestingly, many people don't believe in democracy in the workplace or rather that it can be achieved in the workplace (Kastelle). Beyond this narrow view of the world, some people just prefer structure and for some it is so deeply engrained that they cannot even begin to imagine work or a world without hierarchy (Kastelle). A common rejection of an *Open Organization* is the idea that it is hard to change an organization's structure despite the ample evidence available (Kastelle). Regardless of the excuses given against an *Open Organization*, going *Open* requires changing the way we view human capital in our organizations. In an *Open Organization*, leaders encourage their followers to break out of mindsets by questioning routines, challenging assumptions, and, with respect to appreciating diversity, continually looking at what is going on from variously changing perspectives (Kouzes and Posner, p. 228). When the leader embraces the power behind going *Open*, their organizations benefit in the long run, and the employees are happier and more productive in their work.

An *Open Organization* requires a great deal of self-efficacy on the part of everyone within the system. Self-efficacy refers to beliefs in one's capabilities to organize and execute the courses of action required to produce desired results (Carmeli, et al., 2006, p. 79). Self-efficacy maintains that a person's motivation is determined by a belief that they are capable of performing required tasks and that a given behavior or set of behaviors will lead to a given outcome (Sanna, 1992, p. 774). Together with the goals that people set, self-efficacy is one of the most powerful motivational predictors of how well a person will perform at almost any endeavor and is a strong determinant of their effort, persistence, strategizing, training, and job performance (Heslin and Klehe, 2006, p. 705). An *Open Organization's* high degree of self-efficacy leads its members to work hard and persist in the face of setbacks (Heslin and Klehe, p. 705).

Because *Open Organizations* are considered learning organizations with complex tasks, a high-level self-efficacy causes individuals within the system to strive to improve their assumptions and strategies, rather than look for excuses such as not being interested in the task (Heslin and Klehe, p. 705). A high degree of self-efficacy will improve the employees' capacity to collect relevant information, make sound decisions, and then take appropriate actions, without having to be managed at every step of the way (Heslin and Klehe, p. 705).

Aside from self-efficacy, an *Open Organization* presumes a high degree of self-organization on the part of all members of the system. Self-organization is an individual's ability to build valuable communities and resources and share them over time, without having to rely on formal guidance from any center of authority (McAfee, 2009, pp. 140–141). Like many of the *Open Organizational* concepts presented, this concept does not come naturally to most traditional organizations because of its hierarchy, or predefined and largely stable structures (McAfee, pp. 140–141). Within a classic hierarchy, attributes like authority, expertise, and roles are assigned or conferred (McAfee, pp. 140–141). However, organizations that embrace the concept of *Open* will need to let go of the idea that expertise, authority and roles should be specified up front and never again questioned (McAfee, pp. 140–141).

If an organization is to succeed at becoming an *Open Organization*, they will need to embrace the idea that expertise, authority, and roles are emergent over time, rather than fully specified in advance, and that employees need to interact with one another openly to determine who knows what and who should work together, rather than having these decisions defined or even managed for them (McAfee, pp. 140–141). In fact, self-organization is a spontaneous emergence of new structures, ideas, and forms of behaviors in an *Open Organization* (Allee, p. 266).

An *Open Organization* is a system of inclusivity, where everyone belongs and individuality and differing opinions are essential to its success. An *Open Organization* offers a sense of community and members are motivated by a desire to create a better widget (Brafman and Beckstrom, pp. 94–95). Members believe in the idea of an *Open Organization* and this ideology is the glue that holds the organization together (Brafman and Beckstrom, pp. 94–95). Individuality creates *Happiness* and job satisfaction amongst its members. In turn, higher degrees of efficiencies and success are achieved.

Chapter 12

Beyond *Organization 3.0*

In Chapter 1 we introduced three organizational eras. As we move into the current era of *Organization 3.0*, we have an emerging view of what the future may hold for leaders and organizational structures. While knowing or predicting

Scenario analysis is a skill that human capital must acquire if they are to compete in the twenty-first century.

exactly what will happen in the future is not possible, we can anticipate possible future conditions to better prepare for them (McGuffey, 2012; Cornish, 2004, p. 65). However we find that many leaders are unable to anticipate future possibilities, weigh them against opportunities and risks their organizations may face, and then respond with agility to such possibilities (Cornish, p. 65). This is certainly, to a large extent, a greater challenge for monolithic closed organizations attempting to compete in the new global landscape.

The era beyond *Organization 3.0* will require individuals who are able to develop long-range planning skills and successfully navigate changes in shorter windows of time. The more we consider the unexpected, the greater opportunity we have to achieve success (Cornish, p. 4). Preparing for the unexpected is achieved through many methods: by simulations, games, lists, processes, or techniques. Considering future possibilities helps us better prepare mentally for the eventualities the future may hold.

How we plan for the future beyond *Organization 3.0* is an important exercise to consider. Where will organizations be in 20, 30, or even 100 years from now? What kinds of disruptions will we encounter? What new opportunities await us on the horizon? These are all important questions to ponder as we peer into the future. The organization of the future must be agile enough to not only consider future possibilities, but to navigate around challenges encountered along the way. It is far more challenging to navigate rigid organizations around disruptions because they are optimally designed for lag-thinking and the status quo. It is understood that the future holds great potential for disruptions and the lag-thinking approach is no longer optimal. The organization of the future must engage a viewpoint of foresight and become a future-focused organization ready to meet the challenges when presented. The *Open Organization* provides the best possible design to achieve the most optimal future while dealing with daily real-time challenges the organization faces.

Scenario analysis has emerged as one of the most widely used techniques for constructing plausible futures of an organization's external environment (de Kluyver and Pearce, p. 70). Scenario analysis is a skill human capital must acquire if they are to compete in the twenty-first century. For many, the concept of scenario analysis begins and ends with strategic planning. Strategic planning was originally billed as a way of becoming more future-oriented, even though most managers admit that their strategic plans reveal more about today's problems than the opportunities of tomorrow (Senge, p. 210). This truly is lag-thinking at its best.

Strategic planning has long been seen as the most successful way to prepare for the organization's future. However, creative strategies seldom come from annual planning rituals of the three to five-year plan as the company will likely stick to market segments it knows, even though there may be greater opportunities elsewhere (Senge, p. 214). Because most strategic plans of the past were developed with the three to five-year mindset, they were most often focused only on what they already knew (lag-thinking) about the organization's performance and current direction rather than what could be. Most organizations will put their strategic plans in binders and place them on their office shelves and rarely open them again until the next strategy meeting. Organizations that engage in strategic planning for the future will have to change the way they view and interact with their plans. The organization of the future will require active, daily interaction with their plans and the mindset to question needed changes at an instant to produce the agility required to reach their goals.

Without scenarios organizations may become blindsided by future possibilities (Schoemaker, p. 46). A prime example of an organization missing a future possibility is found in Encyclopedia Britannica. Britannica began in the book business but evolved, nearly overnight, into an information business (Schoemaker, p. 46). In 1989, Britannica was at the top of its industry but by 1994 sales slipped 53 percent as other companies offered more exciting electronic alternatives at a lesser cost and greater ease of consumer use (Schoemaker, p. 46). Emerging technologies made it possible for content providers to update and push out updates at a much quicker rate than that of traditional book publishing companies. Unfortunately Britannica failed to anticipate the future of its industry and by 1996 its sales dropped by 70 percent (Schoemaker, p. 46).

Technology became a disrupter to the company's status quo. Had Britannica considered potential technological scenarios, they would have avoided tunnel vision and overconfidence which ultimately could have been their ruin (Schoemaker, p. 46). Britannica was caught up in focusing on the known and either was unable to or unwilling to step outside of its comfort zone to attack the unknowns, even with opportunities awaiting them (Schoemaker, p. 47). Using scenarios planning and analysis, Britannica could have potentially begun to identify different possible disruptors and drivers of change and consider future alternatives through the process of scenario analysis.

One of the problems we face in the twenty-first century is that most business literature was written in the twentieth century and is focused mainly on organizational strategy and vision rather than the concept of flexible long-range strategic planning known as *Strategic Foresight*. Therefore, many of today's leaders have been trained with a narrow mindset of planning. Rather than the short-range goal-setting process taught in most traditional business schools, *Strategic Foresight* involves the use of techniques and frameworks to hypothetically stand in the future and understand where the organization may find itself (Marsh, et al., 2002, p. 2). *Strategic Foresight* is about creating new perspectives on key issues concerning an organization today through an integrated approach to strategy which results in discovery and articulation of a preferred direction for the organization (Marsh, et al., pp. 2—4). *Strategic Foresight* follows hypothetical cases which describe an organization's response to crisis management, opportunity management, risk management, and potential changes in a given sector (Marsh, et al., p. 11). Leaders may best incorporate *Foresight* methodologies through the framework focused on what would be most critical to an organization's success (Hines, 2006, p. 18). For leaders to determine the strategic direction of their organization, they must look inward, outward, and forward while scanning both the internal and external organizational environments to identify trends, threats, and opportunities for the organization (Daft, 2004, p. 495). *Strategic Foresight* is a skill which enables leaders to anticipate the risks and opportunities they may confront in the future (Cornish, p. xi). *Foresight* permits us to mentally stand in the future and imagine what it might be like and then return to the present day with possible insights to help us understand our potential future (Marsh, et al., p. 2). *Foresight* allows managers to discover and articulate a preferred direction for their organization and then focus on what would be most critical to an organization's success in the future (Marsh, et al., p. 4; Hines, p. 18).

Foresight produces the imagined possibilities, innovation, and the resulting solution to those possibilities. Therefore, *Foresight* is *what* can be expected and innovation is *how* we react to the future. The goal of forecasting is not to predict the future but to tell you what you need to know to take meaningful action in the present (Saffo, 2012, p. 72). Once we stand in the future and look back to the present, issues concerning us now begin to look different rather than unimportant (Marsh, et al., p. 2). The concept of *standing in the future* allows us to create an *unrestricted view* of the future as we are now free to realize that the future is not predetermined and thus something we necessarily need to react to or cope with (Marsh, et al., p. 2). *Strategic Foresight* is a way of thinking, engaging, discovering, and acting as a way to discovering crucial factors and sharing in the exploration of trends and change related to the future and relies on a framework focused on what would be most critical to an organization (Marsh, et al., p. 5; Hines, p. 18). Through the act of forecasting we realize the fluidity of potentials and the imagination of possibilities enhances our ability to act reasonably to the issues before us.

To best prepare for the eras beyond *Organization 3.0* we must consider taxonomies or paradigms in mapping out the terrain of the future through: scanning, trend analysis, trend monitoring, trend projection, scenarios, polling, brainstorming, modeling, gaming, historical analysis, and visioning. These taxonomies rely on modeling to represent or simulate actions and their results (Gary, 2012; Cornish, pp. 70, 78–79). Taxonomies are used to anticipate, forecast, or assess future events (Cornish, p. 78). Considering scenario planning, we look toward trends, strategies, and wildcard events to create awareness of potential future events that may or may not validate the desired course of actions for the organization (Cornish, p. 79). In essence, scenarios help us navigate toward our preferred future outcome. The use of systems and taxonomies create proper decision funnels for practitioners of *Foresight*. Finding ways to assimilate these changes without threat becomes important to organizational growth and change.

Current trends appear to indicate that the future of organizations is best seen through a lens of collaboration. Perhaps the most compelling trend driving this shift is that less than half of the workforce in the industrial world was in "proper" full-time employment by the beginning of the twenty-first century (Handy, p. 31). In fact, in a 2011 Gallup poll, 40 percent of the industrialized world were in full-time positions. As the landscape of employment and human capital changes, organizations must consider structures that account for decreasing numbers of full-time employees and increasing numbers of part-time, temporary, and contract labor (Foster, 2011b, p. 4).

As we look to the future we encounter uncertainty. In fact, the further we look out, the greater this uncertainty. As a result, the approach to strategic planning should include a holistic synthesis of the here and now as well as ten years and beyond. This is facilitated through the process of *Strategic Foresight*. *Strategic Foresight* is a deliberate process of establishing well-informed future-oriented perspectives that help guide innovation, planning, and decision-making at a macro-level. The process of *Foresight* creates competitive advantage by providing a future context for strategy and plans. *Foresight* helps an organization to maintain the view of agility against foreseeable future potentials. Most business leaders are well-accustomed to strategic planning. In fact it is a traditional business function to develop a strategic plan.

Strategic Foresight on the other hand uses a time horizon of ten to 25 years (or more) to look for trends, disruptors, and game-changers which will share our future. The process of *Foresight* will generate insights about alternatives which could affect the organization's future. When this knowledge is applied to the planning process it results in a more robust strategic plan. It provides the ability to mentally *stand in the future* and imagine preferred scenarios and outcomes. This provides insights about actions which need to be undertaken to move forward from the here and now as we head toward our preferred outcomes. In the end, *Strategic Foresight* helps organizations better understand, imagine, anticipate, and prepare for change by equipping its members with tools and resources to challenge assumptions, ask provocative questions, rethink opportunities, reset goals, and explore new alternatives that might otherwise not have been thought of.

An *Open Organization* is in a constant process of *Strategic Foresight* because it constantly tries to understand its environment through the use of environmental scanning, market research, and evaluations. Essentially, working groups regularly search for possible effects of its actions on other groups. It adapts its work to prevent adverse effects on others. An *Open Organization* engages its *Knowledge Workers* in *Strategic Foresight* through its *Knowledge Commons* and constant chats. This is the truest essence of an *Agile, Flat,* learning organization better known as an *Open Organization*.

The *Open Organization* is poised to be the most strategic, future-focused, agile alternative for the organization of the future. It engages human capital, builds community, manages agility, and creates a motivated workforce that is better educated, connected, and strategically minded than in any other era we have known. While the *Open Organization* may not be the answer for all organizational struggles, it certainly is a competitive way to "do business" in the future. It is a methodology that is beginning to take hold and will surely define a new era in leadership and organizational design.

References

Advameg, 2011. *Open and Closed Systems* [online] Available at: http://www.referenceforbusiness.com/management/Ob-Or/Open-and-Closed-Systems.html [Accessed November 23, 2011].

Aitken, A., Negrette, J., and Munro, R., 2003. *Organizational Policies and Open Source* [online] Available at: http://www.olliancegroup.com/opensource/Olliance-Company_policies_and_Open_Source.pdf [Accessed May 7, 2013].

Allee, V., 2003. *The Future of Knowledge. Increasing Prosperity through Value Networks.* Burlington, MA: Elsevier Science.

Ashkenas, R., Ulrich, D., Jick, T., and Kerr, S., 2002. *The Boundaryless Organization. Breaking the Chains of Organizational Structure.* San Francisco, CA: Jossey-Bass.

Authenticity Consulting LLC, n.d. (a) *Benefits of Open Systems View of Organizations* [online] Available at: http://managementhelp.org/misc/orgs-Open Systems.pdf [Accessed May 15, 2013].

Authenticity Consulting LLC, n.d. (b) *What is an Open System?* [online] Available at: http://managementhelp.org/misc/open-systems-benefits.pdf [Accessed May 15, 2013].

Awad, E.M. and Ghaziri, H., 2010. *Knowledge Management. 2nd Edition.* North Garden, VA: International Technology Group, Ltd.

Babcock, C., 2013. *Gartner: 50% of Enterprise Use Hybrid Cloud by 2017* [online] Available at: http://www.informationweek.com/infrastructure/cloud-infrastructure/gartner-50--of-enterprises-use-hybrid-cloud-by-2017/d/d-id/1111769? [Accessed December 17, 2013].

Babel, n.d., *The Silent Language* [online] Available at: http://wwww.babelgroup.co.uk [Accessed February 17, 2012].

Bacon, J., 2012. *The Gamification of Community* [online] Available at: http://osdelivers.blackducksoftware.com/2012/06/06/the-gamification-of-community/ [Accessed December 8, 2013].

Barbour, J.D., 2012. *Leading in Complex Worlds.* San Francisco, CA: Jossey-Bass.

Barbour, J.D. and Hickman, G.R., 2011. *Leadership for Transformation.* San Francisco, CA: Jossey-Bass.

Beitler, M.A., 2006. *Strategic Organizational Change. A Practitioners Guide for Managers and Consultant. 2nd Edition.* Greensboro, NC: Practitioner Press International.

Belosic, J., 2013. *5 Ways a Flat Management Structure Can Empower Your Business* [online] Available at: https://www.openforum.com/articles/5-ways-a-flat-management-structure-can-empower-your-business [Accessed September 5, 2013].

Benko, C. and Weisberg, A., 2007. *Mass Career Customization.* Boston, MA: Harvard Business School Press.

Bennis, W. and Nanus, B., 2003. *Leaders. Strategies for Taking Charge.* New York, NY: HarperCollins Publishers, Inc.

Bernoff, J. and Schadler, T., 2010. *Empowered.* Boston, MA: Forrester Research, Inc.

Bhanot, V., 2013. *How to Change a Company from the Inside* [online] Available at: http://www.theguardian.com/business/2013/dec/15/how-to-change-company-from-inside [Accessed December 17, 2013].

Birdsall, W.F. and Shearer, K., 2007. An Open Model of Organization for Diverse Knowledge Systems. *Interdisciplinary and Transdisciplinary in the Organization of Scientific Knowledge.* Leon, Spain: Universidad, pp. 43–50.

Black Duck Software, 2012. *Introduction to Open Source Governance and Compliance Guide Book* [online] Available at: http://www.blackducksoftware. com/noindex/salesforce/pdfs/Intro_OS_Governance_Compliance-UL.pdf [Accessed September 13, 2013].

Black Duck Software, 2013. *Four Steps for Creating an Open Source Policy* [online] Available at: http://www.blackducksoftware.com/noindex/salesforce/pdfs/Open_Source_Policy_UL.pdf [Accessed September 14, 2013].

Black, J.S., Morrison, A. and Gregersen, H., (1999). *Global Explorers: The Next Generation of Leaders*. New York: Routledge.

Bodo, P., 2004. *Open and Closed Organizations* [online] Available at: http://www.hr-network.hu/szolgaltatasok/open_and_closed_organizations.pdf [Accessed May 12, 2013].

Bolden, R., Gosling, J., Marturano, A. and Dennison, P., 2003. A Review of Leadership Theory and Competency Frameworks. *University of Exeter Centre for Leadership Studies*. Exeter, United Kingdom.

Bowers, A., 2014. *Five Misconceptions about Holacracy* [online] Available at: https://medium.com/about-holacracy/da84d8ba15e1 [Accessed January 12, 2014].

Brafman, O. and Beckstrom, R.A., 2006. *The Starfish and the Spider.* New York, NY: The Penguin Group.

Branch, C., 2011. Retrieved from his posting: Blackboard Dialogues for Doctorate in Strategic Leadership, Regent University, Virginia Beach, VA.

Branch, C., 2012. Retrieved from his posting: Blackboard Dialogues for Doctorate in Strategic Leadership, Regent University, Virginia Beach, VA.

Brooks, C., 2013. *The Thing Employees Want Most from a Job* [online] Available at: http://www.businessnewsdaily.com/5632-employee-happiness.html [Accessed December 22, 2013].

Broudy, J.D., 2009. *Guiding Principles and Why Your Business Should Have Them* [online] Available at: http://www.constructionbusinessowner.com/topics/management/construction-workforce-management/guiding-principles-and-why-your-business-should [Accessed September 12, 2013].

Burke, W.W., 2002. *Organization Change. Theory and Practice.* Thousand Oaks, CA: Sage Publications, Inc.

Burkus, D., 2010. *The Portable Guide to Leading Organizations.* Tulsa, OK: LeaderLab Press.

Burkus, D., 2013. *The Myths of Creativity.* San Francisco, CA: Jossey-Bass.

Burton, R.M., DeSanctis, D., and Obel, B., 2006. *Organizational Design. A Step-by-Step Approach.* Cambridge, NY: Cambridge University Press.

Carmeli, A., Meitar, R., and Weisberg, J., 2006. Self-leadership skills and innovative behavior at work. *International Journal of Manpower.* Vol. 27, No. 1, pp. 75–90.

Caste System, 2013. In World History: Ancient and Medieval Eras [online] Available at: http://0-ancienthistory2.abc-clio.com.library.regent.edu/ [Accessed April 8, 2013].

Chaleff, I., 2003. *The Courageous Follower.* San Francisco, CA: Berrett-Koehler Publishers, Inc.

Chen, W., 2013. *Bosslessness: What It Is and Why It's All the Rage in Silicon Valley* [online] Available at: http://www.entrepreneur.com/article/229977 [Accessed November 27, 2013].

Choi, J., 2013. *How Does Work Get Done Without Managers?* [online] Available at: http://smartblogs.com/leadership/2013/11/04/how-does-work-get-done-without-managers/ [Accessed November 22, 2013].

Clark, D.R., 2004, *Instructional System Design Concept Map* [online] Available at: http://www.nwlink.com/~donclark/leader/leadcon.html [Accessed August 24, 2010].

Cleveland, H., 2002. *Nobody in Charge. Essays on the Future of Leadership.* San Francisco, CA: Jossey-Bass.

Cloud Computing, n.d. *Cloud Computing Defined* [online] Available at: http://www.cloudcomputingdefined.com/ [Accessed September 2, 2013].

Compagne, O., 2014. *Readers Comments on 'Here's Why Eliminating Titles And Managers At Zappos Probably Won't Work.'* [online] Available at: http://www.businessinsider.com/zappos-holacracy-unlikely-to-work-2014–1 [Accessed January 12, 2014].

Cornish, E., 2004. *Futuring. The Exploration of the Future.* Bethesda, MD: World Future Society.

Cummings, T.G. and Worley, C.G., 2001. *Organization Development and Change. 7th Edition.* Mason, OH: South-Western College Publishing.

Daft, R.L., 2001. *Essentials of Organization Theory and Design. 2nd Edition.* Cincinnati, OH: South-Western College Publishing.

Daft, R.L., 2002. *The Leadership Experience. 2nd Edition.* Mason, OH: South-Western.

Daft, R.L., 2004. *Organization Theory and Design. 8th Edition.* Mason, OH: South-Western.

DaSilva, J., 2013. *How the Co-founders of iAcquire Build Culture in a Rapidly Growing Company* [online] Available at: http://smartblogs.com/leadership/2013/11/25/how-the-co-founders-of-iacquire-build-culture-in-a-rapidly-growing-company [Accessed November 26, 2013].

Davis, A.L. and Rothstein, H.R., 2006. The effects of the perceived behavioral integrity of managers on employee attitudes: a meta-analysis. *Journal of Business Ethics.* Vol. 67, pp. 407–419.

de Bree, E. and de Wiel, G., 2011. *Organization 3.0: Unmanage!* [online] Available at: http://www.secondsight.nl/work/organization-3–0/ [Accessed November 12, 2013].

de Kluyver, C.A. and Pearce II, J.A., 2009. *Strategy. A View From the Top. 3rd Edition.* Upper Saddle River, NJ: Pearson Prentice Hall.

DeGraff, J., 2011. *Thoughts on First Principles* [online] Available at: http://www.examiner.com/article/thoughts-on-first-principles [Accessed August 30, 2013].

DeMarco, T. and Lister, T., 1999. *Peopleware. Productive Projects and Teams. 2nd Edition.* New York, NY: Dorset House Publishing Co., Inc.

DeVito, J.A., 1988. *Human Communication. The Basic Course. 4th Edition.* New York, NY: HarperCollins.

Ecosystem, 2001. *Webster's Unabridged Dictionary.* New York, NY: Random House.

Eisenberg, E.M. and Goodall Jr., H.L., 2004. *Organizational Communication. 4th Edition.* Boston, MA: Bedford/St. Martin's.

Elmer, D., 1993. *Cross-Cultural Conflict: Building Relationships for Effective Ministry.* Downers Grove, IL: InterVarsity Press.

Elmquist, M., Fredberg, T. and Ollila, S., 2009. Exploring the field of open innovation. *European Journal of Innovation Management.* Vol. 12, No. 3, pp. 326–345.

Elsey, W., 2013. *Discussion on Leadership and Global Organizations* [telephone] (Personal Communication, June 2013).

Farrell, C., 2011. *Myths of an Aging Workforce* [online] Available at: http://www. kiplinger.com/columns/practical-economics/archives/myths-of-an-aging-workforce.html [Accessed October 23, 2012].

Feller, J., Finnegan, P., Hayes, J. and O'Reilly, P., 2009. Institutionalizing information asymmetry: governance structures for open innovation. *Information Technology and People.* Vol. 22, No. 1, pp. 297–316.

Ferrazzi, K., 2012. *How Successful Virtual Trams Collaborate.* Available at: http://blogs.hbr.org/cs/2012/10/how_to_collaborate_in_a_virtua.html [Accessed May 8, 2013].

First Principles, 2013. *The Free Dictionary* [online] Available at: http://www.thefreedictionary.com/first+principle [Accessed August 27, 2013].

Fletcher, J., 2012. Retrieved from her posting: Blackboard Dialogues for Doctorate in Strategic Leadership, Regent University, Virginia Beach, VA.

Foster, P.A., 2011a. *Open Source as a Leadership and Organizational Model. Presented at the Regent University School of Global Leadership and Entrepreneurship Leading Transformational Innovation Roundtable,* May 14–15, 2011.

Foster, P.A., 2011b. Retrieved from his posting: Blackboard Dialogues for Doctorate in Strategic Leadership, Regent University, Virginia Beach, VA.

Foster, P.A., 2011c. *The Open Organization: Exploring the implications of Open Systems Theory as an Organizational Model and its impact on the structure, motivation, culture and generational differences of the organizational system.* Virginia Beach, Virginia: Regent University LDSL 705, December 4, 2011.

Foster, P.A., 2012. Retrieved from his posting: Blackboard Dialogues for Doctorate in Strategic Leadership, Regent University, Virginia Beach, VA.

Galbraith, J.R., 2000. *Designing the Global Corporation.* San Francisco, CA: Jossey-Bass, Inc.

Galbraith, J.R., 2002. *Designing Organizations. An Executive Guide to Strategy, Structure and Process.* San Francisco, CA: Jossey-Bass, Inc.

Gardler, R. and Hanganu, G., 2013. *Benevolent Dictator Governance Model* [online] Available at: http://oss-watch.ac.uk/resources/benevolentdictatorgovernancemodel [Accessed December 8, 2013].

Gary, J., 2012. Retrieved from his dialogue posting: Blackboard Dialogues for Doctorate in Strategic Leadership, Regent University, Virginia Beach, VA.

Gilbert, J. and Matviuk, S., 2008. *Empirical Research: The Symbiotic Nature of the Leader-Follower relationship and its impact on Organizational Effectiveness.* Academic Leadership [online] http://www.academicleadershiporg/emprical_research/The_Symbiotic_Nature_of_the_Leader-Follower_relationship_and_Its_Impact_on_Organizational_Effectiveness_printer.shtml [Accessed March 20, 2013].

Girod, C., 2013. *King David. In World History: Ancient and Medieval Eras* [online] Available at: http://0-ancienthistory2.abc-clio.com.library.regent.edu [Accessed April 8, 2013].

GitHub, 2012. *Governance Model* [online] Available at: https://github.com/yahoo/mojito/wiki/Governance-Model [Accessed May 7, 2013].

Godin, S., 2008. *Tribes. We Need You to Lead Us.* New York, NY: Penguin Books Ltd.

Goldman, R. and Gabriel, R.P., 2005. *Innovation Happens Elsewhere. Open Source as Business Strategy.* San Francisco, CA: Morgan Kaufmann Publishers.

Gordon, J.R., 1991a. *Organizational Behavior. 3rd Edition.* Needham Heights, MA: Allyn and Bacon.

Gordon, J.R., 1991b. *A Diagnostic Approach to Organizational Behavior. 3rd Edition.* Needham Heights, MA: Allyn and Bacon.

Gorham, S., 2012. Retrieved from his posting: Blackboard Dialogues for Doctorate in Strategic Leadership, Regent University, Virginia Beach, VA.

Grace, D., 2011. Retrieved from his posting. Blackboard Dialogues for Doctorate in Strategic Leadership, Regent University, Virginia Beach, VA.

Griffin, D., n.d. *Open System Organizational Structure* [online] Available at: http://smallbusiness.chron.com/open-system-organizational-structure-432.html [Accessed November 24, 2011].

Griffith, T.L., 2012. *The Plugged-In Manager.* San Francisco, CA: Jossey-Bass.

Groth, A. 2014. *Zappos is Going Holacratic: No Job Titles, No Managers, No Hierarchy* [online] Available at: http://qz.com/161210/zappos-is-going-holacratic-no-job-titles-no-managers-no-hierarchy/ [Accessed January 10. 2014].

Gundykunst, W.B. and Kim, Y.Y., 2003. *Communicating with Strangers. 4th Edition.* New York, NY: McGraw-Hill.

Hackman, M.Z. and Johnson, C.E., 2000. *Leadership. A Communication Perspective. 3rd Edition.* Prospect Heights, IL: Waveland Press, Inc.

Hamel, G., 2002. *Leading the Revolution.* New York, NY: Penguin Group.

Hamel, G., 2011. First, let's fire all the managers. *Harvard Business Review.* December 2001, pp. 48–60.

Handy, C., 1989. *The Age of Unreason.* Boston, MA: Harvard Business School Press.

Hardy, Q., 2012. *Dreams of 'Open' Everything* [online] Available at: http://bits.blogs.nytimes.com/2012/12/28/github-has-big-dreams-for-open-source-software-and-more [Accessed May 7, 2014].

Harf, J.E. and Lombardi, M.O., 2010. *Taking Sides: Clashing Views on Global Issues. 6th Edition.* Dubuque, IA: McGraw Hill Contemporary Learning Series.

Hayes, T., 2008. *Jump Point. How Network Culture is Revolutionizing Business.* New York, NY: McGraw-Hill Companies.

Hearst, H., 2011. *Effective Governance of Open Source* [online] Available at: http:// opensourcedelivers.com/2011/09/29/effective-governance-of-open-source [Accessed April 23, 2013].

Hesline, P.A. and Kleche, U.C., 2006. "Self-Efficacy." *Encyclopedia of Industrial/ Organizational Psychology*. Vol. 2, pp. 705–708.

Hess, C. and Ostrom, E., 2007. *Understanding Knowledge as a Commons—From Theory to Practice*. Cambridge: Massachusetts Institute of Technology [online] Available at: http://mitpress.mit.edu/sites/default/files/ titles/content/9780262083577_sch_0001.pdf [Accessed May 26, 2013].

Hesselbein, F. and Goldsmith, M., 2009. *The Organization of the Future*. San Francisco, CA: Jossey-Bass.

Hewlett-Packard Development Company, 2007. *Best Practices in Open Source Governance* [online] Available at: https://fossbazaar.org/system/files/Best_ practices_in_open_source_governance_lowres.pdf [Accessed May 7, 2013].

Hines, A., 2006. *Strategic Foresight. The Futurist*. World Futurist Society. September–October 2006. pp. 18–21.

HolacracyOne, 2013. *Holacracy Constitution in Plain English* [online] Available at: http://holacracy.org/constitution [Accessed January 12, 2014].

Holman, Z., 2011a. *Customer Support Doesn't Have to Suck* [online] Available at: http://tom.preston-werner.com/2010/10/18/optimize-for-happiness.html [Accessed May 7, 2013].

Holman, Z., 2011b. *From 'Hack' to 'Popular Project.'* [online] Available at: http://zachholman.com/posts/from-hack-to-popular-project/ [Accessed May 7, 2013].

Holman, Z., 2011c. *How GitHub Works: Be Asynchronous* [online] Available at: https://github.com/yahoo/mojito/wiki/Governance-Model [Accessed May 7, 2013].

Holman, Z., 2011d. *How GitHub Works: Creativity is Important* [online] Available at: http://zachholman.com/posts/how-github-works-creativity/ [Accessed May 7, 2013].

Holman, Z., 2011e. *How GitHub Works: How GitHub Works Hours* [online] Available at: http://zachholman.com/posts/how-github-works-hours/ [Accessed May 7, 2013].

Holman, Z., 2011f. *Scaling GitHub's Employees* [online] Available at: http://zachholman.com/posts/scaling-github-employees/ [Accessed May 7, 2013].

Holman, Z., 2011g. *Why GitHub Hacks on Side Projects* [online] Available at: http://zachholman.com/posts/scaling-github-employees/ [Accessed May 7, 2013].

Holman, Z., 2012. *Chat Trumps Meetings* [online] Available at: http://zachholman.com/posts/chat/ [Accessed May 7, 2013].

Homula, M., 2010. *Servant Leadership for Real* [online] Available at: http://www.bearingfruitconsulting.com/2009/07/servant-leadership-not-so-with-you.html [Accessed December 31, 2013].

Howe, J., 2008. *Crowdsourcing. Why the Power of the Crowd is Driving the Future of Business.* New York, NY: Crown Business.

HRMID, 2011. Straight and narrow path to success. *Human Resource Management International Digest.* Vol. 19, No. 2, pp. 5–7.

Hsieh, T., 2010. *Delivering Happiness.* New York, NY: Grand Central Publishing.

ISACA, 2003. *Principles of Governance* [online] Available at: http://www.isaca.org/Journal/Past-Issues/2003/Volume-3/Pages/Principles-of-Governance.aspx [Accessed September 14, 2013].

IT Governance Institute, 2013. *About IT Governance* [online] Available at: http://www.itgi.org/template_ITGIa166.html?Section=About_IT_Governance1andTemplate=/ContentManagement/HTMLDisplay.cfmandContentID=19657 [Accessed September 14, 2013].

Joas, H. and Knobl, W., 2009. *Social Theory: Twenty Introductory Lectures.* Translated by Alex Skinner. New York, NY: Cambridge University Press.

Johansen, B., 2007. *Get There Early: Sensing the Future to Compete in the Present.* San Francisco, CA: Berrett-Koehler.

Johnson, M., 2012. Retrieved from her posting: Blackboard Dialogues for Doctorate in Strategic Leadership, Regent University, Virginia Beach, VA.

Johnson, W., 2013. *Independent Work May Be Inevitable* [online] Available at: http://blogs.hbr.org/johnson/2013/02/independent-work-may-be-inevit. html [Accessed May 8, 2013].

Kanungo, R.N. and Mendonca, M., 1996. *Ethical Dimensions of Leadership* Thousand Oaks, CA: Sage Publications, Inc.

Kastelle, T., 2013. *Hierarchy is Overrated* [online] Available at: http://blogs.hbr. org/2013/11/hierarchy-is-overrated [Accessed November 23, 2013].

Kates, A. and Galbraith, J.R., 2007. *Designing Your Organization. Using the Star Model to Solve 5 Critical Design Challenges.* San Francisco, CA: Jossey-Bass.

Katz, L., 2006. Book Review: Edward T. Hall. The Silent Language. *Leadership Crossroads* [online] Available at: http://www.leadershipcrossroads.com [Accessed February 17, 2012].

Keidel, R.W., 1995. *Seeing Organizational Patterns. A New Theory and Language of Organizational Design.* San Francisco, CA: Berrett-Koehler Publishers, Inc.

Kelly, J., 2012. Retrieved from his posting: Blackboard Dialogues for Doctorate in Strategic Leadership, Regent University, Virginia Beach, VA.

Kerins, J. and Lauster, S., 2006. *The Matrix Reloaded. The Multi-Axis Organization as Key to Competitive Advantage.* Booz Allen Hamilton, Inc [online] Available at: http://www.booz.com/media/file/The_Matrix_Reloaded.pdf [Accessed June 5, 2013].

Kesler, G. and Schuster, M.H., 2009. *Design Your Governance Model to Make the Matrix Work* [online] Available at: http://kateskesler.com/wp-content/uploads/2012/07/Make_the_matrix_work_final.pdf   [Accessed December 8, 2013].

Kirke, D., 2013. *How to Implement and Manage Successful Change Programs* [online] Available at: http://smallbiztrends.com/2013/09/implementing-change-programs.html [Accessed September 20, 2013].

Konnikova, M., 2014. *The Open-Office Trap* [online] Available at: http://www.newyorker.com/online/blogs/currency/2014/01/the-open-office-trap.html [Accessed January 10, 2014].

Kouzes, J.M. and Posner, B.Z., 2002. *The Leadership Challenge*. San Francisco, CA: Jossey-Bass.

Kreamer, A., 2013. *How to Make Your Employees Happier* [online] Available at: http://www.fastcompany.com/3003984/how-make-your-employees-happier [Accessed May 8, 2013].

Krippendorff, K., 2008. *The Way of Innovation*. Avon, MA: Platinum Press

Kuczmarski, S.S. and Kuczmarski, T.D., 1995. *Values-Based Leadership. Rebuilding Employee Commitment, Performance, and Productivity*. Englewood Cliffs, NJ: Prentice Hall, Inc.

Lancaster, L.C. and Stillman, D.S., 2010. *The M-factor. How the Millennial Generation is Rocking the Workplace*. New York, NY: HarperCollins.

Lanier, J.A., 2012. Retrieved from his posting: Blackboard Dialogues for Doctorate in Strategic Leadership, Regent University, Virginia Beach, VA.

Lapakko D., 1997. Three cheers for language: a closer examination of a widely cited study of non-verbal communication. *Communication Education*. Vol. 46, January 1997, pp. 63–67.

Lashinsky, A., 2012. *Inside Apple. How America's Most Admired—and Secretive—Company Really Works*. New York, NY: Hachette Book Group.

Li, C., 2010. *Open Leadership. How Social Technology Can Transform the Way You Lead*. San Francisco, CA: Jossey-Bass.

Li, C. and Bernoff, J., 2008. *Groundswell. Winning in a World Transformed by Social Technologies*. Boston, MA: Harvard Business School Publishing.

Linderman, M., 2010. *Bootstrapped, Profitable, and Proud: GitHub* [online] Available at: http://37signals.com/svn/posts/2486-bootstrapped-profitable-proud-github [Accessed May 7, 2013].

LINFO, 2007. *Scalable Defined* [online] Available at: http://www.linfo.org/
scalable.html [Accessed September 16, 2013].

Liu, I., 2013. *Examples of a Scalable Business Model* [online] http://smallbusiness.
chron.com/examples-scalable-business-model-25576.html   [Accessed
September 16, 2013].

Liu, T.H., 2012. Retrieved from her posting: Blackboard Dialogues for Doctorate
in Strategic Leadership, Regent University, Virginia Beach, VA.

Lunden, I., 2013. *GitHub Hits the 4M User Mark As It Looks Beyond Developers for Its
Next Stage Of Growth* [online] Available at: http://techcrunch.com/2013/09/11/
github-hits-the-4m-user-mark-as-it-looks-beyond-developers-for-its-next-
stage-of-growth [Accessed September 11, 2013].

Marquardt, M.D. and Berger, N.O., 2000. *Global Leaders for the 21st Century.*
Albany, NY: New York Press.

Marsh, N., McAllum, M. and Purcell, D., 2002. *Why Strategic
Foresight?* [online] Available at: http://www.globalforesight.net/
category?Action=ViewandCategory_id=73 [Accessed May 1, 2012].

McAfee, A., 2009. *Enterprise 2.0. New Collaborative Tools for Your Organization's
Toughest Challenges.* Boston, MA: Harvard Business Press.

McCall Jr., M.W. and Hollenbeck, G.P., 2002. *Developing Global Executives.*
Boston, MA: Harvard Business School Press.

McGuffey, C., 2012. Retrieved from his posting: Blackboard Dialogues for
Doctorate in Strategic Leadership, Regent University, Virginia Beach, VA.

Mehrabian, A., 1971. *Silent Messages. 1st Edition.* Belmont, CA: Wadsworth

Meritocracy, 2001. *Webster's Unabridged Dictionary. 2nd Edition.* New York,
NY: Random House, Inc.

Mintzberg, H., Ahlstrand, B., and Lampel, J., 1998. *Strategy Safari.* New York,
NY: First Free Press.

Moore, D., 2011. Overcoming resistance: company stories helping to change
learning. *Training and Development in Australia.* February, pp. 16–17.

Morgan, G., 2006. *Images of Organization*. Thousand Oaks, CA: Sage Publications, Inc.

Morrison, D., 2013. *The One Thing That Truly Motivates Creative Talent—And How to Foster It* [online] Avialable at: http://www.fastcocreate.com/3022240/the-one-thing-that-truly-motivates-creative-talent-and-how-to-foster-it?partner=rssandutm_medium=referralandutm_source=pulsenews [Accessed December 5, 2013].

Myers, D.G., 2007. *Psychology. 8th Edition*. New York, NY: Worth Publishers.

Nadler, D.A. and Tushman, M.L., 1997. *Competing by Design*. New York, NY: Oxford University Press, Inc.

Neath, K., 2009. *It's Not about How Many Hours You Work* [online] Available at: http://warpspire.com/posts/work-life-balance/ [Accessed May 7, 2013].

Neath, K., 2011a. *Build Your Business around an Idea* [online] Available at: http://warpspire.com/posts/idea-businesses/ [Accessed May 7, 2013].

Neath, K., 2011b. *Product Design at GitHub* [online] Available at: http://warpspire.com/posts/product-design/ [Accessed May 7, 2013].

Negandhi, A.R., 1975. *Organization Theory in an Open System*. New York, NY: Dunellen.

Nogan, K., 2009. *Capitalizing on an Aging Workforce* [online] Available at: http://www.pmagroup.com/pdf/PMAInsights/PMAInsightsAgingWorkforce_1–09.pdf [Accessed October 7, 2012].

Northouse, P.G., 2001. *Leadership. Theory and Practice. 2nd Edition*. Thousand Oaks, CA: Sage Publications, Inc.

NuGet, 2013. *NuGet Governance* [online] Available at: http://docs.nuget.org/docs/reference/governance [Accessed December 8, 2013].

O'Mahony, S., 2007. The governance of Open Source initiatives: what does it mean to be community managed? *Journal of Management and Governance*. Vol. 11, pp. 139–150.

O'Toole, J., 1996. *Leading Change.* New York, NY: The Random House Publishing Group.

Olson, G., 2012. *How to Create an Open Source Policy* [online] Available at: http:// opensourcedelivers.com/2012/02/27/how-to-create-an-open-source-policy [Accessed April 18, 2013].

Open Archives, 2011. *Open Architecture* [online] Available at: http://www. openarchives.org [Accessed May 2, 2011].

Open Organizations, 2006. *The Open Organizations Project* [online] Available at: http://www.open-organizations.org [Accessed May 2, 2001].

Ousterhout, J., 2009. *Open Decision-Making* [online] Available at: http://www. stanford.edu/~ouster/cgi-bin/decisions.php [Accessed May 2, 2001].

P2P Foundation, 2008. *Open Organization* [online] Available at: http:// p2pfoundation.net/Open_Organization [Accessed May 17, 2013].

P2P Foundation, 2010a. *Open Business* [online] Available at: http:// p2pfoundation.net/Open_Business [Accessed May 17, 2013].

P2P Foundation, 2010b. *Open Business Models* [online] Available at: http:// p2pfoundation.net/Open_Business_Models [Accessed May 17, 2013].

P2P Foundation, 2011a. *Open Company Models—Foo Associates Model* [online] Available at: http://p2pfoundation.net/Open_Company_Models [Accessed May 17, 2013].

P2P Foundation, 2011b. *Open Enterprise* [online] Available at: http:// p2pfoundation.net/Open_Entreprise [Accessed May 17, 2013].

Penn, A., 2008. *Leadership Theory Simplified.* Little Rock, AR: University of Arkansas.

Peters, S., 2011. *Does Open Source Exclude High-Context Cultures?* [online] Available at: http://stormyscorner.com/2011/09/does-open-source-exclude-high-context-cultures.html [Accessed March 30, 2012].

Piscopo, M., 2012. *How to Develop a Mission Statement and Guiding Principles for Your Business* [online] Available at: http://www.fastbusinessplans.com/business-plan-guide/mission-statement-and-guiding-principles.html [Accessed March 30, 2012].

Pitron, J., 2008. *Followership is Leadership: The Leadership-Exemplary Followership Exchange Model* [online]. Available at: http://knol.google.com/k/dr-john-pitron/followership-is-leadership/12nb17zejmb1w/2 [Accessed December 31, 2013].

Pluralism, 2001. *Webster's Unabridged Dictionary*. New York, NY: Random House.

Politis, J.D., 2006. Self-leadership behavioral-focused strategies and team performance. The mediating influence of job satisfaction. *Leadership and Organizational Development Journal*. Vol. 27, No. 3, pp. 203–216.

Pozin, I., 2013. *Why Employees Shouldn't Have Hours* [online] Available at: http://www.linkedin.com/today/post/article/20130430145142–5799319-why-employees-shouldn-t-have-hours [Accessed May 8, 2013].

Prahalad, C.K. and Krishnan, M.S., 2008. *The New Age of Innovation. Driving Co-Created Value through Global Networks*. New York, NY: McGraw Hill.

Preston-Werner, T., 2009. *The Git Parable* [online] Available at: http://tom.preston-werner.com/2009/05/19/the-git-parable.html [Accessed May 7, 2013].

Preston-Werner, T., 2010. *Optimized for Happiness* [online] Available at: http://tom.preston-werner.com/2010/10/18/optimize-for-happiness.html [Accessed May 7, 2013].

Preston-Werner, T., 2011. *Ten Lessons from GitHub's First Year* [online] Available at: http://tom.preston-werner.com/2011/03/29/ten-lessons-from-githubs-first-year.html [Accessed May 7, 2013].

Prichard, Skip CEO of Ingram Content Group. Personal Interaction on February 2, 2012, LaVergne, TN.

Reeves, S., 2005. *An Aging Workforce's Effect on U.S. Employers* [online] Available at: http://www.forbes.com/2005/09/28/career-babyboomer-work-cx_sr_0929bizbasics.html [Accessed October 23, 2012].

Rider, G.S., 2006. Open Leader versus Traditional Leader. *T+D*, May, Vol. 60, No. 5, p. 62.

Rollag, K., n.d. Chapter 4: Organizations as Open Systems. *Babson Park, MA: Babson College* [online] Available at: http://faculty.babson.edu/krollag/org_site/scott_org/chap4.html [Accessed May 13, 2013].

Rosen, R., Digh, P., Singer, M. and Philips, C., 2000. *Global Literacies. Lessons on Business Leadership and National Cultures.* New York, NY: Simon and Schuster.

Ross, P., 2014. *2014: The Year of Workplace Reinvention* [online] Available at: http://www.huffingtonpost.com/pam-ross/workplace-reinvention_b_4541805.html [Accessed January 10, 2014].

Rothwell, W.J. and Sullivan, R., 2005., *Practising Organization Development. A Guide for Consultants. 2nd Edition.* San Francisco, CA: John Wiley and Sons, Inc.

Saffo, P., 2012. Six Rules for Effective Forecasting. *Harvard Business Review OnPoint.* Summer 2012, pp. 72–80.

Safian, R., 2012. *Terry Kelly. The 'Un-CEO' of W.L. Gore, On How to Deal with Chaos: Grow Up* [online] Avilable at: http://www.fastcompany.com/3002493/terri-kelly-un-ceo-wl-gore-how-deal-chaos-grow [Accessed November 26, 2013].

Sanna, L.J., 1992. Self-efficacy theory: implications for social facilitation and social loafing. *Journal of Personality and Social Psychology.* Vol. 62, No. 5, pp. 774–786.

Savitz, E., 2012. *The Empowered Employee is Coming, Is the World Ready?* [online] Available at: http://www.forbes.com/sites/ciocentral/2012/02/09/the-empowered-employee-is-coming-is-the-world-ready/ [Accessed April 15, 2013].

Schoemaker, P.J.H., 2002. *Profiting from Uncertainty.* New York, NY: The Free Press.

Science Daily, 2012. *Making People Happy Can Be Better Motivator than Higher Pay for Workers* [online] Available at: http://www.sciencedaily.com/releases/2012/08/120806125918.htm [Accessed November 22, 2013].

Scott, W.R., 1998. *Organizations. Rational, Natural, and Open Systems. 4th Edition.* Upper Saddle River, NJ: Prentice Hall.

Sculley, J., 2011. *What are First Principles?* [online] Available at: http://curiosity.discovery.com/question/what-are-first-principles [Accessed May 18, 2013].

Senge, P.M., 1990. *The Fifth Discipline. The Art and Practice of the Learning Organization.* New York, NY: Doubleday.

Signore, D., 2013. *Built to Scale: Why Growth Entrepreneurs Need Structure* [online] Available at: http://www.inc.com/dino-signore/why-growth-entrepreneurs-need-structure.html [Accessed November 12, 2013].

Simoes-Brown, D., 2009. Opening up Innovation in the Workplace. *Training Journal.* September, pp. 50–53.

Simons, T.L., 1999. Behavioral integrity as a critical ingredient for transformational leadership. *Journal of Organizational Change Management.* Vol. 12, No. 2, pp. 89–104.

Simson, N., 2013. *No Time for Fun At Work: Then 'Get a Life'!* [online] Available at: https://www.linkedin.com/today/post/article/20131216235438–1291685-no-time-for-fun-at-work-then-get-a-life?trk=eml-ced-b-art-M-0andut=0swxGfjT2_Pm01and_mSplash=1 [Accessed December 17, 2013].

Sire, J.W., 1997. *The Universe Next Door. 3rd Edition.* Madison, WI: InterVarsity Press.

Southward, B., 2013. *What Makes a Workplace a 'Great Place'?* [online] Available at: http://management.fortune.cnn.com/2013/11/29/what-makes-a-workplace-a-great-place [Accessed December 5, 2013].

Stagich, T., 2001. *Collaborative Leadership and Global Transformation.* 1st Books Library.

Stanford, N., 2009. *Guide to Organisation Design. Creating High-performance and Adaptable Enterprises.* London, England: Profile Books, Ltd.

Stanley, A., 2003. *The Next Generation Leader.* Sisters, OR: Multnomah Publishers, Inc.

Stone, G.A. and Patterson, K., 2005. The History of Leadership Focus. *Servant Leadership Research Roundtable*—August 2005, School of Leadership Study, Regent University.

Sugar, B., 2010. *What are Your Guiding Principles?* [online] Available at: http://www.entrepreneur.com/article/205846 [Accessed September 12, 2013].

Sy, T. and D'Annunzio, L.S., 2005. Challenges and Strategies of Matrix Organizations: Top-Level and Mid-Level Managers Perspectives. *Human Resource Planning*. HR 3799, Jrnl 28.1, pp. 39–48 [online] Available at: http://thematrixco.com/download/i/mark_dl/u/4006983785/4527114385/AT%20Kearny%20Matrix%20Article.pdf [Accessed April 30, 2013].

Tamas, A., 2007. *Geert Hofstede's Dimensions of Culture and Edward T. Hall's Time Orientations* [online] Available at: http://www.tamas.com [Accessed February 17, 2012].

Tapscott, D. and Williams, A.D., 2008. *Wikinomics. How Mass Collaboration Changes Everything. Expanded Edition.* New York, NY: Penguin Group.

Taylor, W.C. and LaBarre, P., 2006. *Mavericks at Work. Why the Most Original Minds in Business Win.* New York, NY: HarperCollins Publishers.

The Library of Alexandria, n.d. *The Ancient Library* [online] Available at: http://www.serageldin.com/ancient_Library.htm [Accessed December 17, 2013].

Theory X and Theory Y, 2013. *WebFinance, Inc* [online] Available at: http://www.businessdictionary.com/definition/theory-X-and-theory-Y.html#ixzz2X8UkeRak [Accessed June 24, 2013].

Theory Z, 2013. *WebFinance, Inc* [online] Available at: http://www.businessdictionary.com/definition/theory-Z.html#ixzz2X8X0AGHp [Accessed June 25, 2013].

Titchy, N.M., 2002. *The Cycle of Leadership. How Great Leaders Teach Their Companies to Win.* New York, NY: HarperBusiness.

Tomayko, R., 2012. *Show How, Don't Tell What—A Management Style* [online] Available at: http://tomayko.com/writings/management-style [Accessed May 7, 2013].

Twenge, J.M., Campbell, S.M., Hoffman, B.J. and Lance, C.E., 2010. *Implications of an Aging Workforce* [online] Available at: http://www.strategy-business.com/article/re00117?gko=9abf5 [Accessed October 23, 2012].

Twitter, 2013. *Open Source Code of Conduct* [online] Available at: https://engineering.twitter.com/opensource/code-of-conduct [Accessed December 17, 2013].

University of Iowa, 2012. Making people happy can be better motivator than higher pay for workers. *ScienceDaily* [online] Available at: http://www.sciencedaily.com/releases/2012/08/120806125918.htm   [Accessed November 12, 2013].

Vago, S., 2004. *Social Change. 5th Edition.* Upper Saddle River, NJ: Pearson Education, Inc.

Valve Corporation, 2013. *We're Always Creating* [online] Available at: http://www.valvesoftware.com/company/ [Accessed September 6, 2013].

Vance, A., 2013. *GitHub Got Silly Rich. Next Step: 'Make More Awesome.'* [online] Avilable at: http://www.businessweek.com/articles/2013–06–20/github-got-silly-rich-dot-next-step-make-more-awesome   [Accessed June 21, 2013].

Vescuso, P., 2011. *Why Governance for Open Source? Alignment!* [online] Avilable at: http://opensourcedelivers.com/2011/09/21/why-governance-for-open-source-alignment [Accessed April 23, 2013].

von Bertalanffy, L., 1968. *General Systems Theory* [online] Available at: http://www.panarchy.org/vonbertalanffy/systems.1968.html [Accessed November 26, 2011].

Walton, M., 1986. *The Deming Management Method.* New York, NY: The Berkley Publishing Group.

Wideman, R.M., 2003. *First Principles of Project Management* [online] Available at: http://www.maxwideman.com/papers/principles/principles.pdf [Accessed August 30, 2013].

Wren, D., 1994. *The Evolution of Management Thought. 4th Edition.* The University of Oklahoma: John Wiley and Sons, Inc.

Yeaton, T., 2012. *Inner-Sourcing: Adopting Open Source Development Processes in Corporate IT* [online] Available at: http://osdelivers.blackducksoftware.com/2012/08/29/inner-sourcing-adopting-open-source-development-processes-in-corporate-it/ [Accessed December 8, 2013].

Yehuda, G., 2011. *Becoming an Open Leader* [online] Available at: http://www.gilyehuda.com/2011/03/16/open-leadership-book-review/   [Accessed May 2, 2011].

Yun, S., Cox, J. and Sims Jr., H.P., 2006. The forgotten follower: a contingency model of leadership and follower self-leadership. *Journal of Managerial Psychology*. Vol. 21, No. 4, pp. 374–388.

Zappos, 2012. *2012–2013 Culture Book*. Henderson, NV: Fanny Chen, Orbitel International LLC.

Zweifel, T.D., 2003. *Culture Clash. Managing the Global High-Performance Team*. New York, NY: SelectBooks.

Index

3D printer, 33, 34, 51
501c3 University, 22

AARP, 132
abilities, 8, 22, 53, 55, 58, 74
accessible, 36, 83, 89, 94
accommodate, 23, 41, 120
accountability, 18, 53, 69, 72, 76, 88,
      106, 107, 137, 144, 147, 149
accountable, 18, 19, 29, 88, 106, 137
achievement, 56, 65, 144, 148, 149
   recognition, 60, 75, 108
   reward, 72
actions, 5, 11, 48, 63, 64, 97, 101, 106,
      107, 114, 152, 156, 157
adapt, 12, 13–15, 17, 24, 28, 41, 42, 44,
      47, 74, 107, 124, 125, 136, 143,
      145, 146, 157
adhocracy, 52, 76
administrator, 12, 43, 76
adopt, 3, 28, 30, 61, 66, 90, 92, 99, 106,
      129, 139, 142, 143, 148, 150
Affinity Network, 45, 52
age, 49, 81, 132, 134
   average, 132
   cohort, 132
   profiles, 13, 136
agile, vii, ix, 14, 15, 17, 18, 28, 44, 47,
      52, 57, 59, 61, 81, 83, 98, 100, 115,
      132, 141, 148, 149, 150, 153, 157
agility, 27, 52, 99, 100, 131, 140, 143,
      157
   framework of, 41
   produce, 154

respond with, 153
under pressure, 13, 44
view of, 157
aging
   labor, 133
   population, 133
   workforce, 132, 133, 134, 135
agreement, 11, 19, 45, 54
alcohol, 43
   bar, 32, 36, 43
   beer, 35
   mixed drink, 35
Alexandria Egypt, 89
align, 12, 14, 28, 58, 67, 69, 81, 122,
      123, 130
alliance, 14, 127
ambiguity, 29, 36, 91
American, 8, 49, 50, 112, 128, 132
   Revolutionary War, 127
   Workplace Report, 50
Apple, 66, 139
APPS (applications), 94
archive, 35, 89, 90, 91, 94
argument, 36, 37, 59, 88, 140, 144, 148,
      149
Aristotle, 3, 89
Asian, 120
assumptions, 6, 7, 8, 12, 41, 113, 115,
      118, 144, 152
   challenging, 151, 157
   core, 66
   examines, 11
   fundamental, 66
   sets of, 6, 7

authority, 4, 29, 37, 60, 75, 76, 91, 97,
    103, 130, 133, 140, 141, 152
  ambiguous, 92
  center of, 152
  formal, 97
  scope of, 104
  traditions of, 13, 136
autonomous, 15, 28, 44, 71, 130
autonomy, 11, 16, 26, 33, 52, 53, 88,
    99, 100, 149
Awesome, 31, 35, 38, 53, 87

Bacon, Sir Francis, 89
balance, 12, 42, 56, 65, 67, 68, 98, 101,
    125, 131
  critical, 42
  natural, 41
  work/life, 33, 49
barrier, 36, 48, 84, 112, 113, 116. 147
  artificial, 22
  breaking down, 58, 113
  cultural, 47, 119
  multiple, 46
  purposeful, 43
*Beer:*30, 35, 90, 93, 141
behavior, 7, 9, 10, 11, 15, 19, 63, 66, 70,
    72, 106, 112, 122, 151
  adaptive, 42
  cultural, 118
  dominant, 45
  employee, 14
  forms of, 152
  misinterpret, 121
  organizational, 10, 24, 32
behavioral
  expectations, 70
  integrity, 11
  model, 7
  perspectives, 9
Bennis, Warren, 52
Bertalanffy, Ludwig von, 6, 17, 26, 57

Bethlehem Steel Works, 8
Boomers, 118, 128, 132, 133, 134
boundaries, 6, 12, 14, 43, 45, 59, 82,
    91, 122, 124, 130, 131, 141
  artificial, 22
  cultural, ix, 17, 41, 111, 125, 128,
    130, 135
  national, 116
  organizational, 20, 21, 72, 84
  purposeful, 43
  system, 6, 26, 72
boundaryless, 45
brainstorming, 156
British Red Coats, 27, 28, 29
bureaucracy, 9, 53, 57
bureaucratic, 29, 43
  layers, 43, 140
  red tape, 28, 41

Caste System, 3
catalyst, 3, 56, 87, 101
centralized, 13, 49, 116, 128, 136
  model, 17, 20
  organization, 28, 44
  relationship, 26
  system, 13, 18. 27
change, 11, 12, 15, 20, 24, 31, 38, 41,
    42, 57, 58, 61, 65, 75, 76, 85, 93,
    100, 105, 118, 119, 120, 127, 128,
    136, 139, 141, 142, 146, 151, 156
  ability to, 100, 145
  adverse to, 145
  constant, 72
  create, 55, 145
  drive, 65
  drivers of, 131, 155
  embrace, 143
  implementation of, 145
  institutional, 142
  introducing, 145
  political, 12

rapid, 28, 143
reason for, 146
resistance, 15, 112, 146
social, 12, 129
threat of, 121
chaos, 27, 41, 42, 43, 67, 91, 98, 99,
    142, 144
charter, 16, 19, 69, 125, *See also*
    Governance
chat, 33, 36, 38, 85, 88, 93, 94, 157
China, 114
Closed, 12, 19, 21, 23, 26, 43, 72, 89, 141
    organization, 21, 22, 141, 144, 153
    philosophy, 22
    system, 22, 23, 43–4, 47, 56, 57, 71, 141
Cloud, 94
    application, 94
    computing, 92, 94, 95
    services, 95
    workers, 95
coaching, 128, 150
Code of Conduct, 70, 71, *See also*
    Governance
    Twitter, 70, 71
cohesiveness, 106, 107, 147
collaborate, 13, 17, 20, 31, 35, 38, 44,
    45, 54, 55, 58, 70, 85, 91, 93, 98,
    129, 146, 156
collective, 7, 22, 59, 70
    action, 101
    belief, 15
    cognition, 97
    decisions, 7
    effort, 30
    intelligence, 20
    knowledge, 21, 107
    survival, 102
    voice, 45
command-and-control, 23, 25, 28, 53,
    98, 99, 101, 103, 104, 141, 142,
    143, 144, 147, 149

commitment, 11, 12, 15, 29, 56, 68,
    73, 78, 81, 112, 114, 115, 123,
    129, 134
    expectation of, 75
    to excellence, 49
committed to
    implementation, 55
    to implimentation, 85
    to preservation, 73
committer, 75, 76
communicate, 14, 17, 36, 81, 82, 83,
    92, 93, 112, 113, 114, 117, 119,
    122, 124, 125, 145
communication, 4, 12, 19, 23, 25, 31,
    33, 35, 36, 65, 81–3, 85–8, 90,
    92, 99, 105, 106, 112, 113, 115,
    117–19, 121, 122, 124, 136
    axiom of, 117
    cross-boundary, 91
    cross-cultural, 48, 112, 113, 114, 115
    cross-silo, 21
    cultural, 117, 120, 122
    High-context, 115
    intercultural, 117, 118
    loop, 113
    mechanics of, 117
    Monochronic, 117
    non-verbal, 48, 114, 117
    Open, 84, 86, 91, 136
    para-verbal, 117
    patterns, 113
    polarized, 122
    Polychronic, 117
    poor, 81
    style, 115, 116, 119
    verbal, 117
    vocal, 117
    words, 117
communicator, 119, 122
community, 10, 28, 30, 41, 45, 70, 73,
    74–7, 85, 92, 93, 134, 144, 157

global, 44
    sense of, 63, 152
commuting
    tele, 92
    time, 51
competency, 48, 85, 114
complex, 4, 5, 15, 24, 26, 30, 35, 41, 42,
        46, 52, 53, 55, 58, 66, 74, 81, 105,
        111, 124, 125, 130, 142, 143, 145,
        152
complexity, 4, 14, 28, 41, 42, 56, 57, 70,
        71, 117, 118, 125
    layer of, 117
    level of, 42
concern, 81, 84, 122, 133, 134, 148
    for employees, 10
    high, 123
    low, 112
    main points of, 86
    moderate, 123
    shared, 92
    voice their, 85, 145
conflict, vii, 8, 21, 56, 64, 71, 81, 86, 87,
        106, 119–24
    approaches to, 119
    avoidance, 120, 124
    benefits of, 121, 124
    constructive, 87
    context of, 121
    cross-cultural, 122
    cultural, 120, 122
    handling, 122
    healthy, 87
    impact of, 121
    impact on, 119
    incidents of, 122
    interpersonal, 86
    nature of, 121, 124
    personality, 87
    preference for, 122
    resolution, 119, 120, 122

resolve, 70, 120
    sources of, 121
    styles, 122
consensus, 7, 20, 30, 54, 55, 67, 73, 76,
        77, 78, 85, 104, 116, 135
constitution, 61, 68, 69, See also
        Governance, See also Charter
constraints, 41, 64
    negative, 68
    time, 51
control, 6, 7, 18, 19, 28, 30, 54, 58, 72,
        74, 77, 98, 100, 104, 131, 137, 143
    cede, 101
    exercise, 4, 142, 143
    foci of, 144
    gain, 70
    give, 25
    implies, 142, 143
    internal, 63
    level of, 54, 101, 144
    losing, 147
    perceived, 51
    system of, 27, 31
    tightening of, 137
conversation, 35, 65, 82, 85, 148, see
        also dialogue
    communal, 122
    process of, 35
    sidebar, 37
cooperation, 91, 102
Covenant, 69, 72
creative, 23, 29, 33, 34, 35, 42, 49, 53,
        54, 65, 90, 150
    process, 50, 87
    strategies, 154
creativity, 7, 21, 29, 33, 50, 55, 64, 79,
        87, 98, 144
    catalyst for, 87
    focus on, 13, 130
    problems with, 57
    promotes, 33

source of, 56
state of, 68
stimulates, 49
zone of, 33
critical thinking, 11, 90
crowdsourcing, 52, 53
cultural, vii, ix, 13, 14, 26, 16, 17, 30,
    31, 41, 47, 107, 111–13, 117–20,
    122, 124, 128, 130, 135, 139
  activities, 118
  codes, 122
  context, 121, 125
  cues, 125
  defaults, 120
  difference, 15, 111, 118, 123
  distance, 15, 16
  experience, 119
  hermeneutics, 121
  indirectness, 119
  individualism-collectivism, 122
  lens, 15, 121, 124, 131
  literacy, 111, 119
  myopia, 15
  norms, 122
  nuance, 14, 117, 118, 125
  origins, 111
  relativism, 121, 122
  response, 119
  shift, 52
  silo, 46
culturally, 14, 111, 112, 117, 118, 119,
    122
  diverse, 42, 111, 130
culture, vii, ix, 7, 13–15, 32–4, 41, 42,
    44, 47–50, 63, 64, 67, 74, 79, 81,
    87–9, 93, 98, 111–14, 116–19,
    121–5, 130, 131, 136, 140, 145,
    149
  adapt to, 15, 28, 32, 125
  complexities of, 14
  differing, 112, 113, 130

High- and Low-context, 114, 115,
    117
High-context, 114, 115, 117, 125
  indirect, 119
  interpretation of, 124, 131
  Latin, 112
  Low-context, 114, 115, 117, 125
  Monochronic, 117
  of power, 87
  organizational, 32, 64, 68, 139, 140
  participatory, 87
  performance, 91
  Polychronic, 117
  shame-based, 119
  Universalist, 122
curiosity, 35, 79, 82, 85, 118, 125

debate, 35, 78, 90, 133
decentralized, 27, 29, 44, 52, 71, 91
  matrix, 15
  organization, 15, 28, 101
  structure, 18, 135
  system, 13, 27, 42, 44
decision-making, 5, 9, 13, 18, 19, 20,
    28, 31, 35, 42, 51, 52, 53, 54, 55,
    56, 57, 64, 73, 74, 76, 77, 90, 91,
    93, 99, 100, 103, 105, 107, 111,
    112, 116, 130, 137, 140, 141, 143
  bottle-necks, 99
  decentralized, 71
  joint, 139
  Open, 35, 82
  transparent, 77
Dell, 46, 57, 135, 136, 137
Denmark, 132
departmentalization, 15, 27
Devil's Advocate, 55
dialogue, 35, 78, 85, 90, 102, 148, *See
    also conversation*
dictator, 4, 5, 8, 75
  benevolent, 74, 75, 77

digital
  age, 81
  marketing, 64
  technology, 140, 141
  world, 82
disagreement, 77, 86, 106
discussion, 25, 37, 76, 78, 84, 85, 104, 107
dispersed, 81, 85, 90, 92, 93, 94, 111, 112, 113, 148
disputes, 77, 101, 121
distributed, 15, 27, 32, 36, 37, 48, 49, 60, 91, 93, 97, 102, 115, 116, 141, 142
diversity, vii, 16, 48, 56, 113, 114, 118, 130, 151
Doll, Brian, xi, 32
Drucker, Peter, 29

ecosystem, vii, 41, 42, 65, 105
egalitarian, 52, 63, 64, 78
ego, 35, 55, 82
Elsey, Wayne, 22
email, 32, 36, 51, 77, 93
empower, 7, 19, 33, 35, 37, 41, 45, 46, 53, 54, 57, 60, 61, 68, 69, 71, 79, 88, 92, 97, 98, 99, 100, 101, 102, 103, 104, 105, 135, 137, 143, 144, 146, 149, 150
encode, 48, 114
encyclopedia, 21, 31, 46
  Britannica, 154
English, 112, 113
entrepreneurial, 44, 74
equifinality, 9, 56, 57
equilibrium, 6, 9, 42, 47
Europe, 127
expertise, 10, 55, 64, 90, 102, 129, 152

Face Time, 37, 94, *See also Skype*
Facebook, 31

face-to-face, 93, 113
feedback, xi, 9, 37, 59, 60, 82, 83, 84, 85, 92
Firefox, 25
First Principles, 32, 47, 59, 63, 64, 65, 66, 67, 68, 69, 71, 73, 74, 75, 77, 78, 79, 84, 88, 90, 97, 98, 101, 106, 107, 139, 142, 144, 146, 147, 149
flat, 41, 45, 46, 57, 59, 60, 61, 87, 98, 100, 127, 129, 130, 131, 140, 142, 145, 148, 149, 150, 157
flexible, 12, 13, 15, 18, 19, 20, 22, 26, 27, 28, 29, 33, 34, 41, 42, 44, 45, 47, 51, 52, 53, 54, 56, 58, 59, 60, 91, 100, 104, 114, 115, 128, 130, 131, 133, 135, 144, 155
Foresight, 154, 155, 156, 157
  methodologies, 155
  Strategic, 131, 155, 156, 157
fun, 33, 34, 35, 46, 49, 50, 65
future, 3, 5, 12, 13, 14, 25, 27, 41, 42, 49, 56, 83, 85, 90, 91, 93, 94, 98, 99, 100, 104, 111, 112, 128, 129, 130, 131, 132, 133, 134, 135, 143, 146, 153, 154, 155, 156, 157
  alternatives, 155
  anticipate, 103, 153, 154
  benefit, 11
  focused, 154, 157
  optimal, 154
  oriented, 154, 157
  plausible, 154
  potential, 155, 156, 157
  predict the, 156
  preferred, 156
  stand in the, 155, 156, 157
  standing in the, 156
  viability, ix
  view of, 153
future-readiness, 129

Gallup, 49, 50, 132, 156
games, 32, 43, 153
Gamification, 107, 108
Gartner Survey, 94
General Motors, 140
generalist, 18, 27
Generation X, 128
geographic, 82, 130
    differences, 46
    dispersed, 93, 111
    divides, 45
    locales, 130
    location, 51, 93
    regions, 58
    separations, 92
Germany, 155
Git, 31
GitHub, xi, 31, 32, 33, 34, 35, 36, 37,
        38, 43, 51, 52, 53, 56, 64, 65, 69,
        74, 77, 82, 84, 85, 87, 90, 92, 93,
        97, 98, 103, 104, 105, 106, 107,
        139, 140, 141, 145, 148, 149
GitHubber, 32, 37
global, vii, 12, 13, 14, 15, 44, 45, 48, 51,
        58, 69, 71, 92, 93, 94, 112, 113,
        114, 116, 119, 124, 125, 128, 130,
        131, 133, 140
    approach, 112
    competition, 93, 133
    context, 14, 48, 112, 124, 130
    expansion, 125
    implications, 134
    landscape, 111, 153
    literacies, 112
globalism, vii, 4, 111
Google, 31, 66
    Hangouts, 94
Governance, 16, 19, 29, 47, 59, 61,
        68–79, 90, 92, 97, 98, 101, 106,
        107, 139, 144, 145, 147, 149, *See*
        also charter: see also Constitution

corporate, 69
Open, 70, 71, 73, 146
organizational, 69, 72, 73, 77, 78,
        79, 142, 144
slack, 78
government, 35, 38, 46, 114, 133, 134, 151
Gray Belt, 133
Great Britain, 115
Greenleaf, Robert, 29
Groupthink, 45, 55, 56, 87
growth, 13, 47, 58, 65, 133, 156
    pathways for, 66
    personal, 102
    platform for, 64
    projections, 137
Guiding Principles, 65, 67, 68

hacking, 33, 34, 36, 51
Hall, Edward, 114
Happiness, 33, 34, 41, 49, 50, 51, 52, 79,
        107, 131, 144, 152
    optimized for, 32, 33, 34, 35, 42,
        49, 50, 51, 108, 112
    hierarchy, 8, 26, 29, 61, 70, 72, 75,
        87, 98, 136, 151, 152
    classic, 152
    rigid, 57
    traditional, 5, 46
    top-down, 8
    vertical, 97, 143
Hofstede, Gert, 115, 117
Holacracy, 60, 61, 150
homogenize, 25, 113
Human Resources, 23

iAcquire, 64
IBM, 140
imagination, 49, 51, 156
immigration, 8, 128
inclusivity, 63, 152
independence, 53, 71, 102

independent, 19, 74, 99, 128, 151
innovation, 11, 13, 15, 23, 25, 41, 50, 58,
        60, 64, 69, 79, 89, 91, 100, 106,
        118, 130, 131, 141, 142, 155, 157
innovative, ix, 29, 49, 52, 53, 54, 57,
        87, 90, 101, 145
innovators, 12, 98, 118
inquisitiveness, 119, 124, 130
insights, 75, 155, 157
integrity, 11, 23, 73, 78, 84
Intellectual Capital, 89
Intrapreneur, 44
irrefutable truths, 64, 66

Japan, 114
Jobs, Steve, 64, 66

King David, 3
Knowledge Commons, 35, 42, 59, 73, 75,
        76, 77, 85, 89, 90, 91, 93, 94, 105,
        106, 131, 157
Knowledge System, 91, 92
Knowledge Workers, 42, 55, 56, 90, 91,
        94, 99, 140, 157

lag-thinking, 28, 153, 154
language, 13, 14, 16, 24, 48, 68,
        112–14, 119, 121, 124, 125
    body, 81, 117
    business, 113
    common, 113
    foreign, 113
    global, 112, 113
    North America, 119
    technical jargon, 136
leader, vii, 3–5, 7, 8, 10–15, 18, 19,
        23–9, 41, 44–6, 48, 53–5, 59, 60,
        68, 69, 75, 77–9, 86, 90, 97–105,
        111, 112, 116–121, 124, 125, 130,
        135, 137, 140, 142–4, 148–51,
        153, 155, 157

authoritarian, 4
Catalyst, 101
classically trained, 98, 102
corporate, 44
cross-cultural, 116
cultural, 124
cult, 87
empowering, 104
global, 45, 48, 112, 113, 114, 119,
        124, 125, 130, 131
leaderless, 19, 41, 57, 59, 68, 98, 99,
        100, 141, 144, 149, 150
leadership, vii, ix, 3– 11, 13, 18,
        19, 23, 25, 26, 29, 31, 37, 46,
        49, 52, 53, 56, 63, 68, 78, 91,
        97, 99, 101, 102, 104–106,
        112, 116, 123, 128, 129, 131,
        136, 139, 140, 143, 144, 147,
        148, 157
    authoritarian, 116
    democratic, 116
    global, 119
    organizational, vii, 99, 130, 148
    top-down, 129
    traditional, 97, 98
library, 89
listen, 48, 54, 59, 68, 86, 102, 112, 113,
        117, 118, 119, 140, 144
loyalty, 124, 125, 130, 132, 134

management, vii, 4, 7, 8, 9, 18, 26,
        29, 31, 37, 38, 42, 43, 61, 71,
        72, 94, 98, 99, 103, 105, 106,
        116, 121, 124, 129, 144, 148,
        151, 155
    boundary, 122
    middle, 53
manager, 6, 7, 8, 10, 12, 22, 26, 32, 37,
        44, 48, 53, 60, 97, 98, 99, 100,
        116, 136, 143, 148, 154, 155
    classically trained, 22, 53, 98, 99, 144

functional, 58
    middle, 46
    mini, 37, 104
managerless, 57, 59, 60, 144, 149
Manpower Incorporated, 140
Matrix, 4, 5, 15, 45, 57, 58, 99
Matrix Guardian, 59, 74, 78
Matrix Organization, 46, 57, 58
Mehrabian & Ferris, 117
Mehrabian, Albert, 81
mentoring, 45, 150
Meritocracy, 59, 60, 73, 74, 75, 150
micromanage, 54, 99, 101
Millennial, 49, 118
the Minutemen, 27
mission, 22, 23, 43, 63, 64, 130
model, vii, 3, 6, 7, 17, 19, 25, 60, 142
    business, 19, 29, 30, 41, 43, 103,
        137, 141
    centralized, 17, 20
    classic, 50
    Decentralized Authority, 29
    Employee-led Team, 29
    Freemium, 31
    Governance, 72, 74, 76, 142
    Open Organization, 17, 20, 51, 58,
        139, 141
    organizational, 11, 19, 47, 130, 135,
        142
    self-leadership, 98
    Servant Leader, 29
    traditional, 8, 14, 151
monarch, 3, 4, 5, 8
morale, 136, 137
mortality, 133
motivate, 13, 49, 53, 54, 135, 137, 140,
    147, 152, 157
motivation, ix, 7, 19, 20, 79, 104, 135,
    151
    intrinsic, 19, 130, 136, 137
myth, 41, 144, 149

Nashville, Tennessee, 46, 135, 136
needs, 5, 12, 13, 15, 17, 19, 20, 23, 24,
    42, 46, 47, 53, 59, 73, 78, 86,
    102–104, 112, 115, 130–32, 135,
    140, 143
    intrinsic, 52, 132
    motivational, 19, 20, 130, 135
Netflix, 31
network, 5, 42, 45, 52, 95, 111, 121, 131
    information, 75
    social, 118
New Millennia, 127, 131
non-traditional, 13, 18, 26, 28, 29, 44,
    97, 136
non-verbal, 48, 113, 114, 115, 117, 118

off-boarding, 42, 56
office, 44, 46, 51, 84, 90, 92, 94, 128,
    135, 141, 148, 154
    formal, 135
    home, 127
    mobile, 94
    Open, 148
    politics, 147
    remote, 92
    virtual, 92
on-boarding, 42, 150
one-size-fits-all, 18, 25, 57, 136, 137
online, 31, 92
    bulletin board, 36
    platform, 91
    storage, 94
Open, 15, 17, 18, 22, 23, 26, 28–32, 34,
    35, 37, 38, 41, 43, 46, 48, 52,
    57, 59, 60, 61, 64–6, 70, 73, 77,
    82, 84, 86, 89, 94, 99, 100, 102,
    114–16, 124, 127, 130, 135–7,
    139–45, 147–52
Open and Closed, 23, 26, 141, 144
Open Governance, 146
Open Innovation, 25, 141

Open Leader, 101, 102
Open Leadership, 101, 102
Open Office, 148
Open Source, 25, 30, 31, 32, 35
    software OSS, 25, 55, 70
Open System, 4, 5, 18, 20, 24–7, 29, 30,
        36, 44, 47, 49, 53, 60, 61, 68, 86,
        116, 119, 125, 130–32, 137, 146,
        147, 149
Openness, 6, 9, 19, 22, 23, 25, 33, 36, 43,
        47, 54, 55, 69, 75, 77, 78, 81, 85,
        103, 119, 139, 141, 147
opinion, 25, 29, 54, 55, 78, 86, 122, 145,
        152
organic, 10, 15, 20, 36, 91, 100, 143
organisms, 6, 17, 21, 41
organization
    aligned, 81
    behavior, 11, 15
    boundaryless, 45
    chart, 28, 32, 99, 100, 112
    cross-cultural, 48, 114
    culture, 42, 63, 67, 145
    decentralized, 15, 28, 101
    design, 5
    distributed, 37, 97
    diverse, 41
    established, 139, 145
    flat, 46
    flexible, 27
    future, 13, 14, 42, 93, 98, 100, 111,
        129, 132, 135, 146, 153, 154, 156,
        157
    global, 13, 94, 113
    hierarchical, 107
    learning, 35, 152, 157
    managerless, 144
    non-traditional, 13, 18, 28, 29, 44,
        136
    objective, 4, 75
    one-size-fits-all, 156

performance, 85, 148, 154
scalable, 47, 49
start-up, 179, 134
structure, 5, 7, 57, 59, 102, 142
Taylorian, 28
team-based, 58
top-down, 8, 53, 144
traditional, 28, 29, 43, 44, 46, 69, 72,
        86, 92, 97, 105, 107, 143, 146, 152
twenty-first century, ix, 14, 15, 42,
        100, 109, 128, 130, 145
values, 10
virtual, 92
Western, 123
Organization 1.0, 4, 7, 8, 9, 10, 14, 18
Organization 2.0, 4, 8, 9, 10, 11, 12, 14,
        18, 19
Organization 3.0, 4, 5, 9, 14, 15, 48, 111,
        131, 153, 156
Organization 4.0, 131
organizational, ix, 9, 17, 20, 22, 36, 41,
        43, 45, 57, 72, 73, 74, 82, 94, 99,
        128, 130, 134, 135, 144, 153, 155
    agility, 52
    attribute, 12
    behavior, 10, 24, 32
    boundaries, 20, 21, 72, 84
    capabilities, 12
    change, 57
    Charter, 125
    compensation, 19
    culture, 32, 64, 68, 139, 140
    decision-making, 13
    design, ix, 12, 13, 14, 18, 25, 29, 44,
        100, 136, 137, 157
    development, 23
    ecosystem, vii, 41, 65
    effectiveness, 100
    efficiencies, 56
    growth, 156
    health, 59

leader, 15
leadership, vii, 99, 130, 148
learning, 72
mandates, 19
mechanism, 20
members, 82
metrics, 28
mode, 19
model, 11, 19, 130, 135, 142
objectives, 76
philosophies, 139
policies, 147
position, 97
process, 10
requirements, 144
risk, 70
setting, 87, 102, 135
silo, 45, 46
strategy, 155
structure, vii, 3, 7, 8, 9, 12, 15, 19,
    20, 23, 26, 29, 41, 42, 45, 49, 57,
    61, 93, 97, 106, 129, 139, 151, 153
struggle, 157
support, 54
system, ix, 3, 6, 13, 17, 41, 42, 91,
    128, 130, 135
talent, 58
theory, 9, 10, 18
transformation, 10, 145
outsourcing, 14, 128
ownership, 16, 74, 84, 103, 149, 150
    of knowledge, 90, 105

participate, 9, 17, 18, 20, 48, 69, 70, 73,
    75, 76, 78, 92, 104, 107, 116, 132,
    144
participation, 4, 47, 53, 71, 73, 78, 107,
    146, 147
    culture of, 87
    Open, 16
part-time, 25, 31

passion, 33, 49, 52, 60, 65
peer, 7, 37, 47, 53, 147, 150
    interaction, 17, 20, 87
    pressure, 102, 106, 107, 149
    review, 87, 88
performance, 9, 20, 44, 45, 52, 55, 58,
    59, 84, 85, 88, 91, 102, 104, 106,
    107, 141, 142, 147, 148, 152, 154
    appraisals, 107
    measures, 59, 130
    standards, 10
Peter, Tom, 29
philosophy, 22, 30, 32, 65, 81, 139
    idealistic, 22
    personal, 67
planning, 11, 52, 76, 92, 154, 155, 156,
    157
    long-range, 153
    rituals, 154
Pluralism, 71
policy, 11, 21, 61, 72, 73, 76, 101, 147
power, 7, 8, 10, 18, 27, 36, 48, 52, 58,
    60, 61, 71, 76, 78, 79, 83, 87, 89,
    90, 97, 99, 102, 104, 115, 139,
    142, 146, 147, 149, 150, 151
    abuse of, 19, 29, 102
    distributed, 102
    distributing, 102
    distribution of, 15, 27, 48, 116
    personal, 103
    positions of, 87
    relationships, 10
    share, 102, 104, 130
    sharing of, 78, 102
    struggle, 26
    transfer of, 69
power-distance, 48, 115, 116, 122, 124,
    125, 131
    High, 48, 115, 116
    Hofstede's, 115
    Low, 48, 49, 115, 116

Preston-Werner, Tom, 31, 32, 34–6, 38, 84, 97, 103, 104
principles, 6, 45, 63, 66–8, 86, 130, 131
    classical, 9
    core, 65
    founding, 145
    moral, 12
    set of, 6
productivity, 4, 32, 49, 50, 51, 60, 74, 95, 121, 124, 147, 148
project, 12, 13, 17, 29, 30, 34, 35, 37, 38, 52–4, 56, 58, 70, 71, 73, 75 –7, 90, 93, 94, 107, 115, 127
    administrator, 76
    assignments, 150
    development of, 75
    engagement, 72
    management, 94
    output, 76
    side, 51
    team, 52, 53, 57
psychological, 120, 122, 142, 143, 148
    contracting, 11
    distance, 15, 102

Reilly, Terri, 150
relationship, 5, 6, 10, 14, 26, 47, 48, 51, 55, 65, 89, 97, 112, 113, 115, 118 –21, 123, 124, 130
    cooperative, 7
    cross-cultural, 48, 114
    developing, 14
    direct, 26
    inter-organizational, 71
    interpersonal, 115
    oriented, 45, 53
    personal, 86
    superficial, 120
remote, 32, 36, 51, 92, 93, 136, 148
    access, 94
    jobbing, 51

research and development, 25, 52
resistance, 11, 15, 28, 112, 146, 147, 150
    managerial, 129
respect, 12, 14, 16, 50, 54, 61, 86, 91, 118, 119, 122, 132, 151
responsibility, 4, 7, 8, 9, 21, 29, 53, 56, 64, 69, 70, 72, 73, 74, 76, 90, 91, 92, 97, 104, 120, 148
retire, 128, 132, 133, 134, 135, 140
    accounts, 135
    age, 132
    full-time, 132, 135
    funds, 134
    plan, 133
    working, 132
reward, 19, 20, 49, 58, 60, 72, 106, 107
    system, 19
rigid, 8, 13, 19, 20, 28, 41, 42, 43, 46, 51, 57, 59, 100, 136, 144, 153
risk, 16, 45, 49, 52, 55, 63, 70, 74, 78, 116, 141, 147, 149, 153, 155
    management, 155
    security, 95
    social, 88
roles, 9, 10, 22, 53, 58, 59, 60, 61, 74, 92, 100, 140, 150, 152
rules, 17, 21, 29, 41, 56, 61, 64, 68, 131, 144, 147, 150
    board, 69
    complex, 74
    driven, 68
    emotional, 66
    for interaction, 113
    functional, 16
    of engagement, 69, 70, 71, 74, 76
    simple, 74
    social, 21
    void of, 68

SAAS (software as a service), 94
Salesforce.com, 94

scalable, ix, 46, 47, 69, 94
scanning, 155, 156, 157
scenario, 19, 43, 48, 84, 114, 129,–31,
        135, 154–57
    analysis, 153–5
    planning, 155–6
schedule, 53, 91
    9 to 5, 52
    flexible, 33, 133
    rigid, 33
    work, 33, 133
self-
    checking, 74
    competing, 43–4
    concept, 10
    confidence, 102
    control, 7
    direction, 7, 60, 93
    discipline, 7
    efficacy, 151–2
    employed, 129
    esteem, 101
    evident, 15, 67
    forming, vii, ix, 36
    fulfilling, 6, 102
    governed, 29
    influence, 104
    initiate, 14
    interest, 20, 147
    leadership, 4, 5, 17, 18, 19, 41, 57,
        59, 68, 97, 98, 100
    led, vii, ix, 17, 33, 41, 59
    managed, 16, 29, 32, 36, 37, 83, 84,
        99, 102, 106, 144, 147, 150
    organization, 152
    organize, 30, 33, 36, 60
    preservation, 21, 44
    regulate, 106
    serving, 105
    sustaining, 45
Semco, 57, 141, 142, 150

shareholders, 50, 59, 144
silo, 21, 26, 30, 45, 46, 52, 72, 84, 92,
        131, 144
Sire, James, 121
skills, ix, 7, 13, 16, 17, 22, 41, 45, 47,
        49, 53, 55, 58, 76, 79, 86, 90, 98,
        103, 117, 118, 125, 128, 130, 135,
        140, 153
    acquisition, 108
    verbal, 55
Skype, 94
Smart Device (SD), 127
smartphones, 94
social, 7, 9, 12, 21, 66, 88, 94, 118, 120,
        122, 127–9, 134
    activities, 69
    conscience, 63
    constructs, 4
    context, 71
    cues, 113
    force, 107
    harmony, 55
    institutions, 7
    interaction, 51
    media, 14
    norms, 134
    patterns, 3
    pressure, 147
    services, 134
    values, 113
Social Security Administration, 132,
        134
software, 31, 32, 70, 92, 93, 94
    as a Service - SAAS, 25, 94
    development, 30
    industry, 25, 38
    license, 30
    programs, 30
    version control, 31
Soles for Souls, 22
Soviet Union, 123

stakeholders, 13, 15, 23, 45, 63, 73, 74, 100, 135, 144, 149
strategy, 11, 15, 22, 48, 60, 98, 112, 139, 143, 148, 154, 155, 157
structural
  concept, 57
  design, 15, 27
  perspective, 9
  realignment, 14
structure, vii, 3, 4, 6–15, 17– 29, 37, 38, 41–7, 49, 50, 54, 57–61, 69, 71–3, 76, 82, 84, 91, 93, 97, 99, 100, 102, 107, 118, 119, 129–32, 136, 139–45, 147, 150, 151, 153, 156
  agile, 18
  circle, 61
  closed, 21, 89
  command, 46, 57
  corporate, 8
  creating a, 60, 92
  decentralized, 18, 135
  departmental, 57
  distinct, 3
  fixed, 56
  flat, 142
  flatter, 5, 145
  flexible, 53
  form of, 6, 26
  formal, 18, 20, 26, 29, 60, 136, 141
  functional, 57
  grid-like, 46
  hierarchical, 15, 25, 27, 141
  Lattice, 58
  Matrix, 58
  network, 131
  new, 152
  nonlinear, 143
  non-traditional, 44
  old, 4
  Open, 59, 124, 130, 147
  organic, 10

product/service, 26, 57
project-team, 57
Rational, 58
rigid, 59
simple, 22
social, 66
Star, 5, 58
traditional, 28, 29, 79, 100, 136
success, vii, xi, 14, 15, 16, 44, 45, 47, 48, 51, 55, 67–9, 73, 82, 98, 100, 111, 112, 118, 125, 129, 131, 135, 146, 149, 150, 152, 155
  achieving, 13, 82, 101, 152, 153
  drivers of, 100
  essential to, 117, 125, 146
  future, 135
  global, 112
  indicator of, 18, 25, 137
  ingredients for, 82
  keys to, 55, 149
  level of, 13, 107
  material, 7
  metrics of, 107
  option for, 20
  scenario for, 19, 130, 135
Sun Belt, 133
supervision, 36, 48, 99, 116
supervisor, 46, 47, 83, 86
system, ix, 3, 5, 6, 8–10, 12, 13, 16–20, 22– 31, 41, 43, 44, 46, 47, 53, 56–58, 61, 63, 67, 68, 71, 72, 78, 81, 91, 92, 100, 112, 125, 128, 130, 135, 141, 143, 150–52, 156
  adaptive, 42
  agile, 47, 52
  award, 107
  complex, 4, 42
  flexible, 47
  hierarchical, 4, 82
  isolated, 12
  legal, 16

natural, 143
opening the, 23
political, 16
sophisticated, 42
status of the, 22
structureless, 29
technological, 91
work, 9

task, 9, 12, 20, 23, 25, 35, 52, 53, 55, 56, 66,
        69, 82, 93, 94, 127, 140, 151, 152
    assigned, 21
    complex, 152
    force, 53
    group, 52
    oriented, 46, 123
Taylor, Fredrick W., 4, 8, 9, 28, 56, 99,
        148, 150
team, 17, 25, 29, 32, 33, 36, 45, 46, 52,
        53, 55–9, 64, 65, 67, 75, 99, 107,
        134, 148
    building, 23
    cohesive, 102, 107, 144, 147
    cross-functional, 27, 93
    distributed, 93
    hierarchical, 20
    high functioning, 88
    high-performing, 26
    members, 147
    self-directed, 93
    self-managed, 102, 106, 150
    self-forming, 36
    spirit, 107, 147
    start-up, 44
    successful, 48, 114
    virtual, 52, 92, 93
    work, 47, 60
technology, vii, 9, 12, 14, 30, 91, 92,
        93, 94, 100, 113, 118, 128, 129,
        130, 139, 142, 150, 155
    adopt, 90

changing, 81
digital, 140, 141
tensile strength, 144
tension, 55, 56, 67, 87
    natural, 26
    release, 121
Texas, 136
The Lord of the Flies, 99
Theory, 4, 5, 6, 11, 24, 49
    behavioral perspective, 9
    Classical, 8, 9, 10, 14
    Classical School, 9
    Contingency, 10, 57
    Decision, 9
    emerging, 24
    Environmental Analysis, 9
    General Systems, 6
    Great Man, 3, 4, 7, 8, 150
    Group Dynamics, 9
    Integrative Perspective, 9, 10
    Leader-Follower, 10, 11, 19
    Leadership, 5, 6, 10, 13
    Leadership School, 9
    Open Systems, 24, 25, 26, 30
    organizational, 10, 18, 131
    prospective of, 9
    Scientific Management, 4, 99, 148
    Scientific Method, 8
    Sociotechnical School, 9
    Systems, 9
    Taylorism, 28, 56, 150
    Technological Analysis, 9
    Top-Down, 11
    traditional, 12
    X, 6, 7, 32
    Y, 6, 7, 32
    Z, 7
Tomayko, Ryan, 37
top-down, 4, 5, 8, 11, 53, 59, 82, 86,
        107, 129
transformation, 9, 10, 116, 120, 142, 145

transparency, 17, 22, 30, 53, 64, 81, 104, 105, 106, 146
transparent, 56, 60, 70, 77, 83, 84, 106, 130
trend, 18, 25, 58, 98, 128, 129, 131, 132, 155, 156, 157
    analysis, 156
    demographic, 98
    emerging, 151
    exploring, 156
    monitoring, 156
    projection, 156
    sociodemographic, 128
trust, 7, 11, 14, 18, 19, 25, 29, 35, 54, 55, 88, 99, 101, 103, 105, 113, 118, 119, 124, 125, 131, 136
    build, 86, 125
    create, 105
    deter, 48
    developing, 124
Twitter, 70, 71, *See also* Code of Conduct

United States, 8, 94, 122, 127, 128, 132, 133, 140, 151
UNIX, 30

value, 7, 10–13, 21, 30, 34, 47, 48, 59, 63, 64, 68, 69, 87, 91, 113, 118–22, 125, 130, 131, 134, 140, 141
    common set of, 150
    core, 23, 47, 49, 63, 64, 65, 119
    intrinsic, 135
    shared, 67, 91
Valve, 41, 53, 139, 145
verbal, 11, 48, 55, 113, 115, 117
video conferencing, 51, 93, 94
video games, 32, 43
vision, 22, 51, 66, 68, 83, 101, 104, 113, 130, 147, 148, 155, 156
    shared, 76, 147

vote, 76, 77
    formal, 76, 77
    majority, 54

W.L. Gore, 46, 57, 98, 105, 139, 145, 150
Wal-Mart, 140
Wanstrath, Chris, 31, 32
Web, 31, 58
    browser, 92
    services, 95
Westerners, 119, 120
Whole Foods, 84, 139
Wikipedia, 20, 21, 31, 45, 90
Wikis, 25, 88, 90, 94
WordPress, 25, 139
workers, 8, 9, 29, 42, 43, 44, 46, 49, 50, 60, 82, 93, 95, 98, 105, 107, 128, 132–5, 147, 149, 150
    aging, 133, 135
    American, 49, 50
    independent, 151
    mature, 133
    remote, 32
    unhappy, 50
    young, 132, 134
workflow, 47, 56, 75, 83, 90, 103, 107
workforce, 14, 24, 30, 44, 50, 53, 54, 105, 111, 128, 129, 133, 134, 140, 144, 151, 156, 157
    aging, 132, 133, 134, 135
    dispersed, 85, 92, 94, 112
    distributed, 32, 36
    diverse, 12, 129
    dminishing, vii, 50
    emerging, 133
    full-time, ix
    global, 93
    graying, 132
    shrinking, 129
    techno-linked, 81

United States, 132   Yammer, 94
    younger, 133
workplace, 8, 50, 118, 151   Zappos, 60, 65, 66, 139, 145
worldview, 13, 15, 16, 28, 48, 111, 112,
    114, 124, 130, 131, 148

If you have found this book useful you may be interested in other titles from Gower

**Smart Flexibility:
Moving Smart and Flexible Working
from Theory to Practice**
Andy Lake
Hardback: 978-0-566-08852-0
Ebook – PDF: 978-0-7546-9208-9
Ebook – ePUB: 978-1-4094-7337-4

**Smart Working:
Creating the Next Wave**
Anne Marie McEwan
Hardback: 978-1-4094-0456-9
Ebook – PDF: 978-1-4094-0457-6
Ebook – ePUB: 978-1-4094-6014-5

**Integral Development:
Realising the Transformative Potential of Individuals,
Organisations and Societies**
Alexander Schieffer and Ronnie Lessem
Hardback: 978-1-4094-2353-9
Ebook – PDF: 978-1-4094-2354-6
Ebook – ePUB: 978-1-4094-6040-4

GOWER

Collaborative Wisdom:
From Pervasive Logic to Effective
Operational Leadership
Greg Park
Hardback: 978-1-4094-3460-3
Ebook – PDF: 978-1-4094-3461-0
Ebook – ePUB: 978-1-4094-7354-1

A Field Guide for Organisation Development:
Taking Theory into Practice
Edited by Ed Griffin, Mike Alsop, Martin Saville
and Grahame Smith
Hardback: 978-1-4094-4049-9
Ebook – ePUB: 978-1-4094-4050-5
Ebook – ePUB: 978-1-4724-0163-2

Building Anti-Fragile Organisations:
Risk, Opportunity and Governance in a Turbulent World
Tony Bendell
Hardback: 978-1-4724-1388-8
Ebook – ePUB: 978-1-4724-1389-5
Ebook – ePUB: 978-1-4724-1390-1

Visit **www.gowerpublishing.com** and

- search the entire catalogue of Gower books in print
- order titles online at 10% discount
- take advantage of special offers
- sign up for our monthly e-mail update service
- download free sample chapters from all recent titles
- download or order our catalogue